The Language of the News

Martin Conboy

D0491666

Routledge
Taylor & Francis Group

LONDON AND NEW YORK

First published 2007
by Routledge
2 Park Square, Milton Park, Abingdon, Oxon OX14 4RN

Simultaneously published in the USA and Canada
by Routledge
270 Madison Ave, New York, NY 10016

Routledge is an imprint of the Taylor & Francis Group, an informa business

© 2007 Martin Conboy

Typeset in Bell Gothic by
Keystroke, 28 High Street, Tettenhall, Wolverhampton
Printed and bound in Great Britain by
Antony Rowe Ltd, Chippenham, Wiltshire

British Library Cataloguing in Publication Data
A catalogue record for this book is available from the British Library

Library of Congress Cataloging in Publication Data
Conboy, Martin.
    The language of the news / Martin Conboy.
        p. cm.
    Includes bibliographical references.
    1. Journalism—Language. 2. Journalism—Social aspects. I. Title.
    PN4783.C58 2007
    070.401′4—dc22   2006036316

ISBN10: 0–415–37202–X (pbk)
ISBN10: 0–415–37201–1 (hbk)

ISBN13: 978–0–415–37202–2 (pbk)
ISBN13: 978–0–415–37201–5 (hbk)

Immer bereit!
Für Simone

Contents

Acknowledgements

I would like to thank the following for giving me permission to use their material: *The Advertiser, The Australian*, the *Daily Express*, the *Daily Mail*, the *Daily Mirror*, the *Daily Star*, the *Daily Telegraph*, the *Guardian*, the *Independent*, *International Herald Tribune*, the *Observer*, the *Sun*, the *Times*, *USA Today* and *The Wall Street Journal*.

This book, as all others, has benefited from the often unwitting support and inspiration of many friends and colleagues who have contributed ultimately to its shape, tone and content. I hope that the resultant work is a fitting tribute. Christy Kirkpatrick first seized the potential for such a book. Since this initial backing, Louisa Semlyen and Nadia Seemungal have been especially helpful in advice towards the publication stage. Nigel Starck provided me with the Australian newspapers and also with invaluable insights into the attractions of lower league football and the art of the obituary. For making the Department of Journalism Studies at Sheffield such a smooth-running and supportive place to work, my thanks go to Cecilia Harvey, Amanda Sewell and Susie Whitelam. In my new academic home, Liz Nice, John Steel, Tony Harcup and Jackie Harrison have provided me with essential sounding boards for ideas and strate-gies – if they appreciate it or not – and John Richardson inadvertently gave me the opportunity of carrying on this work on the language analysis of the press. Alastair Allan has been a constant source of sage advice in the building of research library provision. In bringing to completion a book which aims to succeed as a teaching text, I must thank the numbers of students from Farnham and Sheffield who have helped shape my own thinking and research in this area by their hard work and forensic explorations of newspaper texts over the years. For acting as barometers of academic life through times thick and thin my thanks go to Matthew Rampley, Richard Keeble, David Finkelstein, Bob Franklin, Jane Taylor, Andy Darley and Helen Davis. The work of Teun van Dijk, Norman Fairclough and Ruth Wodak has of course shaped this area of study but, most of all, I must acknowledge a debt of gratitude in memory of Roger Fowler whose pioneering work first stimulated my interest in this area many years ago.

Finally, a word of thanks to Lara for lighting up my life with her continued infectious enthusiasm for all things.

Sheffield, January 2007

1 Language and conventional communities

- Introduction
- Language and society
- The development of newspaper language
- Contemporary newspaper language
- Newspapers as interpretative communities
- Newspaper language content and structure
- Headlines
- Stories
- Objectivity
- Summary
- Suggestions for further reading

Introduction

One of the main aims of this chapter is to emphasize that the study of the language of the news media is not an exercise in exposing the hidden tricks or deceptions of journalists, editors or owners. Rather it seeks to do something which none of these people has time nor often inclination to do: to attempt a systematic study of the patterning of language on various themes across the news in order to further our understanding of the social implications of this language. This approach allows a critical perspective to emerge while respecting the integrity of the work that people do in journalism. Journalists do not have the time to explore such perspectives on a regular basis. Students and consumers of journalism, on the other hand, may allow themselves the time to better understand the ways in which language acts at the heart of this process of public communication. This opening chapter will emphasize that language is a profoundly social activity. It will argue that the success of news as a form of communication over time has been linked to its ability to integrate itself within the social aspects of language. It will look briefly at how language styles specific to a range of news media have become stylized and have shifted over time to become the variety of practices they are today. The overall book will concentrate mainly on the language of newspapers as they have usually provided the template for the development of the language of news but it will also concern itself with exploring how other news media have adapted or altered this language to better match their own specific demands.

Language and society

Language is of a public nature. The self which we conveniently inhabit is to a large extent a social construct and it is constructed within a community of language. Our name, our gender, our ethnicity, our work, all identify us and they do this through a language which we hold in common with others in society. Because of its social nature, we can say that the language through which we make our way in the world, precedes us. Language has always been rooted in social activity. As well as communicating ideas and issuing instructions, it has the potential to signal the social positioning of speaker and listener or writer and reader. The very production of meaning itself in everyday life rests heavily upon linguistic activity (Montgomery, 1986: 42). Language is central to many debates in contemporary society and it is the medium in which those debates are embedded. This is of double significance for a practice such as journalism which reports upon and therefore records the world in which we live. The implications of this social positioning for the study of language is made clear in the following:

> language is a social practice which is one amongst many *social practices of representation and signification*. From this it follows that the study

of language is irreducibly dual, drawing on social and semiotic theories, theories of social forces and relationships, and theories of systems of representation and signification.

(Hodge and Kress, 1993: 202–203)

This study of the news therefore obliges us to consider the style and structure of its language as well as the social and historical networks in which it is located.

 Activity 1.1 o—

Consider the following list and discuss with a partner. In small groups, order the list according to how important you find each of the uses. Compose your own lists of the nine uses of language.

The nine uses of language

    i) to dissipate superfluous and obstructive nerve-force
   ii) for the direction of motion in others, both men and animals
  iii) for the communication of ideas
  iv) as a means of expression
   v) for purposes of record
  vi) to set matter in motion (magic)
 vii) as an instrument of thinking
viii) to give delight merely as sound
  ix) to provide an occupation for philologists

(Ogden and Richards, 1985: 46)

Discussion of the social nature of language is nothing new. In ancient Greece, the writings of Plato and Aristotle triggered intense debate between naturalist and conventionalist interpretations of language. Plato considered that words had originally had a natural relationship with the world they represented while Aristotle believed that words gained their meaning through the conventions of society over time. This debate ensured that the study of grammar and vocabulary developed momentum in learned society particularly with regard to whether language influenced society or whether society influenced language. Nowadays we would tend to conclude that it is a combination of both influences, depending on time and situation. One consequence of the heightened interest in language in ancient Greece was the rise of the Sophists who worked as language teachers and interpreters. As the Greek language spread geographically there was a need to be aware of the different linguistic customs and expressions, legal terminology and manners of polite address which were diversifying over this large expanse of the Greek-speaking world. The Sophists were widely travelled and as students of linguistic variety within Greek, they could help people to select the right words to have the right effect on the right occasion, fitting in with local language use and social conventions and customs. What they taught became known as rhetoric – the art of appropriate communication. This became an essential part of any-body's education who wanted to become active in either politics or the law.

In the contemporary world, we can build on the insights of the ancient Greek philosophers to consider the social implications of the language of news which is, at the same time, didactic and informational, teaching us about the world as well as our own socially constructed place in that world. Analysis of this language can move us beyond sophistry and towards an involvement which may enable us to become better informed actors in our social world, confirming the view that: 'consciousness is the first step towards emancipation' (Fairclough, 1989: 1).

As will become clear throughout this book, language does not merely reflect the world as it is, it interprets, organizes and classifies that world. It therefore embodies theories of how that world is arranged from an ideological perspective (Fowler, 1986: 27). Understanding that helps us to become more active par-ticipants in the world.

The news, in both its elite and popular forms, is extremely important in help-ing us to build up a normative view of the world and set parameters for how we interact with that world. This means that this language has an enormous influence on the ways in which we perceive the world in which we live. This has political implications beyond the narrow confines of party politics. Although this book will touch occasionally on traditional political topics, it will take the broader view that to analyse and to get inside the dynamics of this language is in itself implicitly a political act.

The title of this chapter signals an important element of the above approach. It will insist that in taking a linguistic view of journalism and its social and political roles, we are not subscribing to some form of conspiracy theory. On the contrary, we are claiming that in working with language as a shared social and cultural resource, we are part of a set of communicative patterns which exist outside ourselves as individuals. These patterns help to build a series of commu-nities. Language is part of the process by which we become social participants, understanding and integrating within the wider circle of these communities. We may claim that language is a manifestation of such social integration. This is a functionalist view of language: one which considers how language functions to integrate individual actors within a network of social experience. However, not everyone is happy with the state of society, particularly those who perceive its power relationships to be unjust or unequal. To them a functionalist view of language is merely proof of the attempts which some institutions make to exercise control of social reality through language. In the news media, which act as some of the most influential channels for the definition of reality, this control may not be overt, but it is exercised nevertheless in patterns, habits and structures which have become so commonplace that they no longer are automatically seen as contributing to processes of control but are seen as merely 'reflecting the world as it exists'. The systematic study of language allows us a fresh perspective on some of those patterns of linguistic behaviour and enables us to take a critical look at how the news pursues certain agendas which inevitably contribute to and occasionally challenge patterns of social and political inequality.

The development of newspaper language

The language of the news plays a major part in the construction of what Berger and Luckman have referred to as the 'social construction of reality' (1976). It assists in the creation of a set of public discourses through its selection of narratives and the language it employs to project them. Just as language is a socially constructed form of communication so too is news and its own varieties of language. Just as language continues to vary in its content and structure to adapt to the variety of social and cultural demands made upon it so too has the language of the news.

This language is produced as a set of conventions which carry traces of their historical development. The language of the first newspapers in the seventeenth century was a radical step towards the political involvement of a wider social circle, particularly the rising merchant class. The earliest newspapers gave these readers information, predominantly of the political and economic world which was addressed to them in the local language, the vernacular. This in itself was a departure from the tradition which had seen important communication channelled through the sacred language of Latin and thus restricted to an elite. One crucial factor in the early newspapers' language was their drive to provide factual and reliable information in order to distinguish them from other types of printed matter such as the more controversial broadsides and pamphlets. Lapses in this 'facticity' were what critics of newspapers held against the press, which meant that early newswriters endeavoured to be as accurate as the technologies and communications of the time would allow. Pecke's *Perfect Diurnall of some Passages in Parliament,* published from 1643 to 1649 at the height of the English Civil War, tried strenuously to avoid editorializing for fear of punishment and the diminished reputation of its content. It could be dull fare indeed:

> **Wednesday, March 8 [1647]**
>
> The house of Commons spent the whole time this day in reading and debating of private petitions. They had in debate the wrong sustained by a member of theirs whom rented by lease the Iron-mills in Monmouthshire given to Col. Massie which was referred to a Committee.
>
> They also considered of providing for Reformadoes and widdows of soldiers slain in the war of which there are thousands: They likewise sent a message to the Lords, that they would go on with proceedings against Judge Jenkins.

Newspapers began by assuming that their readership was reasonably homogeneous. This unifying vision helped the rise to power of a middle-class public sphere from the beginning of the eighteenth century across parts of Western Europe (Habermas, 1992). Nevertheless the world that the language of these early papers projected was a bourgeois and a male domain, and both women (McDowell, 1998) and the labouring classes (Harris and Lee, 1978) were excluded from it. Over time it developed a broader variety of register for specifically targeted readerships which came to include almost every social grouping. Their style of language evolved through history because of the constraints of time, space and market.

It is important to remember this great historical diversity in styles as we look at the variety on offer today. Keeble writes that there are 'many journalisms' (1998: 1) but despite this there are certain features which can be identified as forming part of what most people agree are the rudiments of contemporary news language and style. These rudiments have evolved over time because of the changing nature of technological and economic demands on the production of newspapers, and these in turn have made newspapers more dependent on tight, formulaic and stylistic conventions which have emerged as cost-effective solutions to the financial constraints on newspapers as they fight to retain a market share.

Throughout the eighteenth century, news often comprised the contents of letters received, conveying both opinion and information, and the language reflected the letter-writing style of the time:

> **WE HAVE a report here, but we hope without foundation, that his Majesty's frigate Minerva was not lost on the back of the Isle of Wight on Friday night last, when it really blew a hurricane.**

(*London Evening Post,* 31 December to 3 January 1764)

Newspapers depended on such reports for their own content, together with letters from readers to fill their pages. Communication and distribution technologies available at the time still meant that maintaining a regular flow of news was a problem. It meant that the language of the reports which were in regular supply could be more elaborate. Crime news reflected this sedate style as well:

> ON THURSDAY evening last, about nine o'clock, as Mr Henry Foot, of Durham-yard in the Strand, and Factor for the Scotch ships in the river, was going along Market-lane, St. James-market, a villain came behind him and knocked him down with a bludgeon, but some persons coming up, prevented him being robbed; he received a dangerous wound in his head near five inches in length, and still continues very ill.

(*London Evening Post*, 31 December to 3 January 1764)

Newspapers continued to present all forms of news in such language until a point where news was in such plentiful supply and the competition between profit-driven newspapers became so intense that the language became compacted to allow for the maximum coverage and often, particularly in the emergent mass market press, for maximum impact. Economic pressures have meant that the collection and presentation of news have developed to conform to a predetermined style which has increasingly foregrounded brevity and clarity. A central dynamic in this process was the regularity of the appearance of newspapers which increasingly moulded their language into a style which was best suited to the rapid reproduction of a view of the world and the events in it which was straightforward and easy to assimilate. Schudson (1978) has demonstrated, for instance, that the inverted triangle, summarizing the main points of a story at the beginning of a piece, was developed in the USA from the 1880s and marked journalism's shift from record to interpretation. It was largely determined by the technology of the telegraph and was characterized by a tendency for a more truncated and flattened style. This sort of newspaper language culminated in Britain in the New Journalism of the late 1880s which aimed in its language to hit the reader 'straight between the eyes' as T.P. O'Connor (1889: 434) put it memorably of his *Star*. A characteristic of this new discourse of news (Matheson, 2000) was the way that the reporting of facts and opinions, often from partisan perspectives within newspapers, became replaced by the central component of the story (Smith, 1978). With accelerating speed of information delivery and improving technologies of reproduction and distribution it literally paid to be brief, and so newspapers developed a series of patterns which allowed for their language to be composed in the main of short, condensed sentences which presented the news in the sharpest and at the same time liveliest manner. This style had been fully developed by the intense circulation wars of the 1930s in Britain and can be seen in this brief extract from the *Daily Express* which demonstrates the compact language and structure of the sensational, celebrity news values of the popular journalism of that era:

> ### WIDOWED BEAUTY SEEKS AIR SOLACE
> ### MRS HANSON MAY EXPLORE AMAZON
> ### FLYING LESSONS AFTER TRAGEDY
>
> **THE BEAUTIFUL and rich Mrs Ursula Hanson, twenty-one-year-old widow of the City magnate's son who died a tragic death in the Thames at Whitsun is taking to the air – to forget.**

(*Daily Express*, 7 August 1933)

Contemporary newspaper language

What distinguishes the style and content of newspaper language today? Newspapers are 'language-forming institutions' (Bell, 1994: 7) which means that their language informs and is influenced by broader linguistic trends. Much newspaper language is driven as never before by the economic imperative to retain its audience within a densely competitive news media environment. It has to work within an extremely visual popular culture as well as using the attributes of print to their best advantage. The language of other news media also share these challenges and it brings competition to bear on the newspapers themselves.

There are two consequences of these developments. First, newspapers often reduce the complexity of the world and, second, they often lack context because of constraints on space. They provide very much a model of the 'mosaic' culture described by McLuhan (1995). Their language conventions discourage the elaboration of the networks of meanings necessary for a rounded understanding of historical contexts, for example, and the nature of news narratives means that they move on before integration with wider implications can be explored. Peter Preston, himself an experienced newspaper editor, was warning against this reflex of newspaper narratives when he wrote in a recent article on the Madrid bombings: 'It's foolish to try to make instant sense out of senseless events' (*Guardian*, 15 March 2004).

Part of the development of the conventions of news language has been the division of the content of the newspaper into various, not always mutually compatible genres. These can be divided into two main categories. First, the hard news where overt opinion is in general repressed and which includes spot news and the reporting of the routines of politics and public life and, second, those genres such as specialist news, soft news, news features, opinion pieces and editorials where opinion is more or less foregrounded. Van Leeuwen has argued that it is possible that since the social purposes of journalism are contradictory, some being overt such as entertainment, factuality, impartiality and objectivity, while others are covert such as social control, ideological commitment and legitimation, they do not really mesh easily. He considers this is perhaps the reason why such a rich array of generic strategies has developed within the newspaper (van Leeuwen, 1987: 209). It is in the hard news where the 'facticity' (Tuchman, 1978) of the writing is most apparent. The general tendency to omit overt comment in the hard news makes the writing in these sections of the newspaper most institutionalized and closest to the house style of the paper in question (Cameron, 1996). Readers expect this sort of news to be factual, reliable, well-informed and without overt comment from the journalist: objective in the traditional sense. This does not mean that opinion cannot be transmitted in other, less overt ways. This is not to suggest that the production of hard news is a process of conspiratorial manipulation, merely that under pressures of time and within the constraints of tradition, certain patterns of belief are incorporated into even these styles of objective writing and that they vary from newspaper to newspaper in an identifiable fashion. The news values of individual newspapers, together with their approach to ideals such as objectivity, tell us as much about the aspirations of journalism as an institution as about any verifiable reality in the claims to objectivity themselves.

Within specialist sections of the newspaper, sports, fashion and entertainment for instance, there is more latitude for the language to show traces of opinion and even judgement of taste. The opinion pieces, often by prominent and professionally controversial columnists, exist to provoke reaction and response and to generate debate around issues close to the institutional core of the newspaper's own news values. The editorial tends to be the most institutional of opinions, since it is one of the last bastions of anonymity in newspapers. It is here where the newspaper pronounces its own position on what it considers the central political and cultural matters of the day.

In broadcast media the live interview is often the place where opinions are rehearsed or refuted, politicians probed or provoked by searching or sceptical interrogation such as John Humphrys on the *Today* programme on BBC Radio 4 or Jeremy Paxman on BBC 2's *Newsnight*. More populist news programmes, such as *Question Time* or even Five's *The Wright Stuff* or the US-based originator of much audience-based populist current affairs the *Oprah Winfrey Show*, involve the views and questions of the audience itself either in a studio or by e-mail, phone-in or text.

 Activity 1.2 o━ㅜ

List the most common genres within news. What sort of language is used in each of them? Give examples.

Newspapers as interpretative communities

Within the general range of linguistic styles of the news there is a differentiated social target. Each news medium has developed an ideal audience within the language which it uses. Each must look for an opportunity to present its own angle which ties in with a relatively stable identity and lexicon. The language style of each news medium is, in fact, an exercise in audience design (Bell, 1984: 145–204). This style is further differentiated by the division between the two main categories of newspaper, the tabloid and the broadsheet, and their parallels in the broadcast world. We need, however, to revise the categorization of these types of newspaper as ever more broadsheets have changed to a tabloid format while attempting to keep many of their traditional features. Maybe the terms 'elite' and 'popular' may be more accurate for what these still very different styles of newspaper are aiming at. Kitis and Milapedes (1997: 562) claim that the contrast resides in part between the 'neutral' language of the broadsheets and the 'emotionally charged language' of the tabloids. One represents a newspaper of record, the other, a primarily entertainment model. However they both produce ideological perspectives for their audiences. As we will see, any simplistic divisions between the language of these two sorts of newspaper can be misleading. This extract from the *Daily Telegraph*, for example, clearly displays the sort of loaded word selection which critics often assume only occurs in the popular press when dealing with hard news on the front page:

> ### Brown lifts ban on out-of-town stores
>
> **GORDON BROWN has sanctioned an assault on the countryside and the vitality of market town high streets by insisting that the ban on out-of-town shopping centres should be relaxed.**

(*Daily Telegraph*, 22 March 2004)

Social difference is embedded within our language and therefore inevitably within the language of our news media. Our use of language marks us as communal creatures, *homo loquens*, defined as much by our ability to speak as by the social nature of that activity. We belong to communities of media consumption through the distinctiveness of the language of those media. The communal nature of language means that it depends to a great extent on the power of convention. Individuals have difficulty in creating new words or challenging the conventions of language without a wider social acceptance of the changes they propose. We need largely shared understandings of what words mean if language and society are to function effectively. Certain areas of our life, such as the law and medicine and the vocabulary of traffic signs, depend on very precise, shared understandings of language. Misunderstandings can literally be a matter of life, loss of liberty or death. Such conventions do not however mean that everyone is content with the status quo in language and is happy to conform to contemporary practices. One of the most characteristic features of language is that it changes either by gradual social erosion or sedimentation. Language either gradually loses or gains changes in its meanings in social use and this is caused by the changing dialogue about meaning and the use of words, conducted across wide sections of society. Newspapers have always had a central role in such debates and Anderson, for instance, has commented on the material role of newspaper style in creating the 'imaginary communities' (1986) necessary for the birth of the modern nation-state as a continuing component of our contemporary world.

Newspapers have a clear idea of who their reader is. This must be represented in the style and register of language they employ, the stereotypes, both positive and negative which they contain which confirm the social and cultural perspectives of the reader, and the assumptions which are embedded in the truncated style of the newspaper and which have been referred to as 'scripts' (Hall, 1978). In the following headline: 'Police use curfew to control louts' (*Daily Telegraph*, 22 March 2004) the newspaper is employing a word, in this case 'louts' to signal a continuing position on youth crime in urban areas of Britain which makes sense as a form of shorthand within the accepted norms of the newspaper, without having to debate the matter in full. It assumes its readership, affluent and predominantly middle-aged, perceive sections of the younger population to be a threat to their own comfortable lifestyles and uses the loaded vocabulary to reinforce the newspaper's view of them and its support of the police in their attempts to deal with the perceived threat they pose.

All of these features contribute to the production of a textual version of the ideal reader. They are covered by the combination of house style and the distinctive news values of the individual newspaper. News values which represent an unwritten set of criteria which classify events in terms of the interests of the newspaper and its idealized reader are constructed very much in terms of social categories: 'The media do not simply and transparently report events which are "naturally" newsworthy *in themselves*. "News" is the end-product of a complex process which begins with a systematic sorting and selecting of events and topics according to a socially constructed set of categories' (Hall, 1978: 53). An extreme example of this idealization is encapsulated in the reported identification of the ideal *Sun* reader in the 1980s by its then editor, Kelvin MacKenzie: 'He's the bloke you see in the pub – a right old fascist, wants to send the wogs back, buy his poxy council house, he's afraid of the unions, afraid of the Russians, hates the queers and weirdoes and drug dealers' (Chippendale and Horrie, 1992: 148). There are many accounts of the *Sun* newspaper of that decade which claim to be able to identify the traces of that ideal reader in its content (Searle, 1989).

More than any other news media form, the newspaper has an explicitly normative role in how we see the world. Our news is our world to the extent that it contributes enormously to our understanding of what happens beyond our everyday experiences. Above the details of style, the very news contents of different newspapers (Harcup and O'Neill, 2001) are also contributory to differentiated readerships. They act to provide a set of parameters for selective 'interpretative communities' (Fish, 1994). The communication flow of the news is from an organizational top to a viewing/listening/reading base. This means that the views of the institutional and social hierarchy are well and truly embedded in the news values. The audience/readership is often represented statistically by producers of news as the reader/viewer/listener or in the massified data of opinion polls, viewing figures or the Audit Bureau of Circulation figures. It is part of the sophistication of their language that newspapers can embody these elite values while selling themselves to readers as if they embodied these readers' views of the world. This transaction takes place in a language which appeals to them, interpreting the social world in a slightly different and therefore economically viable way and creating categories of insiders and outsiders, our readers and their readers, 'Us' and 'Them'.

 Activity 1.3 o—r

Select two or three newspapers and look at how their combination of overt opinion, selection of particular types of story and emphasis within news stories differ to create a range of different ideal readers, distinct to each of them.

The interrelationship between the newspaper's writing and its typographical features, layout and pictures combine further to endorse an identifiable community of appeal. There is no conspiracy theory about what individual actors in the news process do. Their choices themselves are not necessarily ideologically significant. Yet the communities produced through these networks do tell us significant things about our society and its political orientations and priorities and they do this through the language which is selected and structured to fit with the institutional and social expectations of particular newspapers. The choice of language as well as its layout is always significant in this process.

Newspaper language content and structure

Before considering a range of critical views of the language of the news, it is important to outline and explore what constitute the accepted norms of this language. This section will provide a brief introduction to the conventions of the language of news reporting, from the headline and the inverted triangle to the concept of house style. While these conventions have a logical place within the processes of news gathering and reporting they do not come into existence naturally and they do have ideological implications attached to them. The concept of objectivity, for instance, is structured through particular language devices such as the esteem and reliability of sources, the conventional lack of the personal pronoun 'I' in news reporting, the lack of emotive vocabulary, particularly in the elite news, and the construction of stories from multiple viewpoints. Yet the selectivity which is employed to produce such language can be highly significant in what it prioritizes as significant and what it relegates from view.

Headlines

There has always been some form of headline summary of content in newspapers from earliest times but these have become more sophisticated over time in terms of technologies of layout and more stylized in their linguistic structure in order to maximize their impact on particular readerships. In the same way, there is also much use of headlines in mainstream television and radio news while on some Drive Time bulletins, CEEFAX news pages and text news alerts headlines are all you get. They are the lowest common denominator of the news, the entry portal.

The development of the headline was a central feature of the increasing marketization of newspapers. The first use of tiered headlines was during the USA's Mexican War in the nineteenth century. Here is a striking example of this innovation from the Baltimore *Sun* which combines exclamation marks, both double and single, a sensationalist, triumphalist tone, and the use of capitals as emphasis, all to focus the reader on a particular view of the war report which appears at the top of the next page.

Headlines have developed significantly since this. Yet, still, they serve three functions. First they provide a brief summary of the main news, second they attract attention and, third, they often provide an initial indicator in their content and style of the news values of the newspaper and are an important part of the way in which the newspaper appeals to its audience. This last feature is often apparent when the headline is used humorously as there is no better indicator of social targeting than humour. 'ROD'S NEW LEGGY BIRD – "Emu" spotted at rocker's mansion' (*Sun*, 22 March 2004) refers not as expected in the lexicon of the popular newspaper to Rod Stewart's girlfriend but literally to a bird, a long-legged cassowary, a sort of emu.

Glorious News from the Army

_____

The Campaign opened with Victory!!

_____

MATAMORAS REDUCED TO ASHES

_____

THE AMERICAN ARMY TRIUMPHANT!

_____

700 MEXICANS KILLED!

_____

One American only killed

_____

A General Blockade of the Mexican Ports Ordered

(The Baltimore *Sun*, 19 May 1846)

An Australian newspaper takes a quotation from a member of the public and turns it, without quotes, into a colloquial headline which attempts to use humour to focus the readership's attention on the predictability of the power supply problems in the middle of a heatwave. It has the additional attraction of directly chiming with the speech patterns of its readership and enhances the familiar bond between medium and audience:

Blind Freddy could have seen this coming

(*The Advertiser*, 23 January 2006)

In an American newspaper there is an example of wordplay which recalls in a light-hearted way how twelve Major League baseball players had tested positive for steroids. The light-heartedness builds upon the assumption that the readership targeted are already familiar with the story:

Players stay positive after the positive

(*USA Today*, 25 January 2006)

In the elite press, headlines can flatter the targeted readers' knowledge of literature or history, as in the following example from the *Independent*:

**Ravens, the literary birds of death,
come back to life in Britain**

(*Independent*, 23 January 2006)

This sort of elite referencing can also be deployed to signal key political debates to informed readers:

Senators in need of a spine

(*International Herald Tribune*, 27 January 2006)

Headlines are in themselves a distinctive contribution to the news values of a paper in the ways that their syntactic structure can give patterned evidence of stylistic preference. Consider the way in which the next two headlines combine the contrasting house styles and news values of their respective papers in the language they use. 'Hospital bug hits more children' (*Daily Telegraph*, 22 March 2004) which appears on page 4 of that newspaper is in direct contrast to 'NHS KILLER BUG SHOCK' (*Sun*, 22 March 2004) where the news is broken on the front page in large bold capital letters and plays knowingly on its own 'shock, horror' cliché to deliberate effect.

News actors tend to be placed first in headlines, and Bell (1994: 194) has identified the following as the most common: political figure, official/celebrity, sportsperson, professional or other public figure (e.g. lawyer), criminal or accused, human interest figure, participant (e.g. victim or witness).

Syntactically, stories involving these become condensed to descriptive noun phrases. These phrases are short sequences of words which briefly expand upon a noun where the description becomes a contributor to the 'scripts' of the newspapers, as in the following: Honest Taxpayers, Cancer experts, Soccer ace/star, Health bosses, Bungling cops, Married vicar, First-time buyers, Animal rights protesters, Race fans, America's East Coast millionaires, Persistent fine dodgers. The noun phrases act as a distillation of the news value of the actor to the newspaper in question.

Pressure on space means that newspapers have developed a particular form of language, especially in the headline and lead paragraph. Syntax and vocabulary are both compressed into an intense concentration of communicative form. There is a high reliance on puns, alliteration, reference to proverbs and inversions of popular sayings. Even though newspapers often claim to avoid cliché, they can be easily charged with referring to their own sets of language games and familiar phrases, as in this example of a story about a dog up a tree:

The extraordinary bough-wow determined to keep up with the cats

Jessie, the dog with a head for heights

HER OWNERS are convinced that she's completely barking. And it's certainly true that two-year-old Jessie is one unusual dog.

(*Daily Mail*, 22 March 2004)

Sometimes the humorous effect overrides the meaning as in the following example which on first reading and without further detail makes no sense at all and needs a reader to continue reading the piece (or in this case to key the appropriate number to access the fuller report) in order to understand the headline retrospectively:

BBC Ceefax 20 June 2005: 'Farmers in stew over potatoes'

 Activity 1.4 o⎯ᴛ

Study a newspaper and find evidence to demonstrate how the headlines:

- indicate the preferred meaning of the newspaper
- catch the attention
- give a snapshot of information
- establish/reinforce the reader's identity.

Headlines can also use clichés or commonplace expressions as a reference point for echoes of popular speech emphasizing the humorous element of the content of their stories, as in the case of a wrongly arrested man: 'TAKING THE NICK' (*Sun*, 22 March 2004). The news that a vicar is giving up his ministry to have a sex-change operation is heralded: 'MORE SHE VICAR?' (*Sun*, 22 March 2004).

An elite Sunday newspaper draws comparisons between accusations of institutional racism in both the police and the media by asking: '**So Plod's PC – but are we?**' (*Observer*, 29 January 2006).

 Activity 1.5 o⎯ᴛ

Osama's Greatest Hits

STILL THE DAILY MALE

WEST MUST BRACE ITSELF TO AVOID NIGHTMARE OF NUCLEAR IRAN

First baby for Virgin

Uppity Nats have a beef with the Libs

OUTRAGE

Nonsense in the nursery

Look at the examples above and decide which of them can be described in terms of the following: brevity, omission, exaggeration, humour (puns), strong vocabulary, homophones, word order, alliteration, rhyme. Once you have done this, find your own list of examples for each point.

Stories

As previously mentioned, the staple of newspaper language has become increasingly identifiable as the 'story' since the late nineteenth century. Bell has pointed out the implications for newspapers: 'Journalists do not write articles. They write stories. A story has structure, direction, point, viewpoint' (Bell, 1994: 147). The headline is the first indicator of the content and perspective of the story which follows.

Immediately after the headline comes the lead. The lead, in a news story, is the opening burst of language which summarizes the main story which follows. Leads are complex, linguistically and ideologically, but they are also brief. They succinctly and subtly condense the values and viewpoints of the newspaper.

EU rules to cost NHS work of 3,700 doctors

THE NHS is facing a crisis over medical cover because new EU rules restricting doctors' working hours, which come in this summer, will reduce the work of thousands of junior doctors.

(*Independent,* 22 March 2004)

In this example, the lead expands on the information contained in the headline. When contrasted with many British newspapers, the fact that the EU rules are here reported without negative adjectives is indication enough that the newspaper accepts the jurisdiction of the EU over working hours. Factually, the lead equates the work lost to a crisis, but emphasizes that junior doctors' workloads will be reduced. This in turn, by implication, fits into the broad professional acknowledgement that they work unacceptably long hours.

In the next extract the collective pronoun 'We' is made prominent in the headline, emphasizing the international imperative to combat terrorism. The headline does not mention who has told the representatives of the European Union. The speaker and the more precise details of his address are placed in the lead but the relegation of this information to the lead tends to emphasize collective responsibility.

We must fight terrorism together, EU told

Pressure for greater international co-operation against terrorists intensified last night after Britain's most senior policeman said the Madrid bombings should be a 'wake-up call' to the EU.

(*Daily Telegraph*, 22 March 2004)

Within newspapers, stories tend to follow a set pattern in their exposition and development, from the headline downwards. These follow the so-called 'news triangle' where the most important elements, those which are closest to the news values of that particular part of the newspaper, are presented first, and followed by information in a descending hierarchy of importance to the background material. The *Independent* with its well-publicized opposition to the war in Iraq foregrounds the criticism of Carter in the following story, using the word 'savages' to describe the criticism of both Blair and Bush. This is based on the interview conducted by the newspaper. The chronology which follows shifts from the initial contextualization of Carter as a 'former US president', the fact that he won the 2002 Nobel peace prize, the ambitions of Bush Snr, the opinion of Carter before the war started and his recently published novel. This chronology, unlike chronologies of other narratives, such as conventional novel or mainstream cinema narratives, is very much structured by an inverted pyramid which is determined by the political inclinations of the newspaper and its expectations of the views of its readers.

As with every other feature in the newspaper, the language has its history and its own implications. The language and layout of the newspaper are never simply 'as it is'. One of the consequences of the layout of hard news stories in this conventional pyramid form is that the contextual information is relegated to the end. This is not because that is where it belongs. It is because within the economic and cultural traditions of the newspaper this is how information is prioritized. Newspapers either tend to assume such background knowledge or they relegate

---

Carter savages Blair and Bush: 'Their war was based on lies'

Jimmy Carter, the former US president, has strongly criticised George Bush and Tony Blair for waging an unnecessary war to oust Saddam Hussein based on 'lies or misinterpretations'. The 2002 Nobel peace prize winner said Mr Blair had allowed his better judgement to be swayed by Mr Bush's desire to finish a war that his father had started.

In an interview with *The Independent* on the first anniversary of the American and British invasion of Iraq, Mr Carter, who was president from 1977 to 1981, said the two leaders probably knew that many of the claims being made about Saddam Hussein's weapons of mass destruction were based on imperfect intelligence. . . .

Before the war Mr Carter made clear his opposition to a unilateral attack and said the US did not have the authority to create a 'Pax Americana'. . . .

Mr Carter, 79, has recently published a novel. *The Hornet's Nest* is centred on America's revolutionary war against the British. That period had many lessons for the present day, Mr Carter said.

(*Independent*, 22 March 2004)

it to a subordinate position, the better to concentrate on the shifting focus of public curiosity. There is one striking difference in the newspaper version of the story which is highlighted by Bell and which makes is quite distinct from other narrative forms in our culture: 'The complex time structure – so at odds with the chronological norms of other types of narratives – is a consequence of news obeying news values rather than other narrative norms' (Bell, 1994: 172).

Objectivity

Despite their long reliance on a factual reporting style, as we have seen, newspapers are relatively new to the concept of objectivity as a professional ideal. Eighteenth-century and nineteenth-century newspapers were notorious for their overt support for the political and commercial positions and interests which often subsidized them for that support. Sustained economic success which meant that they did not need to curry direct political favour came relatively late – towards the end of the nineteenth century. This meant that it was only at the start of the twentieth century that newspapers began to consistently adhere to a certain common perception of objectivity as a means of promoting their own professionalism and political independence.

Within the areas of hard news reporting, elite newspapers still maintain a stance of objectivity and, in keeping with the shape of broadcasting conventions, try to avoid the intrusion of editorializing. However, within the routines of source selection and the hierarchy of credibility in witnesses and respondents there is clearly an institutional set of preferences at work. Which story leads? How are the protagonists selected and represented? These are questions which determine the perspective of the newspaper on the relative importance of news issues and actors. One of the chief conventions which signal this approach is that of attribution, which is where the journalist gives the source of the story and implicitly claims authority for the story by referring to this source. This means that despite the fact that an individual journalist does not refer to himself/herself as 'I' in the story and despite the absence of overt commentary, the newspaper has in its selection of the story and the sources used, already provided a viewpoint which is not in any way purely objective. It has been subject to a prior process of selection to match the viewpoint of the newspaper in question. Objectivity is merely an institutional preference. The attribution of sources and the description/titles of the actors in the news both locate and legitimize the values of the newspaper in terms of their selecting of who has something of significance to contribute to public debate. Despite the fact that these belong to established patterns, they can nevertheless carry ideological significance. The conservative *Daily Telegraph* would highlight an alleged split within the cabinet although there is nothing more substantial to attribute than the leak of letters by 'senior ministers' as it serves the paper's own anti-Government agenda and highlights splits, reporting them as factual despite the grey shade of the evidence.

> ## Cabinet is split over new Bill for ID cards
>
> **A new Cabinet split over David Blunkett's drive to introduce compulsory identification cards was exposed yesterday with the leak of letters from senior ministers opposed to the plan.**

(*Daily Telegraph*, 22 March 2004)

> ## Call to ban children from using sunbeds
>
> **Children should be prevented from using sunbeds because of the risks of cancer, health campaigners and industry representatives said yesterday.**

(*Daily Telegraph*, 22 March 2004)

In the example above, the claim of the headline is softened from 'ban' to 'prevent' in the lead paragraph, illustrating a shift in emphasis even within a hard news piece, and the implicit opinion of 'should' is mapped onto the attributed groups.

The traditional if limited commitment to objectivity in the newspaper within one area of its operation is counter-balanced by its overt proselytizing in other areas of its output, such as its commentary and leading articles, opinion pieces and features. This is a further constraint on the objectivity in its hard news.

There is a continuing expectation that despite its sensationalist tendencies which demand that news stories are presented in the liveliest manner appropriate to the particular newspaper, the press is still expected to separate facts from opinion and to report unambiguously and without deliberate distortion in its hard news coverage. Yet under pressure from economic competition from other news media markets and in order to provide a contrast to the bastion of public service ideals and ethics within the style and content of broadcasting news, the newspapers have been increasingly forced into areas where they can compete on different terms of emphasis. 'Newspapers need to "take it further" than T.V. and radio. They need to go beyond the neutral and objective rituals of balance' (Tunstall, 1996: 197–8). There has been consequently an increasing slippage even within hard news as newspapers vie with their language to present a viewpoint that distinguishes them as news media in an era which threatens a bland convergence.

Summary

This chapter has provided an introduction to many of the basic themes of this book. It has established that language is a social phenomenon and that news media work astutely within an understanding of this fact. It has also provided an initial overview of certain of the conventions within newspaper language so that subsequent chapters can engage with analysis in the knowledge of these conventions of style and structure and apply them where appropriate to other news media. Language can then be considered as the site for critical interpretation as a process of active involvement in the worlds that news media interpret and in which they invite us to participate. It is important at all points to remember that the language of the news is not an obligatory sequence but rather a network of choices which are restricted because of the conventions of the institution (van Leeuwen, 1987: 207).

News consists of a set of conventions which create communities of readers through their use of language. The main reason that this has emerged historically is economic. It enables newspapers to identify and sell to a relatively stable readership. However, the choices made within the varieties of newspaper language can also carry meanings which go beyond the purely economic and create communities of belief and opinion with wider ideological implications. It is to these that our analysis will now turn.

Both producers and consumers of journalism are aware of the speed at which the contemporary news environment is formed, digested and changes. This speed risks relegating understanding of language to a blur of superficiality. Analytical practice enables us all to appreciate what is lost if these processes become too fast. It allows us to slow that process down and unpick the ways in which our news is constructed so that we may be able to better appreciate the importance of paying attention to the content of our news media in general. Newspapers are a good place to start this renewal of close reading. We cannot always afford the time but such practice makes us at least more aware of the central role of language and how it can be manipulated and challenged within the functions of the news.

Suggestions for further reading

Conboy, M. (2004) *Journalism: A Critical History*. London: Sage.

Fowler, R. (1991) *Language in the News*. London: Routledge.

Galtung, J. and Ruge, M. (1973) 'Structuring and selecting news'. In S. Cohen and J. Young (eds) *The Manufacture of News: Social Problems, Deviance and the Mass Media*. London: Constable.

Harcup, T. (2003) *Journalism: Principles and Practice*. London: Sage.

Keeble, R. (1998) *The Newspapers Handbook*. London: Routledge.

McDowell, P. (1998) *The Women of Grub Street*. Oxford: Oxford University Press.

Matheson, D. (2000) 'The birth of news discourse: changes in news language in British newspapers, 1880–1930', *Media, Culture and Society* Vol. 22, Number 5.

2 Analytical tools (1)

- Introduction
- Critical linguistics
- The role of the critical reader
- The linguistic turn
- Language and classification
- News values
- Categorization
- The coding of point of view and social values
- Lexical mapping
- Metaphor
- Register
- Narrative
- Campaigns
- Summary
- Suggestions for further reading

Introduction

Even though the language of journalism claims professional and even legal levels of accuracy, fairness and factuality, the process of making the news involves selection and choice which inevitably influence the end product in one way or another. This chapter will provide a brief introduction to an approach to the language of the news known as critical linguistics. This close and analytical reading of the news can reveal regular patternings of language which can be said to represent the dominant social and political positions of the various news media. These patterns are structured according to the ideological assumptions of the news media and these are assumptions which they project onto their readers and expect them to share.

Critical linguistics

Critical linguistics has developed through the work of a variety of academics who have worked closely with the language of the news media, such as Fairclough, Fowler, Hall, Hodge and Kress, Trew, Wodak and van Dijk, among others. It assists critical readers to identify patterns within language which legitimate or naturalize the dominant social order. It seeks to draw attention to the ways in which language is used across news media to create the conditions in which the conventional hierarchies of society are reproduced tacitly and without drawing too much attention to this process of reproduction. Critical linguistics considers language to be one of the main tools of analysis through which knowledge can be gained of the dominant structures of belief within a society at any particular time and place. By studying these patterns of language we can chart the relationship between dominant and subordinate groupings and the strategies which make such representations acceptable to the general public as 'normal'.

The dominant ideas and viewpoints in any society tend to be the ideas and viewpoints of those who have direct political or economic control of that society. The news media, owned as they are by members of those political or economic elites, unsurprisingly reproduce the views of these dominant classes. The language of the news media therefore not only creates a version of the mainstream but it also acts to reinforce and naturalize the categories of people who are deemed outsiders. This process of representation is not a static one, and the news media need to be able to adapt to changing historical or political circumstances. A good example of this was the shift of Murdoch's *Sun* newspaper to overt support for the Labour Party shortly before the 1997 General Election when it had been resolutely Conservative throughout the preceding period. Nor is the process uniform. There are differences within and between news media, dissent from news producers and journalists, and critical voices within the political establishment, which all make the maintenance of the dominant ideas a complex and dynamic one. The news media are demonstrably strong on holding individual politicians and political parties in general to account for their actions and decisions. However, they are less keen to probe the functioning of the political system in general and are generally silent on other key social and economic players such as businessmen, industrialists, entrepreneurs or owners of the news media themselves. Such imbalance in the representation of the activities of such key figures inevitably presents a largely uncritical picture of economic players as opposed to an overwhelmingly negative picture of politicians.

The role of the critical reader

Critical linguistics stresses the active role of the critical reader. In doing so it offers us a welcome antidote to some popular assertions that the news media encourage a predominantly passive and apathetic audience. This chapter will briefly introduce certain linguistic strategies which can be used to analyse the language of the news. It will attempt to show how this language works by giving real examples from the contemporary news media. Once these strategies have been explained and illustrated by reference to news texts, they will then be further drawn upon in subsequent chapters to provide more detailed analysis and further opportunities for students to engage in critical analysis of their own on specific topics. This critical study can thereby provide a form of social and political involvement for an active reader in the analysis of the language of the news: the reader can in this way become more of a questioning, investigating and illuminating participant in the reception of the news.

It is fundamental to this sort of analysis that the language which represents these social hierarchies is rooted in time and place. This means that the language of our news media tells us not only about the world in which we live but much more specifically about the national space which we inhabit and the very contemporary nature of this. The language of the news is not only a means of indicating to an audience its place in the social order of things, it does so as part of a process of national identification, and in doing so goes a long way towards shaping our relationship with the contemporary world from a national standpoint.

The linguistic turn

We live in a period which continues to be dominated by language despite the ever-presence of visual imagery. In fact, the advent of the internet has brought an increased amount of written information onto screens which had hitherto been monopolized by images. In television, news bulletins, where the spoken voice and the image were once dominant, are now much more regularly accompanied by written language, influenced as they are by online news formats. An awareness of the centrality of language to all aspects of human behaviour and social interaction has led to the coining of the term 'the linguistic turn' to describe this modern era. It has seen most parts of human behaviour, such as psychoanalysis and anthropology, being analysed in terms of communication processes, predominantly language. This process has seen various disciplines borrowing terms from language study in order to enable them to better explain themselves. Architecture refers to 'vernacular building styles', psychoanalysis to the 'unconscious being structured like a language', film to the 'grammar of a director' and fine art to the 'vocabulary of a painter'. Critical linguistic approaches to the news media have developed as part of this overall tendency.

Language and classification

This chapter has asserted that the language of the news reinforces the way things are. It can be added that this status quo can only be understood in terms of social hierarchies. News media are directed towards particular groups of people, whether on the basis of their nationality, social standing or educational attainment. The first imperative for any news organization is to categorize which people and which events are of interest for their particular audience. Compare the following brief examples from 27 January 2006:

Hamas victory in Palestinian vote stuns Mideast

More bad Detroit news

Both of these headlines appeared on the front page of the *International Herald Tribune* and clearly appeal to an international audience articulated from an American perspective in the expectation that a blend of international news from the key area of American foreign policy in the Middle East and a story of national significance about job losses in the motor industry back home would strike the balance for its global audience.

In contrast, on the same day the best-selling British tabloid, the *Sun*, had these three stories on its front page:

HANS UP!

German cops over here to nick World Cup thugs

THE BBIG SHOWDOWN

PARKER BOWLES IN A BIKINI

This contrast shows that their audience are not only located in different countries; the social expectations of the two newspapers are so different that their readers could quite possibly be said to inhabit two different worlds. The puns in the language of the popular tabloid demonstrate a difference of appeal between formal and informal English that reinforces the different cultural references which make up the front page; international politics and industrial coverage against show business, football and stories about the British Royal Family. To reinforce its self-awareness of its own particular diet of news classification, the *Sun* continues on its inside page:

Paper that makes the news

Scoop after scoop! Sensation after sensation! That's what you get day after day from your fantastic Sun. . . . The Sun always has the BIG exclusives. The Sun always has the BEST headlines. The Sun is the paper that you dare not miss . . . and you cannot put down.

(*Sun*, 27 January 2006)

 Activity 2.1 ⚷

Identify the differences in the categorization of people and events which are considered newsworthy depending on the political and social agendas of the different newspapers and the social expectations of their readers.

It is often claimed that news media, particularly newspapers, the only exclusively commercial news media, are mainly in the business of delivering consumers to advertisers. The history of successful newspapers independent from formal political influence can be mapped onto the increasing financial independence of the newspapers from the middle of the nineteenth century onwards, a trend which was made possible within the political economy of the era by the ability of newspapers to attract increasing amounts of revenue through advertising. The revenue from advertising was not only used to increase the profitability of newspapers as part of wider publishing companies, it was also used to bring down the price of the newspaper and therefore enable a wider audience to buy them. This advertising needed to be targeted to the income of the audience. The consequence of this was that different newspapers evolved which carried differing forms of advertising, appealing to different income groups. The language of many of these news media is reinforced by advertising which makes a further contribution to the understanding of media audience in terms of social and economic ranking.

 Activity 2.2 ⊶

Look at the differences in advertising in various newspapers. Are there ways in which the advertising matches the language of the newspaper overall and its projected social readership?

Despite concerns that there is a process of tabloidization or dumbing down at work there remains a 'unity of tone' (Engel, 1996) across each of our news media which continues to identify them as targeted towards distinct social audiences. No news medium, no matter how superficially similar the format, shifts easily from the raucous, punning vulgarity of the *Sun* (see below) to the high-brow critical reviews of the *Independent*.

> **ENGLAND soccer coach Sven Goran Eriksson looks as if he has been kicked in the goalies yesterday as he talks about his exit from the job.**

(*Sun*, 25 January 2006, front page and accompanying picture)

The categorization of issues which are selected to form the main news agenda of particular newspapers and the language which matches that categorization can also be seen in the elite British newspaper the *Independent* when choosing to highlight on its front page a particular approach to the debate about the reintroduction of nuclear energy in Britain:

DANGER

Nuclear Waste

BRITAIN has 2.3 million cubic metres of nuclear waste stored around the country – more than enough to fill the Albert Hall five times. Exposure to even a tiny amount of the most potent type could kill an adult within two minutes – and it remains lethal for one million years. It will cost £85 billion to bury all this radioactive rubbish – but our governments have dodged the decision of where to put it for 30 years. As Tony Blair takes the first steps towards building ten new nuclear reactors to plug the looming energy gap, shouldn't we clear up this mess first?

(*Independent*, 24 January 2006)

We can see this unity of tone across different sections of a newspaper or news broadcast. The language and all that contributes to the 'tone' in terms of register and style are all dependent upon an understanding of a relatively stable audience that is articulated in terms of social hierarchy. There may be exceptions in the identities of individual readers but there are few in terms of the structure of the language. This extends to the inclusion of elements of humour in the pages of both popular and elite newspapers. Take for example the 2006 case of the Liberal Democrat MP Mark Oaten, involved in a sex scandal. It was covered in both the *Sun* and the *Independent* but whereas the *Sun* takes a smutty line and refers to the case moralistically, listing names of other MPs who have had their careers wrecked by sexual scandal, the *Independent* chooses, in an opinion column, to dwell, also in the form of humour, on the hypocrisies at work in the world of politics. The *Sun* categorizes Oaten in the characteristic form of a compressed noun phrase 'rent boy shame MP' and alludes to the sexual orientation of the MP in question when it claims that his colleagues are 'BEHIND YOU' in a blend of innuendo and pantomime echo.

Lib Dems tell rent boy shame MP:

WE'RE RIGHT BEHIND YOU

(*Sun*, 23 January 2006)

This is followed by the use of a word 'naughty' in 'THE LONG LIST OF NAUGHTY MPs', which despite the hyperbole of coverage of Oaten's disgrace seems to be trivializing the sexual misadventures of a list of MPs at the same time as forming part of its bathetic appeal.

> IN THE 1920s, when homosexual sodomy could still be punished by life imprisonment, a male prostitute was convicted of the offence. The judge, a rigid puritan, found the whole affair revolting, and decided to take advice to see how severe he could be. He sought out the Lord Chancellor, F E Smith: "My Lord, My Lord, what would you give a man who allowed himself to be buggered?" "Oh, I don't know: 30 bob, two quid, whatever you have on you."
>
> I don't suppose that they are telling many jokes in the Oaten household today.

(Bruce Anderson, *Independent*, 23 January 2006)

News values

One of the ways in which we can identify the social targeting of news is in the news values of a particular newspaper or broadcast. Few events in the world are inevitably news items for every news organization. Even those which are, such as natural disasters and wars involving prominent nations, have different priorities within different news institutions. There are always processes of choice and prioritization in the language selected to represent them to specific audiences. The exploration of these patterns can tell us a great deal about the social and political positioning of the news media. News values already embody a set of categorizations about how the world works and which beliefs structure it. The language of the news fits into these existing frameworks unproblematically. We might consider the way in which a particular newspaper or broadcast places and gives priority to particular stories. This prioritization indicates what the news medium considers of most importance for its audience. In general terms, there is more political news, more economic analysis and more overseas news in the elite press and public service broadcasting and more celebrity news, sport and scandal in the popular varieties of print and broadcast media. There is also a contrast on the whole between the difference in coverage of issues between elite and popular newspapers and the similarities in most forms of mainstream broadcast news. Broadcasting regulations circumscribe to a large extent what tone of language is used and what balance there needs to be in the composition of mainstream news programming on radio and television. Truly popular styles of broadcast are found in programmes away from the traditional news bulletin genre in daytime television and talk radio. Such differences are also often located in the language which the different media use.

Categorization

The first and most obvious ways in which we can observe significant choice at work in the language of the news is in the selection of events and people who are considered worthy of coverage, and how what they say or do is valued. Who gets to speak? How are news agendas structured through categorization? How does the structure of news and running order of broadcasts create hierarchies of meaning and interpretation? Who is the protagonist, the dominant actor in the theme of a story? Who is the first mentioned? Who is given more space? Whose opinions are valued? Who are given more direct and privileged access to the communicative channels of news media? Who are presented as the reliable commentators who reproduce a consensual view of the world as the powerful wish to see it, and how do the news media represent this view to their audience?

 Activity 2.3 ⊶

Compare one television bulletin and one newspaper of the same day. How is the order of the news structured? What is given most prominence? Which speakers are given most priority? What conclusions can you draw about the different news values and priorities of the particular newspaper and broadcast bulletin on that day?

The language of the elite news media represents politics through the prism of the institutions of political representation and through expert political commentators which is a process that tends to close politics down to the parliamentary debate and to sideline more local and unpredictable involvement in politics. In this they use a set of formal conventions as to who speaks and who is interviewed, and what constitutes the parameters of acceptable commentary. Politics is often represented as merely a clash of personalities within the media, even in the elite press.

> **Blair agrees Tory terms for pact on education**
>
> TONY BLAIR seized an offer of support from David Cameron on education reform yesterday in an attempt to avoid a messy compromise with Labour MPs opposed to new trust schools.
>   Mr Blair accepted the Conservative leader's conditions for backing his scheme, pledging not to water down plans for self-governing trusts.

(*Times*, 26 January 2006)

This personalization of politics is reinforced on the same page by a comic sketch of the same story using an extended metaphor of a circus act. Their proximity serves to further undermine the authority of the politicians involved and to add to the flavour of personalization.

Roll up, roll up for the amazing Tone 'n' Dave show

Parliamentary sketch

TONY BLAIR seems serious about this highwire act. He was such a show-off yesterday that he must be practising at home. It really is only a matter of time before he comes to PMQs in his leotard (make no doubt that he has one, for all acrobats do) and starts chalking up his hands.

The big news is that he has a sidekick. Incredibly it is David Cameron. Yesterday the two of them flew through the air with the greatest of ease. Labour MPs watched from the cheap seats with faces of stone.

Tone 'n' Dave are becoming a great double act. They spark off each other and even laugh at each other's jokes.

There are already suspicions that Tone is grooming Dave to take over his act. He would deny this, but actions speak louder than words. Yesterday we could all see that they were flirting like mad . . .

(*Times*, 26 January 2006)

In the elite press there tends to be a much more defined split between the reporting of politics and commentary on it, even when it comes on the same page as in the above example, whereas in the popular press the two are often conflated, and language is regularly used to effect this within the same article where report and opinion are blurred and underlining and capitalization are used emphatically to hammer home what the newspaper considers to be the key facts of the case.

Prescott big bully

One in ten workers in John Prescott's department say they have been BULLIED at work it was revealed yesterday.

(*Sun*, 27 January 2006)

Increasingly, on mainstream television bulletins, in an attempt to liven up political discussion, the reporter is used to complement the anchor's story by lively commentary, personalized yet informed opinion and a sprinkling of restrained wordplay and even humour. It is said that this was pioneered at the BBC by Andrew Marr as political editor and continues now across all British public service news bulletins to a large extent.

 Activity 2.4 o—r

Watch an evening television bulletin. How does the news reporter emphasize the story? How does he/she respond to the anchor's questions from the studio? Are there visual effects which are used to emphasize the report? Does the anchor ask for an opinion from the reporter and if so, how is it delivered?

All news media categorize on the basis of certain well-defined categories of news value. These have been analysed by Galtung and Ruge (1973) and more recently by Harcup and O'Neill (2001). Of particular interest to us is how these news values can be distinguished as an important part of the linguistic identity and the social coding of the news medium in question. The meaningfulness of a story, for instance, can only be assessed in terms of a clear understanding of what social audience it is aimed at. It must have a cultural proximity to its readers and to their lifestyle and of course be couched in a language which reinforces that proximity. Next, there is the expectation that the news values will match the expectations of what constitutes the national interests of its readers and how these are articulated. For all news media, located nationally as they are, this is the most important characteristic of the identity of the news. Britain is the elite nation which determines the newsworthiness of stories which would by any other criteria be rather uninteresting. The protagonists in these stories are sometimes abbreviated to 'Brits':

BRIT'S WIFE AND BABY SHOT DEAD

COPS are hunting a British Dad after his wife and baby daughter were found murdered.

(*Sun*, 25 January 2006)

5,000 Brits face Taliban

More than five thousand British troops are to wage war against the Taliban and Al-Qaeda in Afghanistan, the Government said yesterday. Specially trained Paras will lead the £1 billion two-year operation in response to a resurgence of Taliban and terrorist militancy in the lawless Helmland Province.

The past year has been the deadliest in Afghanistan since US-led forces ousted the Taliban government in 2001. Ninety two US personnel died in the country last year alone.

(*Daily Mirror*, 27 January 2006)

The second story here indicates that beyond the story of the predominant elite nation, Britain for British readers, there is a second set of nations which are considered to share elite status with Britain. In this case, the nation is the USA and it is the casualties of that nation which are emphasized in this story and which have a direct significance for the targeted readership as these are allies of the British. It is significant that the numbers of enemy casualties is not referred to in such stories and even when they are, they are not aggregated over the time of the conflict.

Within this national framework there is an expectation that the news values will match a notional list of elite characters who differ to an extent between elite and popular media.

Two Britons die in frozen waterfall climb

(*Times*, 23 January 2006)

Celebrities recognizable to a specifically national readership are often foregrounded on the front page of popular tabloids:

KATE: I WILL FACE POLICE

My Corrie hell after boss said: You're axed
JANICE BATTERSBY EXCLUSIVE

IS YOUR DIET KILLING YOU?

DR GILLIAN McKEITH JOINS THE MIRROR

(all on front page, *Daily Mirror*, 23 January 2006)

With regard to celebrity news, it is often in the language of the report as much as in its relative prominence where the difference can be seen between elite and popular. Negativity, the old maxim that bad news is good news, or the reversal of normal expectations in patterns of behaviour such as in the 'Man Bites Dog' reversal are also framed in language which portrays the political and cultural expectations of particular audiences. Certain newspapers will treat a story as negative because it plays to a particular aspect of the social expectations of its core readership and this helps to reinforce the classification process.

For a different readership, Conservative leaning, hostile on principle to Labour, an elite anti-hero in the person of Ruth Kelly, a close political ally of Blair, in combination with the revelation of her family connections to an IRA member is clearly something which has a high priority:

> ### Ruth Kelly's grandfather was interned IRA quartermaster
>
> THE grandfather of Ruth Kelly, the embattled Education Secretary, was an IRA officer who was interned by the Northern Ireland Government 80 years ago on a notorious prison ship during a terror campaign in the fledgling state.

(*Times*, 23 January 2006)

The language of the news therefore helps in the processes which frame and classify the events and people who are selected as newsworthy, and in what terms they are described. It is used to emphasize and give value to the stories which serve to construct a particular worldview based on the cultural, political and national expectations which the news media embed in their stories for a particular and well-designed audience.

 Activity 2.5 o—r

Who are the people that particular newspapers favour and disapprove of? How can we identify this in terms of language used, especially adjectives which indicate favour or rejection, and the proximity of particular characters to the political or cultural positions of individual newspapers?

Activity 2.6 o—▼

Select a quality newspaper, a popular newspaper and any mainstream radio or television news programme and compare and contrast how their differing sets of news values are represented in the stories which they run on an average day.

News is a process of selection in which events are prioritized according to a range of socially organized categories. This process is one which already tells us a great deal about the political positioning and the belief systems in specific news media. The news values which structure selection are based on assumptions about the world, who and what is important in it and for which particular media audience they hold this interest. The maintenance of those categories of newsworthiness or even the pace and direction of change in them is a matter of social and political preference. A newspaper such as the *Daily Mail* has a traditional, conservative perspective across its pages whereas a newspaper such as the *Independent* has been a constant opponent of the war in Iraq. Certain items and characters remain stable over a period of time. We can see an uncritical appreciation of the Second World War as a constant touchstone of national meaning across nearly all British newspapers and this seeps into other coverage of national military memorials such as D-Day or Trafalgar Day. Other values shift on a more regular basis, such as in the case of celebrities who are favoured one month and then demonized once a scandal story can be unearthed. In the popular press this can often be seen in the shuttling from back page to front page of celebrities such as sports players as their sporting prowess is succeeded by fleeting notoriety, and then back to the back pages again once the hue and cry have died down. Both shifts and stability must retain a coherence with the targeted audience and be able to place themselves within the preferences of the particular news medium.

The coding of point of view and social values

Each newspaper, in a competitive market, produces its own set of viewpoints which remain fairly constant. This forms part of a marketing strategy to enable the newspaper to appeal to a stable community of readers who get what they expect from their chosen medium. A newspaper like the *Daily Mirror* with a strong connection to Labour politics can be seen in the following extract to be emphasizing the legacy of the years of Conservative Party dominance in British politics in its treatment of contemporary Britain. The opening claim sets the scene as it brings the reader into a collective community and highlights the identity of this community as a national one. The perennial theme of troubled teenagers is given an emphasis which is specific to the expectations the newspaper has of its readers' politics, and editorially points the blame. The news value is highlighted from the opening words as referring specifically to the interest in the readers' own nation and is therefore of the highest priority. The collective pronoun 'we' draws the readership into an assumed identity of interest with both nation and social perspective which the community is presumed to share.

> As a nation, we are finally reaping what we sowed in the '80s. This is the legacy which Thatcherism has bequeathed . . . An underclass dislocated economically by the greed and materialism of the '80s has taken gross self-interest to its ultimate, ugly conclusion – social isolation and breakdown . . . Thatcher's monstrous children . . . Hoodies and ASBO teenagers are a menace.

(*Daily Mirror*, 3 June 2005)

Lexical mapping

After the facts of selection and prioritization embodied within news values, we move to a lower textual level, that of the words used. Choice is manifest in the language of the news in the variety of vocabulary used to present various stories across the media. Each news medium has an almost infinite choice of words and combinations of words which it might use in order to present a story to its audience. The nouns, adjectives and verbs used in conjunction with the main protagonists and themes of the day play a significant part in reinforcing the initial classification and structuring of the news and direct it towards a clear idea of audience. The dominant, preferred vocabulary sidelines other potential readings of a story. In addition, what is left out or marginalized can be just as important for analysis as that which appears in the main body of the news report. In order to begin to assess how vocabulary might demonstrate a set of prioritizations in the news media we need to be aware of the difference between denotation and connotation. Denotation is the literal meaning of a word in its usual setting and one which is acceptable to the readership of a particular newspaper.

We also need to be able to locate vocabulary within a broader semantic field. This is where connotation comes into play. Connotation is the set of expectations and associations which become attached to a word over time within a particular culture which may be either positive or negative. This aspect of a word's meaning goes beyond the literal and into the dimension of symbolic association. Different newspapers, because of their differing takes on the world will develop slightly different ranges of connotation around certain vocabulary so that the readership will understand aspects of the news differently, depending on the development of connotation over time.

Puns (wordplay) can be a significant factor in creating an impression through language. They are usually deployed for humorous effect and the aspects of the news which are depicted in such a light can reveal much about how the newspaper approaches particular issues. The *Sun* for instance signals its opposition to a decision to allow German police to come to Britain to prevent hooligans from travelling to the World Cup in Germany:

NEIN, NEIN, NEIN

(Sun, 27 January 2006)

The death of a whale on the Thames is reported as:

On squid row

Experts reveal Whaley died hunting for deep water food

(Daily Mirror, 26 January 2006)

A diplomatic argument over the activities of British agents in Moscow using hi-tech stones as bugging devices plays on popular knowledge of that most famous fictional British spy 007:

SPY SCANDAL

RUBBLE-O-SEVEN

(Daily Mirror, 24 January 2006)

Yet there are certain stories which are considered too serious in certain newspapers for comical wordplay, and broadcast journalism tends to avoid it altogether because of its commitment to a more considered perspective.

It is however not sufficient to simply compile a list of words in order to fully explore the impact of the lexical elements of a news medium. First, we need to acknowledge that the words form part of a pattern of connections which are important in establishing a news medium's priorities and news values. They are woven together into a coherent agenda by linkage with political preference, the views of dominant communities, celebrities, spokespeople from inside or outside the establishment. This is called lexical cohesion.

Cohesion distinguishes audience-directed news from a random set of sentences. It refers not only to the way that sentences or individual words fit together into one whole package but also to the ability of extended texts to fit into a consistent worldview and longer narratives of social belonging and identification. Lexical cohesion explains how vocabulary forms part of a broader set of categories which are important in establishing news values. Let us return to the *Daily Mirror* and its story of the youth of today, in itself a potentially clichéd topic for a news story. Yet the following extract uses a range of words which fit together both across the article and across the political opinions of the paper to construct a particular viewpoint on behalf of its readers. It builds a sense of lexical cohesion throughout the article by the patterning of words chosen to depict the young people in the form of nouns – 'sociopaths', 'hoodies', 'monsters', adjectives 'feral', 'menacing', 'terrifying' and verbs 'haunting', 'hang around', 'blight'. All of this culminates in the antithesis of this lexical portrait of moral decline on a national scale; the community threatened by these young people is 'Britain's law-abiding citizens'.

Children without a soul

. . . the underclass of young sociopaths haunting Britain today. . . . feral youngsters. . . . Look into their eyes and you see something more terrifying than anger, hatred or evil. You see nothing . . . they are the menacing 'hoodies' who hang around street corners. . . . We've bred a generation of monsters who blight the lives of Britain's hard-working, law abiding citizens.

(*Daily Mirror*, 3 June 2005)

 Activity 2.7 ⊶

Explore a number of stories across a particular newspaper. Choose one topic covered in two newspapers over a week. You can list words used in various reports over a week to map differences and similarities between various news media. Concentrate particularly on adjectives used to describe the main actors in the news to see how a lexical cohesion is built around a particular issue such as young people.

Categorization within news values is a multi-layered feature of news. At the most basic level we have the selection of vocabulary which can begin to build a picture of the world that matches the overall viewpoint of the news medium and its audience. This is one level of lexical cohesion; how it makes sense for a particular audience. Later we will consider how these words, through connotation and metaphorical allusion, are connected into a broader set of cohesion in terms of narrative and how the structure of language builds its own syntax of how the world is arranged. The individual words themselves must be fitted into a syntactic pattern to fully appreciate how the vocabulary represents particular newspapers' views of the world.

Metaphor

Metaphor refers to the description of one phenomenon in terms of another: a condensed and implicit comparison. When the *Guardian* writes **SPURS GO TO WAR OVER ARNESSEN** (6 June 2005) this does not mean that the football club is literally going to war but that they are acting in a manner which is as hostile as if they were. It enables the newspaper to exaggerate for the sake of emphasis. Most aspects of news coverage can be couched in metaphorical terms. It is a tendency which, given the emotive nature of much metaphorical association, calls into question the objective and neutral claims of newspaper language. Some linguists go so far as to claim that non-literal language, including metaphor, is the rule not the exception in news language in general. They consider metaphorical language as acting as a bridge between the factual world and the world of ideological persuasion, and according to this hypothesis metaphors have an important role in establishing powerful commonsense associations within newspaper texts, associations which do not seem to require much in the way of justification or explanation. Some would also argue that the background of references to military metaphors as in the case below actually naturalizes war and acts as a banal form of everyday acceptance of that normality so that it becomes easier to step into the real thing when it occurs. Consider the weight of metaphorical allusion to war and aggressive conduct in the following, from the sports pages of one issue of the *Independent*:

FA in fight to save Eriksson

Bent seizes on Chelsea's complacency to plunder rare point from the Bridge

Souness rolls with the punches but is living on borrowed time

Wenger cries foul at Moyes' 'bully' tactics

Goals camouflage Warnock worries

Watford resilience heartens Mackay for battles ahead

The hordes of Hades gorge on Sale's flesh

Diamond's depleted Sarries in disarray after six-try blitz

(all in the sports pages of the *Independent*, 23 January 2006)

The level of shared assumptions on behalf of an audience involved in the use of metaphor make it highly significant in terms of the belief framework of the news. Metaphor demonstrates how these assumptions are channelled into expectations of how events can be interpreted in terms of already positioned comparisons which, as is the nature of metaphor, remain implicit and are not overtly stated. As we will see in subsequent chapters, ideology is most strongly characterized by its tacit assumptions and therefore metaphors fit well within its framework.

Politics are often depicted in metaphorical terms in newspaper language in general. This can add to the personalization and emotive emphasis within political reporting which plays down political processes to better concentrate on the less demanding issue of the people involved:

Let Willets the owl and Davis the vulture do battle for Tory leadership

(*Times*, 6 June 2005)

Register

A further way of exploring the way in which the vocabulary of the news attempts to appeal to a particular audience is in terms of the register used. Register refers to the use of a particular type of language in a particular context. Register can reveal as much about the media institution as it can about its perceived audience because it articulates a version of the language of its target social grouping. Cohesion and worldview are both embedded in the language selected and therefore assumptions about what the audience knows in terms of lifestyle, education and politics. Register can include aspects of language which match a specific appeal to lifestyle, age group or professional identity. Register can be observed in the formal/specialist vocabulary of certain parts of the elite press, for instance in its financial pages or in the assumptions it makes about the political knowledge of its readers. In contrast, popular media often reduce the complexity of such stories by associating them with soap opera storylines with which they assume their audience are familiar or by producing a guide to a story as a context, for instance, in the '10 Things You Didn't Know . . .' format. Popular register can also rely on informal language, slang and conversationalization as encapsulated in the following headline announcing a story of political pressure on Deputy Prime Minister John Prescott:

Prezza gets sacks over gypsies

(*Sun*, 1 June 2005)

The use of colloquial phrases is not restricted to popular media, however, as can be seen in the following:

Bush slaps down Brown's plan to double Africa aid

(*Daily Telegraph*, 3 June 2005)

In a more extended version we can contrast the following two extracts on educational policy. The first involves the politics of teaching reading in schools. The *Sun*'s register is characterized by 'U-turn', 'face the axe', 'trendy teaching techniques'; strong and simplistic rhetoric while championing the plight of the supposed victims, 'generations of children let down by the system'. The 'system' is a popular tabloid version of authoritarian and abstract control which fits into the worldview that the popular media often present to their audience. It is a worldview in which the readers are excluded from decision-making processes and discussion of policy; a world of policy swings represented in the language of sudden shifts. The second article appears in the *Guardian*, with its assumption of a readership more familiar with the professional subtleties of the debate, even in its drawing upon a former Secretary of State for Education, Estelle Morris, as a guest writer to criticize plans for the formation of controversial academies in inner cities. The first draws on a register which has disempowered parents and children inscribed within it. The second appears to draw more on a register informed by a professional concern for those disadvantaged. The contrast is between populist and professional registers – both papers know their readers.

U-turn by Kelly over 'old-style' teaching

Schools were told to go back to old-style teaching methods yesterday in a bid to boost reading standards. Trendy techniques introduced in the Sixties face the axe and teachers' leaders welcomed the news last night. But the move comes too late for generations of children let down by the system.

(*Sun*, 3 June 2005)

Another round of structural change won't by itself achieve universally high standards. Worse than that it could be a distraction. In five years' time, whose children will be going to these new academies? Will choice and market forces once again squeeze out the children of the disadvantaged?

(Estelle Morris, *Guardian*, 13 September 2005)

Narrative

The vocabulary of the news media fits into a more general set of patterns which allow the audience to make sense of the world in a consistent way. One such patterning is narrative. From Homer's epics to the folk tales which emerged from the medieval German forests, from African plains and Indian jungles and the 'outback' of indigenous Australia to the contemporary urban myth, narrative has existed across time and cultures. Carl Jung also identified the building blocks for all narrative deep in the human mind as archetypes. Narrative, we might say, is a universal expression of humankind. However, universal as narrative may be, specific narratives are always rooted within time and place. Furthermore, narrative is also bound by social and political contexts which give priority to certain narratives over others, which present different 'sides' of the story, which chose different heroes. This cultural positioning of a narrative and the selectivity of its content mean that narratives play an important part in shaping the world in which we live rather than simply describing it. The narratives act upon the world and can be considered as types of speech act, which means that the forms of language used act on the world in material ways. Narrative becomes a site where different versions of the real can be played out and relayed to a general audience or where conflicting versions can be brought to reconciliation.

Bal (1997) explains the different layers which build to form a narrative, all of which can be directly applied to the narratives of the news. First there is the 'fabula', the material for a story in chronological or logical sequence. This could be seen as the answer to the classic journalist's questions, Who? What? How? Why? When? Then there comes the 'story' itself which involves the arrangement of the 'fabula' into an order which will provide the necessary emphasis, for instance the 'inverted triangle' of the traditional hard news story, or the scene-setting of a more evocative piece, creating perspective and even giving characters context and character. Finally, the narrative adds to these layers the generic choices which can give the story its rounded cultural associations and preferences. News narratives emphasize the elite people and communities which are the dominant characters of the news media version of everyday life. The popular tendency for journalists to refer to their products as stories has a good deal of critical accuracy. Commentators on journalism have often stressed that journalists do not compile reports, they tell stories. The factual events of the world are turned into news by a process of selection, mapped onto news values which can be seen as longer-term narratives in themselves. These stories then become inserted into the news media in ways which enable the audience to make sense of how they fit in culturally. This involves stories fitting into various news types and being allocated to different locations in the newspaper. Politics, sport, international news, home news, celebrity news all have their space within newspapers. They are made to fit into the designed audience of the newspapers by fitting both with the house style as well as the taxonomy of news in particular publications. Consider the following examples. Look at the ways in which Bal's construction of the narrative can be demonstrated. Analyse how they fit into the patterns of newspaper storytelling. Look in particular for the hierarchies of credibility which are built into the narratives by the selection of witnesses, and consider what the ordering of the stories means.

Europe 'ignored detention of prisoners by the CIA'

European governments turned a blind eye to the illegal transport and detention of prisoners by the CIA, an investigator from Europe's main human rights watchdog will argue today.

Dick Marty, a Swiss parliamentarian, will release interim findings from his inquiries on behalf of the Council of Europe, assessing a host of allegations concerning secret flights across EU airspace and illegal prisons. However, the inquiry is not so far thought to have uncovered any new evidence on the most sensitive of the allegations – the location of secret prison sites.

Instead, Mr Marty's report will focus on cases already in the public domain, including those of the Egyptian cleric Osama Moustafa Hassan Nasr, also known as Abu Omar, allegedly kidnapped from Milan in 2003; and a Lebanese-born German, Khaled el-Masri, who was allegedly abducted in Macedonia last year and flown to Afghanistan where he was held for four months.

Today's report marks the start rather than the conclusion, of European efforts to get to the truth of CIA flight claims, which first surfaced last November.

The secretary general of the Council of Europe, Terry Davis, has invoked article 59 of the European Convention to ask all his 46 member nations to reply to a series of questions on the claims by 21 February. And last week the European Parliament agreed to set up a separate but parallel committee of inquiry which, though it will not be able to subpoena witnesses, has the power to embarrass governments by holding public hearings and making it clear who is refusing to cooperate.

European states have been reluctant to press the US on the issue, leading to speculation that many were complicit in the CIA's activities. Yesterday, René van der Linden, chairman of the Council of Europe's parliamentary assembly said he "would like to see some parliaments [stand up to] the governments".

Mr Marty has been promised imagery of possible detention sites from the EU's satellite centre at Torejon in Spain, though this has not yet been delivered, nor has he received flight log bookings from the Brussels-based air safety organisation Eurocontrol.

The allegations fall into two categories. The first and most serious is that prisoners were detained secretly in two east European countries. Human Rights Watch identified Romania's Kogalniceanu military airfield and Poland's Szczytno-Szymany airport as possible sites for secret detention centres, basing its claims on flight logs of CIA aircraft from 2001 to 2004. Both governments deny involvement.

Mr Marty has conceded that he faces an uphill battle in proving these allegations, since the facilities for which he is searching are likely to be small, and have probably been closed.

The second set of claims centres on secret CIA flights. Across the continent, governments have been forced to reveal possible involvement with the flights. Sweden says at least one plane has landed in its territory. Denmark has identified 14 suspect flights, while Norway pinpointed three. And Austria's air force is investigating allegations that a US transport plane containing suspected terrorist captives passed through the neutral country's airspace in 2003.

(*Independent,* 24 January 2006)

'Father Flash' in hiding as cousin reveals pregnancy

HE WAS known as 'Father Flash', as famous for his fast cars, expensive clothes and holidays as much for any spiritual advice dispensed on the Hebridean island of Barra.

But yesterday Father Roddy MacNeil, a close friend of Frances Shand Kydd, the late mother of Diana, Princess of Wales, faced being formally defrocked after his cousin told a newspaper that she was pregnant with his child after a tempestuous affair.

Hilda Robertson, 41, whose mother is Father MacNeil's aunt, was apparently so besotted with the priest that she tried to take her own life after suspecting that he was seeing other women. She is believed to have been airlifted to hospital last October after taking an overdose. News of their alleged affair, said to have been leaked in an anonymous letter to the local bishop, was still being digested by the Roman Catholic Church last night. But Father Paul Conroy, general secretary of the Bishops' Conference of Scotland, said that moves were likely to be taken to strip Father MacNeil, 46, of his priesthood.

Father MacNeil and his cousin are said to have embarked on their affair when she sought comfort after the death of her brother last year.

She separated from her husband, moving out of the family home in Larkhall, South Lanarkshire, and seeking refuge on Barra, where Father McNeil has been the parish priest for several years.

Islanders asked questions after Mrs Robertson appeared to move into the priest's home but he said that she was 'family' and that he was helping her through a difficult time.

Days before Christmas the Right Rev Ian Murray, Bishop of Argyll and the Isles, announced that Father MacNeil had been suspended from his post and was taking time out "to reflect on the future of his priestly vocation". No reason was given.

The tiny island, home to 1,300 people, was still in shock last night as parishioners faced up to the reality that Father MacNeil was unlikely to be returning. Councillor Donald Manford said: "There will be many people here who will be hurt and upset by what has happened. Roddy was very popular on Barra but we must now all move on."

Neither Mrs Robertson nor Father MacNeil could be reached for comment yesterday. Mrs Robertson, who is expecting the child in June, is staying with relatives in Glasgow. It was reported that Father MacNeil may have gone abroad.

Mrs Robertson's brother, Ewen MacLeod, said: "We'll stand by her, no matter what. At the end of the day Hilda is my sister, and I'll be there to support her through all this."

(*Times*, 24 January 2006)

Campaigns

Within the language of the news, aspects such as 'scripts', 'frames' and even 'ideologies' have their narrative elements as too do the highly idiosyncratic campaigns of the various newspapers. In fact, one of the most recognizable of news narratives is that of the campaign. Newspapers used the campaign from the middle of the nineteenth century as a device to identify their priorities and often to reinforce their claims to being representative of their readers' concerns. The *Daily Telegraph* ran a famous moral crusade through its letters pages in the 1860s on the controversial issue of prostitution and middle-class men. In the USA, Gordon Bennett ran famous campaigns on behalf of the 'ordinary man' in his *New York Herald,* and closer to the end of the century Joseph Pulitzer drew populist credit from his support for the building of the Brooklyn Bridge. The characters of campaigns are explicitly embroiled with the worldview of particular news media and their assumptions of the concerns of their audience. The *Daily Mail,* perhaps as a reflection of its long interest in popular science, has taken a particular stance on the debate over genetically modified crops which it routinely refers to as 'Frankenstein food'.

Particular social anxieties, embedded in abbreviated 'scripts' by a particular vocabulary can emerge regularly across newspapers and become an understated, implicit sort of campaign. The acronym ASBO (anti-social behaviour order) is one such trigger for the 'script' of moral decline and the stigmatization of social outsiders, as too is the vocabulary of 'youth' and 'thug', forming the vocabulary of a very specific set of contemporary narratives from the point of view of the moral majority threatened by something which is presented as the constant menace of violent outsiders:

Youth on ASBO admits killing

(*Times*, 3 June 2005)

Thug killed a dad 8 days after ASBO

(*Sun*, 3 June 2005)

So prevalent has the acronym become as an abbreviated reference to a particular script that, on a brighter note, a newspaper can even pun on the acronym in a good news story about a young man who has been released from the terms of his order:

He's ASBO.K

Praise for ex-drug dealer first to have Order lifted

(*Daily Mirror*, 25 January 2006)

Another significant narrative is what many newspapers signal as 'political correctness' and here the *Daily Express* seeks to give context and additional perspective to the narrative of how the moral majority appear to be besieged by a 'politically correct' conspiracy: the newspaper cites selectively to seek to prove the patterning to this sort of behaviour and to tie it explicitly with contemporary debate about the place of Islam in British society:

Don't blame Islam for the religious meddling of the politically correct

Just over two years ago a primary school in Batley, West Yorkshire, made national news after the head teacher sent a memo to her staff instructing them not to use books using pigs when teaching the under seven classes in her school where two-thirds came from a Muslim background. . . . The following year Father Christmas was replaced by a woman in Telford, Shropshire, to help 'recreate the figure in a more maternal image'.

(*Daily Express*, 7 June 2005)

Campaigns are not unique to newspapers, although their need to crusade on a particular issue makes them a more suitable vehicle than broadcast news media which are more traditionally identified with a more even-handed presentation of news. However, television news programmes do occasionally chose to highlight a particular story over a few days and sometimes return to stories with a self-referential flourish announcing that they did cover a certain story previously and are now returning to it. In March 2006 a story in a regional news bulletin about a local Yorkshire woman who had visited survivors of the earthquake in Pakistan was revisited when it was found that she was aiming to raise more funds in order to return once again to help people in the region worst affected. The contemporary story was narrated over footage of the original pictures of her first visit.

 Activity 2.8 o—ᴛ

Select a campaign from any newspaper and identify how it fits in with both its target audience and its editorial identity. Are there any significant features of the language or presentation of the campaign which you can identify which can be used to demonstrate how the campaign fits in with the 'unity of tone' of the newspaper in question?

Summary

In this chapter we have considered the role of critical linguistics in enhancing an engaged readership. We have furthermore considered how this form of critical activity fits into the general dynamic of the 'linguistic turn'. We have begun to explore some of the tools which can assist in the analysis of the language of news media as they seek to address specific audiences. This started with a discussion of news values and then moved on to concentrate on the level of vocabulary. It then explored register and metaphor and how these fit into the larger patterns of narratives in the news. The final area discussed was that of narratives and campaigns and how they too fit into the patterns of audience expectation within particular news media. We will continue to consider these aspects of language throughout the book as we examine how, in combination, they provide a judicious blend of information and indications of power.

Suggestions for further reading

Knowles, M. and Moon, R. (2005) *Introducing Metaphor*. London: Routledge.
Van Leeuwen, T. (2004) *Introducing Social Semiotics*. London: Routledge.
Barker, C. and Galasinski, D. (2003) 'Tools for discourse analysis'. In Barker, C. and Galasinski, D. (eds) *Cultural Studies and Discourse Analysis: A Dialogue on Language and Identity*. London: Sage.

Barthes, R. (1974) *Mythologies*. New York: Wang.

Curran, J., Douglas, A. and Whannel, G. (1980) 'The Political Economy of the Human Interest Story'. In Smith, A. (ed.) *Newspapers and Democracy: International Essays on a Changing Medium*. Cambridge, MA: MIT Press.

Entman, R.M. (1993) 'Framing: toward clarification of a fractured paradigm', *Journal of Communication* 43 (4): 51–58.

Harcup, T. and O'Neill, D. (2001) 'What is News? Galtung and Ruge revisited', *Journalism Studies* Vol. 2, Number 2: 261–280.

Toolan, M.J. (1998) *Narrative: A Critical Linguistic Introduction*. London: Routledge.

3 Analytical tools (2)

- Introduction
- Verbal processes
- Actional and relational verbs
- Transactive and non-transactive
- Transitivity
- Transitivity shifts
- Active and passive
- Modality
- Nominalization
- Compressed noun phrases
- Declaratives
- Presuppositions
- Summary
- Suggestions for further reading

Introduction

In the last chapter we considered how language affects the selection of news and how the vocabulary of the news can build up a picture, both of the news medium and also the audience it is directed towards. We also considered how the vocabulary can be observed to fit into patterns of metaphor, register and narrative which also tell us about the social and cultural location of the news. In this chapter we move on from this vocabulary-based view of the language of the news to look at how this language takes on meaning through its grammar, the syntax of the news. To this end we will introduce and illustrate certain ways in which the use of verbs can give priority to one set of meanings over potential alternative meanings.

Verbal processes

Just as there are choices to be made with regard to which vocabulary is used in a news story, there are also options how to structure sentences in terms of how verbs are employed. Verbs are words which denote action or feeling, or establish relations between people or things. They can also be used to express preferences or opinions either overtly or covertly, as we will see. The most common verbal structure for a sentence can be expressed as follows:

Agent – Process – Affected – Circumstances (adverbially expressed)

The Agent is sometimes referred to as the Actor and is the main protagonist in the sentence. The process is expressed through a verb and often stands in relation to the Affected or achieves a Goal within the sentence. Sentences are often complemented by adverbial phrases which indicate the time, location, situation, etc. of the action expressed or the participants in the sentence. In the following examples, we can see these processes at work. The Agent and Affected are the participants in the sentence and they are either nouns or pronouns, while the process is expressed as a verb.

Man (Agent) Bites (Process) Dog (Affected)

Damiola forensic team (Agent) missed (Process) vital evidence (Affected)

5,000 Brits (Agent) face (Process) Taliban (Affected)

3,300 British troops (Agent) head into (Process) Taliban territory (Affected) for the first time (Circumstances, adverbially expressed)

IRISH ECONOMY (Agent) SURGES AHEAD OF (Process) UK (Affected)

The sorts of processes which verbs can express can include material processes which involve action and intention, the mental processes of perception, reaction, cognition, relational processes, existential processes and behavioural processes. Examples of the first three can be seen in the following report from the *Daily Mirror*:

> **[Material:] Gun cops <u>arrested</u> over 'table leg murder'**
>
> **[Mental:] PC Fagan <u>believed</u> officers were about to be shot**
>
> **[Relational:] The 46-year-old decorator <u>was</u> 'slightly the worse' for drink after a pleasant afternoon . . . Mr Stanley <u>was</u> weary as he trudged home.**
>
> (*Daily Mirror*, 3 June 2005)

Clearly, however, we need more than one way of ordering a sentence or else our communication would become very boring indeed. Language needs variety in order to express a range of meaning, and in this variety there is also the potential to subtly alter emphasis or even meaning. Relationships between objects and events can be expressed in a variety of ways. This means that there are choices open to a speaker or a writer when they put together a sentence.

Actional and relational verbs

Syntax, the grammar of a language, can and does encode some of the most significant ideological meanings of a text. Verbs can be classified into two main categories. Actional verbs and relational verbs. Actionals involve activity and relational verbs involve the relationship between two or more entities. Actional verbs which express an action done by the Agent to the Affected are called 'transactives' while actional verbs which only involve an Agent are called 'non-transactives'. Relationals, are very clear in apportioning responsibility and expressing explicit opinion, and are a strong indicator of the position of a news institution, as in the following statements:

> **Mr Oaten <u>is</u> an able man**
>
> **TONY Blair and Jack Straw <u>were</u> last night under increasing pressure**
>
> **<u>He's</u> a troubled man leading a very troubled life**

In general terms, actions which might be considered controversial by the news media are reported in an acausal way if the emphasis is on the victims, whereas actors in the news who are encoded as performing actions which the newspaper approves of are placed firmly in the reader's attention and within broader patterns of agency which match the scripts and news values of the newspapers concerned through the use of direct actional verbs. In the first example below, we see how the focus of the story is the death of a British soldier which fits within the national interests of the newspaper. The closest that the opening sentences of the story get to apportioning blame is to simply indicate that it was a bomb which blasted the convoy and that 'A roadside bomb killed a British soldier'. The Agent is the bomb, and the person who has laid the bomb or exploded it has been taken from the story, partially because of the anonymity of the assailants and also because this representation further emphasizes the British soldier at the heart of the attention of the reader. The process of impersonal representation of the conflict tends to highlight the individual loss of British personnel while obscuring the potential reasons why such an asymmetrical war is being waged against them.

British soldier dies as bomb blasts convoy

A roadside bomb killed a British soldier and badly injured four others yesterday when it exploded next to their patrol in Iraq.

(*Daily Express*, 30 May 2005)

In the following extract, the Agents who are directly referred to are the 'yobs' who have attacked an innocent victim. They fit lexically and thematically with one of the main cultural and social anxieties of the newspaper so that their elevation to the lead position as Agent in this story and the actional relationship between them and the Affected (him)/the victim highlights the emphasis of the story on the 'yobs'.

---

one of the yobs turned on him and slashed him across the face with a six-inch kitchen knife.

(*Daily Mail*, 23 January 2006)

Transactive and non-transactive

There is also significance in the selection of transactive or non-transactive verbs. A non-transactive sentence is one in which there does not seem to be an explicit agent involved in effecting a particular action. It can be used merely as a variety in the news media to avoid monotony but more importantly it can be used to obscure or indeed hide one participant in the story: 'Trial jury is told of crucial errors in murder investigation'. This might be for legal reasons, or reasons of ethics, i.e. not revealing a source, but it might also be as a means of drawing the reader's attention away from an important political factor for reasons to do with the political preferences of the particular news medium concerned.

Non-transactives are often used to obscure the source of a story and are a common device in political news stories: 'it emerged yesterday'; 'it was revealed last night'; 'sources close to the Prime Minister claimed'.

> **As Labour is revealed to reward three out of four party donors . . . it emerged that Tony Blair has axed a watchdog designed to prevent political donors being rewarded with knighthoods and peers.**

(*Daily Mail*, 6 June 2005)

Shifts between transactive and non-transactive verbs can show the preferred shape of the news agenda and political nuance within a particular newspaper at a very subtle level. In the above example, at first we can see that the piece prefers to open with a non-transactive verbal construction, 'Labour is revealed'. This obscures the agents who have revealed this news, and the conspiratorial tone is continued as the impersonal verbal construction, 'it emerged' follows. The contrast between this sort of obscure agency and the strength of the metaphor used in the following transactive verb which uses Tony Blair as the agent could not be more telling. Blair has 'axed' the very 'watchdog' which would have made these rewards more easily traceable. The balance between what is obscured in the choice of non-transactives and that which is emphasized in the metaphorical strength of the transactive matches the editorial perspective of the *Daily Mail* towards the Labour administration in general and Tony Blair in particular.

As transactive verbs display agency – who is doing what to whom – non-transactives can conceal agency. The *Sun* headline 'Saddam trial soon' is a good illustration of how a non-transactive headline has the potential to highlight the person on trial but not the more awkward political details of who exactly is trying him and possibly why he is being tried. The whole issue of the role of the USA in setting up the trial and questions of jurisdiction in post-invasion Iraq are obscured by the conflation of the process to the truncated version of 'Saddam trial'. The non-transactive removes the agency from the trial process and leaves the former ruler of Iraq as the main focal point of the story with all the accumulated negative connotation which has built up around him.

Hodge and Kress have commented on the general tendency of this verbal form across the news media:

This ambiguity and vagueness is clearly functional. We can hypothesize and suggest that, since language functions to deceive as well as to inform, every component of the grammar will contain one set of forms which allow the speaker to avoid making distinctions which are primary and another set where these distinctions have to be made sharply and with precision. . . . Thus transactives on the one hand distinguish absolutely between causer and affected, whereas non-transactives blur precisely this distinction. Similarly the causer-process relation is coded precisely in the transitive and blurred in the prepositional variant of that model.

(Hodge and Kress, 1993: 125–126)

In journalism, this is not often a set of conscious strategies or even strategic choices but part of an accepted patterning of language almost as second nature, honed within the pressure of commercial deadlines. Yet this reasonable explanation does not mean that the language has no wider social and political implications beyond the newsroom.

Norman Fairclough has explored the relationship between the language of contemporary politics and the language of the news media. Transitivity and agency are key to this relationship as he points out in an analysis of one of Blair's speeches – New Labour's (1998) 'Building the Knowledge-Driven Economy', cited in Fairclough (2000):

'In the increasingly global economy of today, we cannot compete in the old way. Capital is mobile, technology can migrate quickly and goods can be made in low cost countries and shipped to developed markets.'

The following 'transformations' can be read in the text of the speech which have implications for how this sort of political language can prioritize or obscure agency:

- 'capital is mobile' transforms a transitive action into a relation
- 'technology can migrate quickly' ascribes agency to technology itself
- 'goods can be made in low cost countries' and ' [they can be] shipped to developed markets' are transitive actions processed without agents.

Fairclough (2000)

Transitivity

Language is never simply as it is. It always represents the outcome of a series of choices, whether implicit or explicit. This makes language always part of an intervention in the world. Journalists' use of language may be swift, efficient and highly constrained in terms of conventions but it is this very set of limitations which gives their language such an important role in the construction of our everyday world and our expectations of it through the patterns of its representation. One of the central processes of language is in the organization of how participants act in and on the world. This organization is therefore an important part of the news media's narratives about the world as it helps classify and make sense of events in the world for an audience which is specifically targeted in terms of social and national contexts. Transitivity is an umbrella term with regard to the verbal structure of a sentence. It refers broadly to who does what to whom, and how. Another verbal choice involving agency is between expressing a sentence as transitive or intransitive. A transitive sentence has the agent acting upon the affected, whereas the intransitive option uses a verb which does not have an affected. Transitivity allows options and, as we have already seen, any process which allows choice in this way in the news media can often be ideologically significant in its preferences. In the first example below, Iran clearly 'accused' Britain. The transitive construction allows the adverb 'angrily' to be attached to the accusation without consideration of whether this anger was justified or having to quantify the anger or demonstrate why its accusations were effectively angry. In the second example, a politician's vice is viewed as 'surfacing' of its own accord, as if such things are driven without reason or the control of the Agent. The intransitivity of the verbal expression assists in the placing of the Circumstances, 'inevitably' to further enhance this view of a flawed politician as someone driven by irrational and uncontrollable urges. The politician is literally not in the position of Agency, not the subject of his own life.

> **Iran yesterday angrily accused Britain of helping bombers who killed eight people**
>
> **Such selfishness will inevitably surface, to the detriment of their party, their person and their family.**

In the following example, the 'British soldier' is the affected and elevated to the beginning of the sentence because the perpetrators of the explosion are anonymous and the news value of a British death is significant. The adverbial phrase 'in the troubled region of Amara in south eastern Iraq' is also significant and therefore prioritized in its euphemistic reference to 'troubled' to mask the true extent and possible political causes of the fighting in the area. It may be interpreted as playing down the potential for panic-mongering in news stories and is clearly within the restrained tradition of an elite, liberal newspaper like the *Guardian*.

> **A British soldier was killed by a bomb blast in the troubled region of Amara in south eastern Iraq yesterday.**

(*Guardian*, 30 May 2005)

Considering any alternative agency would be awkward without entering into speculation. Even assuming the perpetrators are unknown, the significant agent in the story from the perspective of the news agenda remains the single British soldier. News values even within a liberal newspaper determine that a single British death is more worthy of coverage than for instance, the killing by anonymous agents of an Iraqi, which would be so routine as to warrant no mention at all.

In the next example, the Secretary of State for Education, Ruth Kelly, is represented as being in command of the reported situation. She 'has ordered trials'. This presents her as a powerful figure, single-handedly bringing about an examination of controversial reading techniques in schools although it is an examination which the *Sun* claims has been brought about by its own campaigning intervention. Her position at the head of this sentence, combined with the choice of verb 'ordered' indicates in its transitivity a preference for strong action by politicians on issues supported by the newspaper in question.

Ms Kelly has now ordered trials of the phonic system.

(*Sun*, June 3 2005)

The key point about transitivity in relation to the news media is that it confirms that language offers choices in the ways in which an event is represented. In choosing one option over another we have suppressed one way of telling a particular story and determined the dominant point of view within the story. Of course, the choice is not made by an individual according to their own idiosyncratic tastes. The language used by newspapers and other news media conforms to wider social expectations and cultural traditions. It might be the final decision of a sub-editor rather than the journalist but ultimately such choice derives from the patterns of preference operating within that news medium at that time. Individual choices must fit that patterning and conform to the 'house style' or ideological preference of the news medium.

Transitivity shifts

There are often shifts in the pattern of transitivity from the headline to the main paragraphs of a story which may mitigate or otherwise contextualize the ideological proposition of the headline, but it may well still be the tone of the headline, with its power to provide the initial foregrounding, which retains the privileged impact. The function of the headline and its transitivity is especially important in the congested media environment where often a reader will glance at many headlines and read fewer entire stories, which means of course that there is the possibility that the headline is taken as the whole story. This is a tendency which is also prevalent in television news bulletins or rolling news programmes where the headlines are repeated three or four times. It is important therefore both for the political preferences of the news medium and for its assumed audience that the preferred reading of a story is contained within the initial emphasis and pattern of the headline.

The sort of choice which is available in the syntactic and semantic selection which goes to form a news story will demonstrate a significant amount of ideological preference in both institutional terms (the news medium), political preference (party/nation) or socio-cultural orientation (reader/audience). As well as lexical choice, which can inflect the connotation of a story, the transitivity can also work within the same parameters of objective facts yet give a story a different trajectory, depending on the political or the social orientation of the news medium in question.

Rio in bar brawl

Soccer ace Rio Ferdinand was headbutted in a bar fight, it was revealed yesterday. The £29million Man Utd and England defender was set upon by a customer after a row over a photo according to onlookers.

(*Sun*, 30 May 2005)

In the above headline the footballer Rio Ferdinand, referred to because of his fame or even notoriety simply by his first name, Rio, is implicated as an agent in the bar brawl. The brevity of the headline omits any mention of a third party and therefore Ferdinand seems to be cast in the leading role. The subsequent article reveals that he 'was head-butted . . . set upon by a customer' in a reversal of the transitivity of the headline, presumably because the headline was seeking to maximize the role of the football celebrity to emphasize the correlation of the story to the newspaper's celebrity agenda.

It is instructive to consider how the perspective of an elite nation is constructed for British readers of the two newspapers quoted below, using transitivity, actional and relational verbs. In both stories selected, the Agents are either the British troops or John Reid, the Defence Secretary. No Afghanistani Agents are in a transactive position and none are specifically mentioned. The only time the Afghanistani president is referred to is in a sentence where his government is the recipient of the assistance of the British military, 'to back up President Karzai's Government in Kabul'. The Affected are always Afghanistan in general and never groups or individuals. Even when the subject of heroin production is raised there is only one mention of the farmers who will be persuaded to adopt different livelihoods, although these are not mentioned specifically. The area of Helmand seems to be spontaneously responsible for heroin production and no Agent other than the province is referred to.

Both pieces are full of the rhetoric of numbers, seeking to persuade readers by simply citing statistics, often repeating the figures quoted by the British Defence Secretary without any context or wider frame of reference. Relationals are used to make the specifics of the situation in Afghanistan clearer and even simpler to readers: 'Helmand province, an area notorious for producing a large proportion of Afghanistan's opium for the heroin trade and formerly the heartland of the Taleban'. From the perspective of the British troops, 'One role for the troops will be to help the Afghan government to tackle the opium trade'.

The sort of military-strategic language noted by critics such as Chilton (1982) and Keeble (2005) is apparent in the two stories in phrases such as 'insurgency group', 'robust battle group', 'inaugural operational outing', and 'provincial reconstruction'. The most infamous recent adoption of a military euphemism into the language of the news media has been the uncritical use of the term 'collateral damage' to denote the death of innocent civilians at the hands of British or American troops.

The soldiers themselves are almost always the Affected within sentences, a linguistic choice which reinforces the fact that they are told to go to particular places and which takes away any idea of operational discussion between politicians and military: 'The force is to be deployed', 'will tomorrow be ordered', 'are being sent'. This is clearly a perspective which prioritizes the political over the military within the Afghanistan campaign.

3,300 British troops head into Taleban territory for first time

BRITISH forces in Afghanistan will number 5,700 when soldiers are sent to the Taleban's heartland in the south for the first time.

John Reid, the Defence Secretary, announced that Britain would expand its military commitment in Afghanistan significantly by the summer, with a pledge to stay for three years.

There are 1,000 British troops in the country at present, based in Kabul and Mazar e-Sharif in the north. After Cabinet approval for the deployment yesterday, Mr Reid said that the reinforcements would include a 'robust' battle group of 3,300 soldiers from 16 Air Assault Brigade for the south.

This force is to be deployed in Helmand province, an area notorious for producing a large proportion of Afghanistan's opium for the heroin trade and formerly the heartland of the Taleban with their al-Qaeda supporters.

For the first time the British troops will be backed up by eight Apache attack helicopters from 9 Regiment Army Air Corps. It will be the inaugural operational outing for these aircraft, 67 of which have been bought for £4 billion.

One role for the troops will be to help the Afghan Government to tackle the opium trade, which supplies 90 per cent of the heroin that ends up in Britain. Although it is not clear what action the troops will take, a renewed effort is to be made to persuade the opium farmers to adopt alternative livelihoods. Britain is to donate £20 million a year as compensation for the farmers who agree to stop growing poppies.

Underlining Britain's renewed commitment to Afghanistan, Mr Reid said the troops would stay for three years at a cost of £1 billion.

(*Times,* 27 January 2006)

4,000 TROOPS OFF TO AFGHANISTAN

Tough Paras lead 'No 1 danger zone' mission

THOUSANDS of Britain's fiercest troops will tomorrow be ordered to the world's most dangerous region.

Defence Secretary John Reid will reveal that up to 4,000 soldiers from the Air Assault Brigade and the Parachute Regiment are being sent to a lawless province of Afghanistan.

Officially their role is 'provincial reconstruction' to make southern Afghanistan governable again.

They will help the country's authorities retake control over the wild Helmand area, where a new insurgency group has formed. Their task is **NOT** to hunt down al-Qaeda cells, Taliban extremists or terrorist training camps – though commanders have been warned to brace themselves for violent clashes . . .

(*Sun,* 25 January 2006)

 Activity 3.1 o—

Look at the following examples and consider how transitivity, and the use of transactive and non-transactive or relational verbs are used to present different emphases in the account of the investigation into Damilola Taylor's death.

> **Damilola's blood on kid's trainer for 5 years . . . but police experts MISSED it**
>
> (*Sun,* 25 January 2006)

Dami's blood found on boy's trainer

MURDERED schoolboy Damilola Taylor's blood was found on the trainer of one of the three youths accused of killing him, jurors were told yesterday.

Yet experts who examined the shoe in the initial probe failed to spot it the court heard.

(*Daily Mirror*, 25 January 2006)

Bloodstain 'linking boys to Damilola was ignored'

Vital evidence allegedly linking two boys to the murder of 10-year-old Damilola Taylor was missed during the initial police investigation, the Old Bailey was told yesterday.

(*Independent*, 25 January 2006)

Damilola forensic team missed vital evidence

Trial jury is told of crucial errors in murder investigation

CRUCIAL clues to the identity of the killers of Damilola Taylor were missed by forensic scientists and finally uncovered after a 'painstaking' new investigation, the Old Bailey was told yesterday.

Laboratory staff failed to spot vital bloodstains on a trainer and a sweatshirt, linking two brothers, now aged 17 and 18, to the 'callous and brutal' murder of the 10-year-old boy.

(*Times*, 25 January 2006)

Active and passive

Another way of varying the presentation of news which may have significant implications for the preferred views of the newspaper in question is the choice of active or passive constructions. Active constructions make the Agent the theme/subject of the sentence. Passive constructions put the focus on the Goal or the affected participants, and shift the Agent out of prominence in this part of the text. Although such a choice may simply provide a stylistic variation to stop prose becoming monotonous, passive constructions can also offer an opportunity to represent an event without reference to an agent. This is called 'Agent deletion'. When Agents are deleted there can be the impression that the process erupts spontaneously into the world. Deletion can serve the purposes of economy and/or distortion. There are other functional possibilities, such as the register of language usually used in certain papers to report bureaucracy (in itself a form of ideologically inflected deference) e.g. 'it was revealed', 'It was announced'. The Agent is deleted from the process, with the potential for shifting blame onto depersonalized forces or even the victims themselves. On occasions the Agent can be absent from such sentences. This Agent deletion can have very significant implications in the news. It can mask responsibility just as a non-transactive verb can. Agents can be deleted 'for various reasons – perhaps because they are obvious, but also as a way of obfuscating agency or respon-sibility' (Fairclough, 2000: 163). Passive constructions may be the marker of a particular register, such as a scientific report or academic paper where indi-vidual agency is traditionally subordinate to evidence or argumentation via sources. The question *Who did it?* is implicit, with the Agent deleted, and can only be deduced from the broader understanding of the world and events in it by the reader, and to a large extent the assumption is that the reader shares this framework of knowledge through the news medium and the silences and com-monsense understandings of the world which are implied in their relationship.

At least 200 Taliban have been killed in clashes with American and Afghan forces over the past ten weeks.

(*Daily Telegraph*, 2 June 2005)

France delivers its judgement, and Europe is plunged into crisis

(*Guardian*, 30 May 2005)

In the first example, the fighters asserted to be 'Taliban' have been killed but they have been killed in apparently agentless 'clashes' with the vaguely iden-tified 'American and Afghan forces'. The process of their deaths is deliberately obscured, the status of the perpetrators is unclear and the whole process is part of a systematic euphemistic treatment of this conflict. In the second example, a more subtle process is engaged in. There are two clauses. The first is active and the second passive and apparently agentless. The voters of France, abbreviated and personified in the concept of 'France' have delivered their judgement in fact on the proposed new EU constitution and have rejected it in a referendum. Europe itself, the institutions and organizations of the European Union them-selves, have been plunged into crisis and by implication, although there is no Agent in the second of these clauses, it is plain that the crisis has been triggered by the result of the French ballot.

Modality

Modality provides an opportunity for comment and opinion in the verbs and adverbs of the news. It is used to make claims for preference, truth, obligation, approval, normality and much more beside. It is an excellent illustration of language being deployed as a speech act (Austin, 1962) since within the news media such language use is deployed to actively form opinion among readers and it therefore has at least the aspiration of acting on the world. Modal verbs include *may, could, must, should, will* (and the negation of those verbs, *may not, could not, must not, should not, will not*), adverbial equivalents such as *probably, hopefully, surely* and adjectives which express the probability, desirability and certainty of some views or decisions over others. Such modality is often used (but not exclusively so) in the leading article of newspapers, where it is traditional to include explicit opinion-forming commentary in line with a newspaper's political perspective. In the first example below, 'pitifully' is clearly a modal adverb and the solution is referred to as 'obvious' which is also a judgement on the desirability of one solution.

How pitifully the Royal Mail responds when the regulator Postcomm orders it to cap price rises over the next five years. . . .
Governments of both stripes have ducked the obvious solution – genuine privatisation.

(*Daily Mail*, 2 June 2005)

In the following examples the modality is mainly expressed through verbs:

Flu vaccine for under-twos could cause 'immunisation overload'

(*Daily Mail*, 23 January 2006)

Yesterday it was confirmed that Prince Harry <u>could</u> face frontline service in Iraq or Afghanistan when he joins the Household cavalry.
. . .
The Blues and Royals, who were deployed at the start of the Iraqi conflict, <u>are expected</u> to be sent to Afghanistan in the future and <u>possibly</u> again to Iraq. . . .
The Defence Secretary is <u>likely</u> to stress that the British effort <u>would</u> be geared towards counter-narcotic operations and the establishment of a provincial reconstruction team in Helmand.

(*Independent*, 26 January 2006)

Fatah wins, Hamas gains in Palestinian election

The reality on the ground <u>suggests</u> a more nuanced – and pragmatic – policy <u>may</u> loom, though. . . . The effort <u>is expected</u> to be marked by intense coalition negotiations among his Fatah party, Hamas and the scattering of independent parties.

   If Hamas joins Mr Abbas's new government, it <u>will</u> have an enormous impact on the future contours of the Israeli-Palestinian conflict and any resolution of it. . . . The same discipline, many analysts say, <u>could</u> prove more useful than Fatah in upholding a future cease-fire agreement that both sides have been gently speculating about in recent weeks.

(*The Wall Street Journal*, 26 January 2006)

The way in which modality can be delayed until well into a particular story may have a significant effect on the perspective of a piece. It is one way in which preferred opinion can be subtly woven within the columns of hard news. Delayed modality can be observed ten paragraphs into this following piece which leads on the strongly assertive thesis that the Hamas victory unquestionably damages peace prospects for the region. The first hint of uncertainty comes in the modal adverb 'potentially'.

Hamas win threat to peace

. . . Hamas's strong showing now stamps it as a dominant player in Middle East politics and potentially shelves the US-sponsored road map to peace that Fatah had pledged to reactivate.

(*The Australian*, 27 January 2006)

There is also a typographic form of modality in the use of inverted commas not just as a means of condensing a story but as a way of privileging one particular reading of a story from the outset while refusing to be drawn into any definitive comment. Condensation of debate such as this nearly also has implications for meaning and emphasis:

Bali Nine 'leader' to face death penalty
AWB 'knew of' UN breach
Refinery 'exposed 3000 to asbestos'

(*The Australian*, 25 January 2006)

Activity 3.2 o—r

Find examples of modality and explore how they privilege certain opinions.

Nominalization

Nominalization is a linguistic shift, a transformation, which enables a process to be described as an entity, for instance 'globalization', 'obesity epidemic'. In other words, it turns verbs (and adjectives) into nouns. It deletes certain participants in a process, has a tendency to make complex processes much more simple, takes events out of historical context and can heighten abstraction. News discourse is crammed with nominals – 'insurgency', 'extraordinary rendition', 'collateral damage', 'democratization', 'the reconstruction [of Iraq]'. A defining feature of the discourse of the news is how it needs to fit language to a finite amount of space or air time. In many ways summarizing and abbreviation are at the very heart of journalism's language. However this economy of space/ time relations within journalism masks the operation of a more subtle set of pressures on language as it is fitted into this restricted space in order to tell particular sorts of stories. The economy of space/time is very much part of the political ideology of information flow. This is particularly true of elite news. It deals more in abstractions and nominals as they are literally abstracted from more complete contexts. It expects more contextual knowledge from its audience.

Much is deleted in the transformation involved in nominalization – history, participants, modality. The use of nominalization makes for abstract reporting, distant from concrete events and real people. It constitutes a highly ideological abbreviation of narratives so that they can fit the preferred agendas of news media without the distractions of long sidetracks to give details of individuals or assumptions which have already been made. Nominalization, by acting in this way, can hide the agents of decisions because events appear to be spontaneous and self-explanatory. It can also mask the circulators of rumour and the processes which may have led to a particular situation or state of affairs. It presents the world ultimately in terms of 'already known' categories and is therefore key to the processes of the news media. Nominalization may simplify a process, make the relationship between cause and effect invisible to rational argument or make a problematic and contested situation a matter of fact, thus naturalizing events and taking them out of their social and historical contexts. Reports can hide the agents of decisions, the founders of rumours, the processes which have led to a situation. In the first example below the 'revitalization' implies a rejuvenation, a rebirth almost of the company through severe job cuts. The decisions are driven impersonally by 'Ford', 'Ford Motors', the 'Automaker', the 'plan' and it is 'jobs' and 'facilities' which will be cut. There are so many abstractions here that it is easy to forget that the implications are people without livelihoods, and yet it is all in the cause of the 'revitalization' which takes the decisions out of history and even out of the economy and into a quite different metaphorical range, thereby attempting to establish a base for a very particular way of interpreting these economic developments.

Ford acts to stem U.S. losses

Automaker to slash 25,000 jobs

Ford Motor announced a sweeping revitalization plan Monday aimed at shoring up its sagging U.S. business.
 The plan includes cutting 25,000 to 30,000 jobs and closing 14 facilities, seven of them assembly plants, by 2012. The moves will reduce Ford's U.S. automaking capacity by 26%.

(*USA Today*, 24 January 2006)

These same economic processes of sacking workers and protecting profits for large corporate concerns in a global economy can also be represented in a similarly abstract fashion as 'restructuring':

More Detroit bad news

restructuring efforts . . . restructuring plan for GM Motors faced with largest yearly loss since '92.

(*International Herald Tribune*, 27 January 2006)

Nominalization reifies. It turns processes into things. These things then can be used as a set of categories which are then superimposed onto the world of events. This abbreviation of the complexity of the processes at work in the world can be used to map this framework onto the assumed pre-existing ideological map of the reader. The news becomes the known. It confirms the sense of social solidarity and consistency of belief within this mediated community. 'Democratization' against 'insurgents' seems to have become, within the patterns of nominalization in the news media, a key battle of known quantities. 'Democratization' is clearly, in the first example below, synonymous with the foreign policy aims of the Bush administration which, because of the use of the nominal, deflects any critical enquiry and invites the reader into a set of political assumptions concerning the nature of democracy, its potential to be exported to other countries and the role of America as its champion. The second abbreviated extract shows the dependence on the term 'insurgent' as a nominalization which acts as a shorthand for the varied and complex opposition to the American invasion of Iraq and, because of its lack of historical detail, falls short of probing the link between America's presence in Iraq and the very 'insurgency' itself.

Bush calls election result rebuke 'to the old guard'

Bush's comments seemed to reflect the sense that Hamas posed a clear threat – and perhaps a fatal blow – to the administration's push for democratization in the Islamic world.

(*International Herald Tribune*, 27 January 2006)

Enemy in Iraq may be splitting

U.S. officer cites local–foreign rift

. . . radical foreign-led fighters and Iraqi insurgents . . . the top U.S. intelligence officer in Iraq said. . . . Sunni insurgents . . . insurgents loyal to the local tribe . . . Al-Qaeda insurgents . . . hard-core Iraqi fights . . . [plus six other mentions of insurgents]

(*USA Today*, 26 January 2006)

 Activity 3.3 o—ⲧ

Can you find examples of nominalization in the press? How are the examples you find significant in the way that they compress information about the world and assume knowledge in their audience?

Compressed noun phrases

The compression of noun phrases to fit as much information into as small a space as possible is one of the chief identifying features of newspaper English. This simply places a number of nouns together to create an abbreviated narrative which relies upon a great deal of implicit understanding on behalf of the reader. The headline below clearly refers to a doctor who has made a mistake, and we presume that the compression indicates that the story is well known enough among readers of the *Daily Mail* to allow for this sort of compression.

Blunder doctor allowed to work alone

(*Daily Mail*, 26 January 2006)

Activity 3.4 o—

Can you add to the list of examples of compressed noun phrases below?

Sex beast   Afghan forces
US campaign   Osama support
Mideast fundamentalists   Riot cop backflip
Enron trial   Postcode lottery

The transformation of individuals or groups of civil servants into institutions or personifications of Britain is also a manifestation of the process of nominalization. In the following example, their advice becomes the nation state itself and the process of civil servant briefings becomes synonymous with the Foreign Office:

Britain prepares to ditch treaty

. . . The Foreign Office was more bullish in private.

(*Guardian*, 31 May 2005)

Declaratives

Declaratives are some of the most explicit forms of intervention by the news media. They can be abrasive, witty and political but they will always conform to what they think their particular community of consumers will find acceptable. These features, which can certainly be considered as speech acts in their intention to intervene materially in the world, are nearly always to be found in headlines or in the opening sentences of a news item, and more often in print media than in their more restrained broadcast equivalents.

Revealed: the new scramble for Africa

(*Guardian*, 1 June 2005)

What now for Europe?

(*Independent*, 2 June 2005)

Don't pump us dry

(*Daily Mirror*, 2 September)

Paras 'beat boy to death'

(*Sun*, 6 September 2005)

Get back to work, a million benefit claimants are told

Ministers will try to sound the death knell of the sick-note culture today by unveiling plans to take a million people off incapacity benefit at a saving of up to £7 billion.

(*Times*, 24 January 2006)

 Activity 3.5 o━┳

Find your own examples of declaratives and discuss what they tell us about the relationship of a newspaper with its readers and what view of the world they privilege.

Presuppositions

Nominalization and noun phrases comprise condensed, existing views of relationships and causation which match the tacitly agreed preferences of both reader and newspaper. There are further methods of inscribing accepted conventions within news reports which endorse the status quo. These can include certain verbal choices. The use of verbs which describe a change of state such as 'begin', 'continue' or 'cease' assumes a prior situation with which we are assumed to agree. The questions so characteristic of journalism – 'why', 'when', 'who', 'what' and 'how' – are only posed once we can be safely assumed to agree with the validity of any other questions which are implicitly answered in order to move to these 'basic' questions. For instance, 'When will British troops be withdrawn from Iraq?' assumes that the reasons for their presence there form part of a consensus from which we can proceed. Beyond the verbal patterns, definite articles and possessive articles assume agreement over the priorities and ownership within the story. The first example below uses a definite article 'the' to presuppose that there is a significant challenge for Britain and that it is one which the newspaper can articulate on behalf not only of its reader to which it is principally addressed but beyond this to the whole of the country. It furthermore presupposes that we agree with its central view that successive governments have acted on our behalf without concerning themselves to find out what 'our' views actually are. It presupposes that the readers are entirely disaffected with the process of government.

> **The challenge for Britain now is to disengage from many of the obligations that successive governments have entered into, unasked, on our behalf.**

> (*Daily Telegraph*, 2 June 2005)

The *Daily Mail*'s use of the extremely emotive word 'Gestapo' in 'the health 'n' safety Gestapo' (6 June 2005) draws upon a popular knowledge of the unsavoury and brutal methods of the Nazi secret police during the Second World War. In aligning the work of the Health and Safety Executive with the Nazi secret police the newspaper presupposes not only a knowledge of the reputation of the Gestapo but also a level of sympathy with the view expressed here that the Health and Safety Executive can be legitimately or provocatively associated with it.

Summary

This chapter has built upon the introduction to the analysis of texts of earlier chapters. It has demonstrated that beyond the vocabulary of the language of the news there are patterns within the use of verbs which can dramatically alter the way in which a text is intended to be read. It has outlined different ways of structuring a sentence around verbs in terms of transitivity and in terms of actional verbs and relational verbs. It has looked at the implications of the deleting of agents from certain news stories as well as how the use of modal verbs can encode preference or opinion. The linguistic analysis of news media can therefore be of a semantic or syntactic nature. Raising questions does not equate to definitive proof in these sorts of analysis. It is more important to simply raise the questions and to suggest that what we take for granted can have meaning beyond the obvious and that we can begin to deduce this meaning from the patterns which it creates.

Suggestions for further reading

Fowler, R. (1991) *Language in the News: Discourse and Ideology in the Press.* London: Routledge.

Hodge, R. and Kress, G. (1993) *Language as Ideology.* London: Routledge.

Kress, G. (1983) 'Linguistic and Ideological transformations in News Reporting'. In David and Walton (eds) *Language, Image and Media.* Oxford: Blackwell.

Reah, D. (2002) *The Language of Newspapers.* London: Routledge.

Trask, R.L. (1998) *Key Concepts in Language and Linguistics.* London: Routledge.

4 Overt and covert persuasion: argument and rhetoric

Introduction

So much emphasis is placed in the study of journalism on the conventions of its hard news and the critical analysis of this part of its output that little attention is paid to the conventions and structure of its explicitly opinionated writing. Both sorts of writing aim in different ways to persuade readers to adopt a particular viewpoint. This chapter will consider the role of the language of features, opinion pieces and editorials, and how they fit into the specific environment of particular papers. All newspapers include: editorials, where the official, institutional opinion of a newspaper can be found; commentary, where more personalized, individual opinion is sanctioned but still within the broad frame of the newspaper's editorial identity and finally columnists, who are sometimes used as provocateurs to generate debate and even to test the borders of the tolerance of the readership on particular issues. The role of Julie Burchill in the Saturday *Guardian* was particularly interesting in the controversy she generated and which was demonstrated each following Saturday by the vehemence of reaction or support for her idiosyncratic views on topical issues. This chapter will also consider the moments when the language of persuasion is more subtly woven into pieces which are more traditionally expected to be objective, such as that news traditionally referred to as 'hard news'. One of the traditional functions of journalism has been to present the news in a way which claims a legitimacy as unimpeded by direct party political considerations. However, this chapter will demonstrate that there is a dynamic two-way flow between opinion-formation and information-transmission in the news, and that this can be more generally political without having a consistent party-political orientation.

Rhetoric

Rhetoric in the language of the news does not refer to features of high-flown style but simply to any linguistic feature which has, as its chief function, the persuasion of the audience to adopt a particular point of view. As we have already considered, a significant part of this process of the construction of viewpoint is performed before the news is presented in its final version by the processes of classification, selection and editorial preference. Once this is achieved and we have the published or broadcast version of the news, we can observe the strategies used to persuade an audience to adopt particular viewpoints and at the same time to reinforce their sense of constituting an audience through this shared community of opinion. These strategies depend upon rhetoric. Rhetoric functions as a means of appealing to a symbolic consensus of ideal readers and this is based on what the newspapers assume are the common sense and shared experience of their readers. There are explicit forms of rhetoric as well as some more subtle variations. It is the explicit forms which we will be considering for the most part in this chapter.

The most immediate form of rhetorical device comes in the typography of the headlines. The enlarging of the words of the main stories is a call for attention, a manifestation of what the newspapers consider most important within their own view of the news on any particular day, and often furthermore an expression of the supposed idiom and identity of its core readership.

150 PAEDOS IN YOUR SCHOOLS

(*Sun*, 20 January 2006, front page)

BURN THE BITCH ON THE STAKE SHE IS PURE <u>EVIL</u>

(*Daily Star*, 13 May 2004)

How can a call centre in Bendigo be geared for a crisis in Adelaide?
<u>FIX THIS</u>

(*The Advertiser*, 24 January 2006, front page)

Iraq kickbacks 'close to bribery'

(*The Advertiser*, 24 January 2006)

State of the Union? Not so good, most say

(*USA Today*, 27 January 2006, front page)

Beyond the bold capital letters, we can also see how other typographical devices can reinforce these rhetorical manoeuvres. Italics, underlining, inverted commas can all be used as specific rhetorical devices, either in headlines or within the text of articles, especially editorials, to emphasize the editorial stance of the newspaper.

Activity 4.1 ⚷

Choose a selection of front page headlines from a range of newspapers from the same day. How does the language of these headlines serve to reinforce the identity of the newspaper and its core readership, and are there devices such as puns, exclamation marks or typographical features to emphasize the newspaper's take on the news?

The conventional 'factuality' of the news can be deployed as a rhetorical device. Constrained by the law and by tradition to stay within the bounds of truth, newspapers can present their own point of view without contravening this basic expectation. Presenting something potentially ambiguous as categorically one thing or another is a characteristic device used within the language of hard news. This is eloquently summed up by Matthew Kieran, who emphasizes that elements that are often considered as reason and fact are as much matters of persuasion as anything else, thus highlighting the rhetorical obligation on the journalist in the delivery of a story when he writes: 'a journalist's news report should aim to persuade the audience that his or her description and interpretation is the rational and appropriate one' (Kieran, 1998: 27).

Numbers can be used as a rhetorical device. Consider the way in which the *Daily Mirror* used a photograph of a tachometer to monitor the days which had elapsed since the search for the alleged 'Weapons of Mass Destruction' in Iraq had begun. This daily repetition of an ever-increasing number on the tachometer served to diminish the credibility of one of the main reasons why the Bush–Blair coalition had invaded Iraq in the first place, as well as simultaneously indicating the position of the newspaper for its readers on this matter. A different point was being made in the *Independent* when it ran a first page with ninety days marked and crossed out, as if a record of time scratched on a prison wall, to underline its opposition to the introduction of ninety days detention without charge for suspected terrorists, which had been proposed by the Government. Such a graphic representation moves beyond reasoned debate to a much more emotive demonstration of the potential effect of such legislation in the opinion of the newspaper. On other occasions, the weight of statistical evidence presented can crowd out any wider discussion of the underlying theme of a story. The statistics are literally left to speak for themselves and tend to perpetuate uncritical views of official reports:

Attacks in Iraq jumped in 2005

Insurgents widen aim to Iraqi forces

The number of insurgent attacks against coalition troops, Iraqi security forces and civilians increased 29% last year.
  Insurgents launched 34,131 attacks last year, up from 26,496 the year before, according to U.S. military figures.
  Car bombs and suicide bombings have increased dramatically. The number of car bombs more than doubled to 873 last year from 420 the year before. And the number of suicide car bombs went to 411 from 133.
  The U.S. military also reported an increase in the number of attackers wearing suicide vests, which went to 67 last year from seven the year before.

(*USA Today*, 23 January 2006)

Sometimes the condensed language of a headline can be used to provide a snapshot of an opinion close to the editorial preferences of the newspaper which is reinforced in its rhetorical appeal by its ability to map onto a familiar phrase. The *Times* uses a neat inversion to emphasize at the same time as summarizing its view of government proposals to impose some sort of road pricing by mileage:

Drive the poor off the road – that's rich

(*Times*, 7 June 2005)

The front page is also increasingly the place where contemporary elite newspapers appear to flag their ambitions to be both informed and populist. The *Independent*, for instance, had a strapline on the top of its front page which read:

WHY MEN ARE CRAP

(*Independent*, 25 October 2005)

Although the strapline referred to an article in the features section of the newspaper, its prominence on a page usually dominated until very recently by hard news in the elite press is an indication of how popularized that space has become, and how the newspaper increasingly assumes that its readers will be as interested in magazine-style opinion pieces as the latest from the world of politics or economics.

Another favoured rhetorical device is the exaggeration for the sake of emphasis, or hyperbole. In the next example, the legacy of Margaret Thatcher is said to have been derided to such an extent by what the newspaper calls 'Labour propaganda' that she appears to be classified by her opponents as belonging in the same category as two cardboard cut-out villains from history. This hyperbole seeks to ridicule criticism of Thatcher as treating her as a mass murderer or totalitarian dictator. The piece rhetorically contrasts this exaggeration with the actual memories, not only of ordinary people, but of the readers of the *Sun* newspaper:

> **Millions of Sun readers did well in the Thatcher years of the Eighties. Today, thanks to years of Labour propaganda, you only have to mention the name Thatcher to get gasps of horror as if you had summoned up the ghosts of Stalin and Jack the Ripper.**

(*Sun*, 6 June 2005)

A further characteristic rhetorical device is very close to the ambitions of any newspaper's editorial identity: the claim to appeal to the 'people', as being synonymous with its own readers. Interestingly, this is not the exclusive preserve of the popular press but can also be found in the elite newspapers as they too seek to explicitly identify their readership:

Putting power back in the hands of the people

We do not, as a newspaper, endorse all these proposals. But we warmly applaud the philosophy and spirit that infuse the programme, and think it worthy of consideration by all political parties, not just the Conservative leadership contenders.

(*Daily Telegraph*, 6 June 2005)

Here we see the 'people' being addressed, not in a popular tabloid newspaper but in the only remaining daily British broadsheet newspaper, which is an elite newspaper, targeting an elite readership in its editorial and its advertising. Furthermore, it considers itself to be, with its long historical trajectory, a newspaper of record, yet it can still find it useful to broaden its appeal across all political parties in this appeal to its readership and beyond as the people. In contrast, the implication of the following piece introducing some reflections on the plight of Africa in the global economy, in the *Guardian*, one of the foremost liberal newspapers in Britain, appears to be castigating not only its own readers but aspects of its own tradition, playing with an echo of the proverbial 'blind leading the blind':

The naive leading the naive in a campaign of liberal guilt

(*Guardian*, 6 June 2005)

Using the front page to publicize a populist campaign to reduce or abolish inheritance tax in Britain is a good way of demonstrating how one newspaper establishes common ground with its readers. Having given campaign car stickers away, the *Daily Express* then produces a photograph on the front page of one of its stickers in the rear window of a car to bolster the impression that the campaign has struck a popular note. It uses the personal pronoun 'you' to directly address its readership and thus reinforce a concern shared by both newspaper and readers. It uses the short slogan 'INHERITANCE TAX IS THEFT' in bold to encapsulate the basic premise of its campaign and calls on the Chancellor, in familiar first name terms, to take action, thus implying a personal proximity between the Chancellor and the newspaper on behalf of the readers.

YOU ARE SHOWING YOUR CAR STICKERS WITH PRIDE

DAILY EXPRESS CRUSADE

INHERITANCE TAX IS THEFT

GET USED TO THIS VIEW GORDON: Our readers are sending the Chancellor a clear message.

(*Daily Express*, 7 March 2006, front page)

Argumentation

Argumentation is also essential to the effective formation of opinion. To study argument as a whole we need to consider features such as the context of the argument, the status of those putting the argument forward, and the power implications in the position of the speaker/writer towards the subject and towards the audience, as well as the stylistic devices used. The context of the argument is very important for the news media. This is informed by the type of newspaper and its political and social preferences. The context of an argument reflects the contemporary positioning of the news medium with regard to the traditions of that medium and whether it is arguing for a continuation of a political preference or for a change of preference.

This was dramatically demonstrated in 1997 when the *Sun* newspaper broke with decades of unqualified support for the Conservative party to swing behind Tony Blair's New Labour. It switched its editorial line unequivocally on 18 March 1997:

> The Sun Backs Blair. . . . a leader with vision, purpose and courage who can inspire and fire the imaginations. . . . The Tories have all the right policies but all the wrong faces.

This may have caused problems for certain of the editorial staff who were used to writing in support of most of the Conservative party's policies and in equal measure to opposing those of the Labour party, but the decision to call on readers to back Labour was an argument which the paper based on reliable indications that this was the direction in which the readers' views as voters had been heading for some time. The argumentation within the context of that particular newspaper at that time was the result of a pragmatic shift behind Labour as popular support among readers for the Conservative party dwindled. The *Sun*, quite simply, did not want to be on the losing side.

Arguments are the statements and strategies which a writer or speaker uses to persuade someone of the validity of their position. Much argumentation within the news media, although sometimes presented as personal opinion, is in fact part of the overall position of the news medium within which it is located. Even dissenting opinion is used to reinforce the impression that a liberal tolerance of a range of viewpoints is accepted and even encouraged from readers as well as from columnists. This was most notable in the *Guardian* in the run-up to the invasion of Iraq in 2003 where the diverse opinions of readers and journalists were allowed considerable scope within the paper.

Argument can use separate or combined strategies to position the writer of the news or commentary on the news in the best possible way in order to win or retain the approval of the imagined audience. These strategies include dialectic, logic, emotion and reputation. Dialectic is the construction of a conclusion based on the consideration of a variety of conflicting positions with one position being demonstrated as the correct one. Logic is the deployment of deductive or inductive argument to lead the reader to the preferred conclusion. Deductive arguments use a series of statements in order to generate a chain of reasoning and are finished off with a statement of conclusion based on these. Inductive arguments use a series of examples or comparisons (analogies) to build to a conclusion which the reader is invited to share. Emotion suggests that the reader can be persuaded by a direct appeal to fear, pride, enjoyment or any other emotional state thereby bypassing rational appeal. Reputation stresses the experience or character of the writer and the direct experience and authority of the source or those the writer chooses to name as supporting the argument presented.

Once an approach to building an argument has been selected, arguments can then be made up of premise, warrant and claim. The premise states the grounds on which the argument is based, either implicitly or explicitly. The warrant is what justifies the premise being linked to the claim which the argument makes (Toulmin, 1958).

A good example of the use of dialectic is to be found in the next piece, which charts and rationalizes the shift in Australian public life to embrace the celebration of Australia Day. It starts with the premise that the national holiday is something to enjoy. The warrants are the historical contexts which have led to liberal guilt about the past in Australia, and the claim is that through a democratic reassessment, as expressed through the ballot box, Australians have decided to warmly embrace their own shared sense of national pride. The dialectic pits the ambiguities and difficulties of Australia's colonial past and continuing link with the imperial power, Britain, against a political rejection of those anxieties which the piece claims are part of a 'politically correct introspection'. Interestingly though, this rejection depends more on an emotional appeal against 'political correctness' than a rational explanation for the political shift. Flawed in rational terms but dialectically persuasive in appealing to the emotions, the piece celebrates the return to fashion of the Australian Public Holiday:

Come let us rejoice

Celebrating Australia Day is back in fashion, so grab your flag and start waving, writes **Stuart Rintoul**

THERE was a time when Australians, if they were at all good-hearted, were obliged to agonise on Australia Day.

If we had to celebrate a national birthday, the argument went, then we ought at least to reflect, however briefly, on the cost of establishing the nation as well as its achievements. We should be conscious that Aboriginal people regard January 26 as Invasion Day and reflect on the illogicality of a nation founded by a British governor and still tied to Britain's monarchic apron strings. It was, all in all, a troubling kind of celebration.

Sick to death of this politically correct introspection, Australians elected John Howard and almost 10 years later are again blithely celebrating the simple joys of being Australian, according to some of the nation's most savvy market researchers. As a result, flag makers are reporting bumper business.

(*The Australian*, 26 January 2006)

This rhetorical patriotism can be reinforced, as in the following colloquial address to readers:

It's our day, so let's celebrate

OUR wide, brown land was crowded and colourful yesterday, as South Australians celebrated Australia Day with a mixture of pomp, ceremony and fair dinkum fun. . . . thousands of backyard barbies . . .

(*The Advertiser*, 27 January 2006)

In the next example, Francis Wheen's personal and professional reputation are explicitly prioritized in order to demonstrate just how bad the European polity has become. This is a good example of the use of reputation to construct an argument. In fact, a great deal of news media language makes use of the personality or reputation of correspondents, and this is most clearly seen in the roles of television correspondents as opinion brokers. Readers, in the example below, may not immediately be aware that Wheen is a well-known left-liberal commentator and a former columnist with the *Guardian* as well as being the author of a sympathetic and well-received biography of Karl Marx. In case they didn't know these facts, the opening sentence makes clear the paradox. Wheen, to reinforce his liberal reputation on such issues, refers to himself as 'an ardent Europhile' in order to strengthen his case against the 'Brussels lie machine' which in itself is a clear example of how, in a brief strapline, an emotive premise which will chime with the views of readers of this particular paper can be declared as the basis for the rest of the argument.

Why I, an ardent Europhile, toast the French and the Dutch for rejecting the Brussels lie machine

(Francis Wheen, *Daily Mail*, 3 June 2005)

The key mechanism of argument in the news media is how the warrants are made to fit into the commonsense assumptions about the world which the audience is expected to share. In this way they act as a normalizing element within the argument and therefore have highly ideological implications as they frame what is expected to be acceptable to readers of that particular news medium. The 'come let us rejoice' piece assumes a commonsense rejection of what it claims is 'political correctness' in order to dialectically quote aspects of what, in the past, Australians had found difficult about their national identity, and to then sweep away these points by siding with a readership that it assumes is fully in tune with a conservative shift in political opinion which allows them to enjoy and celebrate the day. Thus the warrants fit into the audience design of the newspaper.

Deductive argument, drawn from the personal and professional observations of a celebrity psychologist can combine emotive language with a shape of reasoning built upon a chain of probability. The next piece opens using the word 'toxic' and echoes this emotive vocabulary in the final line by the use of the word 'poisonous'. In between it builds the argument. The premise is that 'toxic chemistry' 'can' occur but it is restrained in its use of the modal verb 'can'. It further qualifies that modality by using the word 'probably' to assess the possibility that children lose their sense of reality by being exposed to violent scenes on television. It then moves on to consider how this grasp of reality can 'loosen' before moving to the claim that 'we should not be surprised if . . . fantasies become reality'. Oliver James is using a subtle gradation of deduction to argue that copycat crime is not an inevitability but he is rather considering the possible consequences of a sequence of social and emotional factors on some particular individuals 'from time to time'. It leads the reader, via a series of qualified warrants, to the conclusion that there is substance in social concerns characteristic of a conservative readership that there is a direct correlation between television violence and the behaviour of young people.

A toxic chemistry can occur when gangs of pre-teen youngsters are left unsupervised by adults, which they are more likely to be today, when truanting or after school, with parents still at work. . . .

It is probably extremely rare that a child loses grip on reality so completely that it watches a scene on TV and simply re-enacts it soon afterwards. But the suspension of disbelief when viewing almost certainly loosens what can already be a weak grasp of the difference between fantasy and reality in vulnerable children.

We should not be surprised if, from time to time, the fantasies become reality and we reap the poisonous harvest that they sow.

(Oliver James, *Times*, 3 June 2005)

 Activity 4.2

Select two examples of commentary from the newspapers and show how the argument is formed, evidence presented, and rhetorical devices deployed, and how these combine to provide an exercise in persuasion.

Editorials

The most obvious and the most traditional place for newspapers to express their collective or editorial opinion is in their leading articles. This is where the newspaper takes a stance on what it claims are the most important issues of the day. These pieces are persuasive in tone but so in keeping with the overall political and cultural positioning of the newspaper that there is little actual persuading going on. It is more a process of confirming the identity of the newspaper and in so doing the identity of the idealized community of readership. On the occasions that a leading article does feel that it is moving away from the constructed consensus of its own traditions and consensus with its readers then an explicit reference to such a gambit will often be inserted: 'We have always been of the opinion . . . but . . .'.

A vital duty

READERS may ask why Britain is sending 4,000 crack troops to Afghanistan when we are already stretched in Iraq?

The answer is critically important.

The Afghan people are courageously taking the first steps towards democracy.

Despite problems, the overwhelming majority are desperate for peace, stability and, with luck, prosperity.

It is vital that the West ensures that this fragile process takes firm root.

Our Boys face a dangerous mission. They will confront the world's most vicious armed fanatics.

There will inevitably be casualties.

But the world cannot risk abandoning this troubled nation or allow it to fall back into the hands of al-Qaeda and the evil Taliban.

(*Sun*, 25 January 2006)

This measured and deductive piece from the British popular paper the *Sun* demonstrates many of the linguistic strategies of a successful editorial piece and demonstrates that despite their often raucous tone in news reporting, popular tabloids can be as eloquent and considered along their own political and demotic lines as any of the elite press. The piece starts off by asserting an elliptical premise: 'A vital duty'. It provides a series of statements which move the reader via the warrants towards the claim of the piece. The opening question attempts to frame the targeted reader's concerns and to offer a direct answer to this question. It flags the British soldiers as 'crack troops' in order to generate respect for their professionalism and to enhance a feeling of vicarious satisfaction in having such high quality military personnel at the disposal of the country. It moves from the troops to the more inclusive personal pronoun 'we' when referring to the level of deployment, thus merging the British troops, national interest and readers in this small word. The next statement almost seems to ask for renewed attention from the reader: 'The answer is critically important', and the newspaper is going to explain it in direct, didactic terms. The Afghan people, the ordinary people the 'overwhelming majority' are praised for their willingness to take the 'first steps towards democracy' and these are counterposed to the 'world's most vicious, armed fanatics'. 'Our boys' a familiar popular tabloid descriptor, are held up as the representatives not only of the British and the 'Afghan people' but of the world, and therefore casualties (implicitly British casualties not Afghan casualties) will be the inevitable price of fulfilling this 'vital duty'. It is a strong and persuasively structured piece of writing which fits into, as well as develops, the concept of the ideal reader which it is aimed at. It represents an editorial position which can be drawn from in order to understand many other aspects of the paper's political opinions and what it expects the opinions of its readers to be. On occasions like this, where the paper feels that there is a doubt that the readers might not move with it on important contemporary issues, then it goes out of its way to make the case in as persuasively deductive a manner as possible.

 Activity 4.3 o—r

Take one editorial piece from any newspaper and see if you can match the opinions in that piece with other items in the same issue of the newspaper. For instance, you may want to look at the way the subject is covered in the news section, whether there are any opinion features on that piece of news or whether there are any letters to the editor which deal with that particular story.

Liberal Democrats

No time for recriminations

The weekend revelations about the Liberal Democrat home affairs spokesman are a personal tragedy for Mark Oaten and a very public setback for his party. Mr Oaten is deserving of some sympathy. It is true that paying a prostitute for sex is not wise behaviour for any politician, let alone a member of the front bench. And it is legitimate to point out, as some have, that Mr Oaten in the past used his image as a settled family man for political gain. But, at heart, this was a private matter. And it would have been preferable had it remained so. Now Mr Oaten has resigned from front-line politics, he ought to be given adequate space and time to sort out his domestic situation.

What makes this even more of a pity is that Mr Oaten was a promising politician and a rising star of the Liberal Democrats. He had given serious thought to the position of his party in British politics and had a clear idea of the direction in which it ought to head. As a home affairs spokesman, he provided robust and necessary opposition to the Government's anti-terrorism legislation. And although he was unlikely to have emerged victorious in the leadership contest (something that he acknowledged by pulling out last week), his departure is a real blow to the Liberal Democrat front bench. We hope that this affair does not spell the end of Mr Oaten's political career.

These are turbulent times for the Liberal Democrats. In the space of little more than two weeks they have had to deal with the public revelation of their leader's alcoholism and his subsequent resignation. Then came the admission from Lord McNally, the party's leader in the House of Lords, that he too has battled with a drink problem. And now there is this sex scandal. What must make this succession of damaging headlines more difficult to bear is that they come less than a year after a general election in which the party gained its highest number of seats since the 1920s. Hopes were high for further progress. Instead, the party has gone backwards.

Although there is still much bad blood over the manner of Charles Kennedy's departure, the Liberal Democrats must resist the temptation to indulge in a period of score-settling. That would be wholly counterproductive, especially as the media spotlight is now shining on them intensely. What the party's latest troubles serve to underline is the need for it to choose a leader who can both unify and reinvigorate the MPs and the party in the country. The march of the Tory leader David Cameron on to traditional Liberal Democrat territory means that they do not have the luxury of time. This latest scandal to rock the party makes the need to choose the right leader all the more urgent.

(*Independent,* 23 January 2006)

In the editorial piece above, we have the *Independent*'s view of the discovery that Mark Oaten has been embroiled in a sex scandal and the subsequent end of his political career. In the second line of the piece comes the premise that it is 'No time for recriminations'. It then moves into a series of dialectic concessions, 'deserving some sympathy', 'It is true', 'And it is legitimate', 'this was a private matter', 'And it would have been preferable'. These concessions are followed with one of the key warrants. Despite all of the furore over the scandal and the way it became public knowledge, from the political perspective of the *Independent,* the main shame is that 'Mr Oaten was a promising politician and a rising star of the Liberal Democrats'. It sees the loss as predominantly a political one and moves to a preliminary assertion that, 'We hope that this affair does not spell the end of Mr Oaten's political career'.

There then follows an argument within an argument which is contained in a paragraph outlining the premise that, 'These are turbulent times for the Liberal Democrats'. The warrants are then listed and the claim is produced at the end of the paragraph that, 'the party has gone backwards'. This is followed by the final paragraph where the dialectic continues using concessions to the bad feeling within the party in phrases such as 'bad blood', 'score-settling', and it moves to counter these impulses by referring to them as 'counterproductive'. The premise is to 'choose the right leader' someone who can with double emphasis 'both unify and reinvigorate the MPs and the party in the country'. We have here a carefully balanced argument outlining the damage done to the Liberal Democrats and accepting the reasons why some might be tempted to involve themselves in the settling of feuds, but using these contexts as explanations why the party needs to move on and unify around a strong political leader.

Activity 4.4

Using the commentary on the editorial above and drawing on the linguistic tools which have been introduced up to now in this book, write a commentary on the following piece. How does it construct its argument? Try to deduce the differences in the newspaper's politics and what it imagines are the politics of its readers in contrast to the *Independent*.

A NOT-SO-SECRET LIFE

The sad saga of Mark Oaten is a salutary warning

The personal and political humiliation of Mark Oaten is a self-inflicted tragedy. Mr Oaten is an able man who had sought to move the Liberal Democrats in a more realistic direction. Yet what he describes – in something of an understatement – as his 'error of judgement' has not merely destroyed a career, but inflicted dreadful pain on his family.

Sympathy for Mr Oaten has to be balanced against the extraordinary recklessness of his behaviour. He was seen to be, if temporarily, a candidate for the leadership of his party despite having a not-so-secret life that was destined to discredit him. As a senior Liberal Democrat spokesman, it was naive to think that he was not well known enough to be identified. To assume that if he won the leadership, he might be able to rely on the polite silence of those who sell themselves for sex was an example of being 'in denial'. If he had obtained the position that he sought, the embarrassment would have been even worse for a party whose leader has just resigned over a long-denied drinking problem.

In fairness to him, he is one of a long line of (invariably male) politicians of all parties who have worked on the assumption that their lives could be secretly compartmentalised. The blunt truth is that this can never be the case. Furthermore, voters are entitled to reach conclusions about how those who would lead them conduct themselves in the shadows. Some in the House of Commons might look at Mr Oaten's fate and contend that their shenanigans are a 'private matter'. Such selfishness will inevitably surface, to the detriment of their party, their person and their family.

(*Times*, 23 January 2006)

Columnists – 'Viewspapers'

As newspapers have become involved in a more competitive fight for readers with the increase in the number and accessibility of news media, there is evidence that they have become relied upon more for their activity in confirming the major events in the world rather than as initial sources for information and second, but just as importantly, as sources for commentary on events. Negative criticism has coined the expression 'viewspapers' to describe this tendency, yet there appear to be very sound reasons for newspapers to be increasingly taking this position. Readers appear to approve of newspapers as places to turn to, not just for reports on what has happened – most of this is available at least a day earlier through other channels – but for explanations from trusted sources, the columnists, of what the news means, and to suggest a range of appropriate opinion for their readers to engage with. The columnists have an important part to play, not just in this opinion brokering but also in engendering controversy and eliciting correspondence from readers to generate further opinion and debate within the paper as part of its communicative cycle. They are nearly always the highest paid and highest profile staff on the newspaper. Richard Littlejohn, for instance, who has moved between various British newspapers is reputedly the best-paid columnist in the country.

 Activity 4.5 ⊶

Select two columnists from two different newspapers and analyse how they construct their arguments, paying particular attention to how they use emotive language and appeal directly to the reader for their support.

Opinion in hard news

Beyond the expression of openly political opinion in editorials, commentaries and features, there are also a range of covert strategies in newspapers' coverage of traditional hard news which assist in constructing viewpoints. This is not explicit in the content, but more evident in the structure and selection of news, the hierarchy of informants used to lend credibility to a particular perspective and the ways in which such selection and hierarchies contribute to the representation of a preferred view of the world. Strategies of argumentation, the selection of sources, the ordering of the story to privilege one perspective before introducing another, vocabulary, patterns of metaphor and house style can all play a part in the covert persuasion of a readership and contribute thereby to the maintenance of the identity of a newspaper. Because of the economic imperative for newspapers to maintain a stable target audience their content tends to at least delimit any dissent against perspectives which are contrary to their traditional positions. Newspapers tend to be relatively conservative in their views of the world and this trait is no different in other news media. Consider, for instance, the way in which there has always been a uniformity of tone to the reporting of protests against the G8. Any protest which calls into question the fundamentals of the right of the wealthiest nations in the world to make economic and political policy on their own terms does not tend to gain much in the way of a sympathetic hearing in any of the mainstream media. Newspapers are profit-making organizations and are unlikely to be sympathetic to protests which appear to challenge global capitalism.

One way to inscribe opinion into a hard news story is through the use of exaggeration for the purpose of emphasizing a particular perspective. This is called hyperbole. The initial implication of the next extract is that Australia forms part of the 'West' and has shared political and military concerns with this entity. Of course, only a politically driven rhetoric could claim that Australia forms part of the West, and in many other areas of the Australian news media it is clear that it sees itself in much more of a global location, with access to and interests in the politics and economics of Asia and the Pacific Rim. The second word of the piece is a modal verb, 'must', which insists that the only way to avert a confrontation with Iran is to prepare for war. The preparation is expressed in terms of 'brace' as if impact as in a collision is inevitable, and Iran's alleged move towards a nuclear arsenal is categorized as a 'nightmare'. The impact of the metaphorical 'brace' is underlined when the article proper starts and the less emotive 'get ready' is substituted. The confrontation is then heightened when the 'West' is articulated positively in terms of relational verbs as being, 'free-speaking, free-thinking' and the absence of descriptors for Iran leaves us to draw the conclusion that they are the opposite to this. However, the piece goes on to highlight the deficiencies of such liberal traditions, claiming that they can lead to 'hand-wringing, finger-pointing and second-guessing'. The piece concludes by returning to the hyperbole and draws upon monsters familiar with readers to make its emotive, though hardly politically or historically accurate, analogy:

West must brace for war to avert nightmare of a nuclear Iran

The unimaginable but ultimately inescapable truth is that we are going to have to get ready for war with Iran.

Being of a free-speaking, free-thinking disposition, we generally find in the West that hand-wringing, finger-pointing and second-guessing come more easily to us than cold, strategic thinking. . . . We must ready ourselves for what may be the unthinkable necessity. . . . If Iran gets safely and unmolested to nuclear status, it will be a threshold moment in the history of the world, up there with the Bolshevik Revolution and the coming of Hitler.

(*Weekend Australian*, 28–29 January 2006)

In the next example, we can see a similar range of linguistic strategies which mark this front-page hard news as identified with a particular perspective. This is evident in the geopolitical interests of the newspaper in question and the audience which the newspaper also assumes shares its nationally based perspectives on world politics, The brevity of the headline encodes a nominalization in 'fundamentalists'. The definition of what constitutes a 'fundamentalist', the political and historical genesis of positions opposed to Western interests and the labelling of these as 'fundamentalist' are all necessarily obscured in the abbreviation. Their ascendancy is marked by 'rise', an actional verb but an intransitive verb and one which has no adverbial circumstances attached to it. The headline creates an impression of a spontaneous emergence of fundamentalists in a particular region. This sort of presentation of a vague and politically contentious area, the 'mideast' spontaneously producing political effects which are antagonistic towards American interests, takes away blame or even historical context from such opposition. It is a common 'script' within Western news media so it is no surprise to see it encoded in the all-important opening headline of such a story. Yet, the hard news story here develops this implicit antagonism much more explicitly in the lines that follow. Instead of giving more context to the possible reasons for such antipathies, the story reinforces the binary distinctions, and privileges the national interests of the USA. The winners in the elections are defined as 'at odds with U.S.' and then in the next line, those 'who oppose US interests in the Middle East'. The presupposition is that the readers understand that 'US interests in the Middle East' are their own interests and not in need of further identification or clarification. There is furthermore a binary opposition constructed here between the 'Islamic fundamentalists' whose political position is implicitly driven by religious concerns and an altruistic 'Bush administration' which 'pushes for democracy as a benefit to the region and to the United States'. It is interesting in contrast to note the general lack of reference to the well-documented Christian fundamentalism of the President of the USA. Here we have the geopolitical goals of the US and the region aligned as identical to each other and this by implication reinforces the view that the fundamentalism is irrational, irrevocably linked to the region and possibly irretrievably bound up with religion.

Mideast fundamentalists rise

Groups at odds with U.S. gain in politics

Islamic fundamentalists who oppose US interests in the Middle East have made political gains in free elections while the Bush administration pushes for democracy as a benefit to the region and the United States. . . . Hezbollah . . . branded a terrorist group by the State Department for kidnapping and killing Americans in the 1980s.

(*USA Today*, 25 January 2006)

In the run-up to these elections, emotive language was used in hard news stories to further confirm categorizations of political figures from parties opposed by Western interests. One such figure was Martin Barghouti, a Palestinian running for election from his Israeli prison. He is named in the *Times* (23 January 2006) as a 'firebrand' and a 'voluble populist' and his television address is an attempt to 'woo' Hamas. It is interesting that all of these words tend to highlight the irrational appeal of this political figure rather than explore the rational nature of the appeal of a convicted prisoner and why he represents a credible political figure to voters in that region.

A different political election also provides examples of how language within a hard new story can be used to present a preferred reading. In the first example which follows, there is the word 'humiliated' to describe the outgoing premier of Canada and this must be judged against the more moderate report that the country has moved 'cautiously' to the right which follows in the next sentence. There is also the use of what has been referred to before as modal inverted commas, which serve the purpose of making an accusation which needs not be substantiated, is the opinion of somebody else or supports one opinion among many which the newspaper would like to selectively draw the reader's attention to; in other words a preferred reading once again. The second example uses a metaphor to reinforce its own observations of the victory of the conservatives in the Canadian poll which is clearly more indicative of being impressed by this victory than if the headline had simply reported the fact that they had won the election.

Martin is humiliated as Canada throws out 'arrogant' Liberals

Canada has moved cautiously to the right . . .

(*Independent*, 25 January 2006)

Right wing storms back after years in wilderness

(*Times*, 25 January 2006)

In the following three examples, all from popular tabloid newspapers, we see how familiar, colloquial phrases can be deployed to discuss the politics of a move to reduce the costs of incapacity benefits. In its headline, the *Daily Mirror* uses the colloquial term 'THE SICK' and calls it a 'shake-up'. The *Sun* refers to the benefit first as a 'PAYOUT' and next as a 'handout' both of which reinforce the impression that these are not benefits from a social security system to which recipients and tax payers have actively contributed but obscure this in its use of language to favour a view of the benefits as something rather more passively received. The final example comes close to explicitly acknowledging the underlying impression in the language of all the reports. The reform is marked as a 'crackdown' which implies by connotation that the current practice is something which borders on the illegal or at least unacceptable and needs strong intervention to eradicate. The issue of the expense of the benefits is referred to in terms of a long-running script within this particular newspaper, drawing, it assumes, on the populist views of its readers and reinforcing those views through its choice of language. It refers broadly to the existence of a 'sicknote culture' confident that the insertion of this presupposition into a hard news story will find a sympathetic community of like-minded readers.

Taking one million off the sick will save £7bn

Blair unveils benefit shake-up

TONY Blair yesterday pledged to save £7billion by taking one million people off incapacity benefit and getting them back into work.

(*Daily Mirror*, 25 January 2006)

Sick payout bid 'doomed'

A DRIVE to slash Britain's sick-pay handouts by £7billion a year is doomed, critics warned last night.

(*Sun*, 25 January 2006)

Crackdown? The 2.7m on welfare won't lose a penny

TONY Blair unveiled his long-awaited crackdown on Britain's sicknote culture yesterday with plans to get a million on benefit back to work.

(*Daily Mail*, 25 January 2006)

Activity 4.6

Find examples of how opinion or preferred readings are inserted into hard news stories in both popular tabloid and elite newspapers.

Another way of foregrounding aspects of political perspective within a hard news story is to take out a quotation and highlight it above other aspects of the story or other comments from those involved in the story or interviewed as part of it. As part of the next extract, for example, the words of Nick Herbert, Shadow Police Minister, which were quoted late on in the article, were repeated, promoted to form a stand-alone quotation, prominently enlarged in the centre of the first column: 'On this test, the Government is clearly failing the public.'

The newspaper could have chosen to highlight the rather more conciliatory remarks of the Home Secretary, also quoted, but the choice of Herbert's words is significant as they fit better within the news values of a newspaper which sees opposing Government positions on law and order as less newsworthy or less politically supportable than the views of the Opposition.

Muggings and violent attacks up by more than 10%

MUGGINGS and violent attacks on people soared by more than 10 per cent in the third quarter of last year as the police struggled to contain street crime, according to figures published yesterday.
Street robbery is rising at its fastest since Tony Blair demanded action three years ago by the Home Office and police to tackle the issue.

(*Times*, 27 January 2006)

Broadcast news

Traditionally, broadcast news has had to adhere to more stringent standards of impartiality. This is particularly true of public service broadcasters but even when commercial broadcasters are considered to be moving too much in the direction of politically informed opinion there has been considerable unease among broadcasters and audiences, as the controversy over Fox Television's reporting of the invasion of Iraq in 2003 indicated.

Yet all is not straightforward in the language of broadcast news. The language may not be as clearly indicative of politically partisan positions as the press but there tends to be a sceptical perspective on contemporary politics as well as a conservative perspective on questions of general political economy. In recent years, however, certainly under the influence of increasing reliance on the ethos of entertainment in other parts of the media and in an attempt to maintain market share within this general entertainment business, broadcast news has moved more towards enlivening political reporting in particular by using tactics designed to elicit more opiniated perspectives. It is not however inscribed within the voice or language of the news anchor or presenter. The role of persuasion is shifted from the news anchor to the commentator on the spot who is asked, on the face of it, for analysis but this is often couched in terms of opinion, and acts very much as such.

Overall, some might argue that the most consistent persuasive message of broadcast interviews, especially on political programmes, is to arouse suspicion or even total distrust in the word of politicians.

Opinion is shifted sideways in broadcast news, to special correspondents who are asked for their view outside the confines of the official speaker of the news who appears to present simply a selection of facts. These correspondents are asked relatively open questions about the matter in hand and their opinion is based on their position of expertise rather than as individual commentators. The news anchor is not drawn in any way to this enunciation of informed opinion but draws the audience back into the mainstream of facts and the news agenda as soon as the opinions have been elicited. Another, more complex form of shifting opinion sideways within the discourse of broadcast news is by inviting partisan protagonists to share a physical or virtual platform where the news anchor asks them provocative questions, thereby allowing her/him a modicum of opinion without it being able to be construed as an enunciation of individual or even institutional opinion on behalf of the news anchor. Blumler and Gurevitch (1995) have shown how this can often be used to create an impression of political news as circus or media confrontation. In some television and radio news programmes, notably *Newsnight* and *Today*, the interviewer can move from presenter of facts to confrontational protagonist within the live interview. This live interview is one important feature which distinguishes broadcast from printed news as it is most often omitted or elided in the latter format.

 Activity 4.7 o—ᴇ

Can you find any examples of news correspondents on mainstream television news offering opinion to the news anchor? What language indicates that the correspondent is dealing with opinion rather than hard fact?

Activity 4.8 o⊸

Watch two political interviews on mainstream television or listen to two on radio and consider whether there is any indication in the way that the questions are formulated which may confirm the view that political interviews are used not to provide information but to provoke scepticism and even cynicism about the motives of politicians in the viewers/listeners?

Summary

This chapter has considered the strategies used in the language of the news to emphasize opinion. In an era where technologically we have access to rolling news and internet news sources, the traditional role of newspapers and to a certain extent public service broadcasters to simply provide the latest information about the world is undergoing a transformation. These news media are increasingly being relied upon by their audiences to provide information with commentary and opinion very much integrated within them. This chapter has shown how opinion can be an explicit part of the function of news in leading articles and columnists as well as being more subtly integrated into the conventions of hard news. It has provided examples of the ways in which the selection of vocabulary, the choice of metaphor and verbal construction can all reinforce the preferred meaning of news stories and maintain credibility with an audience which wants its view of the world confirmed at the same time as it wants to be informed.

Suggestions for further reading

Bell, A. (1991) *The Language of News Media*. Oxford: Blackwell.
Hall, S. (1973) 'Encoding/decoding'. In S. Hall, D. Hobson, A. Lowe and P. Willis (eds) *Culture, Media, Language*. London: Hutchinson.
Fairclough, N. (1989) *Language and Power*. London: Longman.
Tuchman, G. (1978) *Making News: A Study in the Construction of Reality*. New York: Free Press.

5 Social semiotic and ideology

Introduction

This chapter will look at semiotics, how language takes on meaning as a complex system of signs. The social aspect of meaning is extremely productive in enabling us to understand how the language of the news generates wider networks beyond the limits of its own pages. The relative stability of meanings produced by news media leads us to combine an analysis of semiology with one of ideology. We have mentioned ideology briefly before but this chapter will explore it more fully and explain how it can shed light on the workings of the language in the news. Ideology is the process by which belief systems become established as common sense, habitual patterns. The constant use of familiar references in daily communication such as within the language of our news media can be seen to reinforce dominant patterns of belief in society, and this has implications for the power structures of that society.

Semiology

Semiology was defined in 1916 by the Swiss academic, Ferdinand de Saussure (1974), who coined the word as meaning the scientific study of signs. For the purposes of semiology, a sign is something which stands for something else. An American academic at the same time, Peirce, referred to his similar investigations into the process of meaning as semiotics.

Signs, put simply, stand for something else. For our purposes words, as signs, stand for objects and concepts. According to semiological analysis signs are filled by intent. This means that the choice of which language to use is highly significant, as that choice tells us about the social location of the speakers and what they expect their audience to understand. Communication, therefore, always works within the constraints of social meanings and conventions. Semiology also emphasizes that meaning comes not from a sign itself but from the place which a sign has within a system of communication and therefore its relationship with other signs.

Semiology encourages us to create a distance from the everyday routines of language to allow us to see language in a de-naturalized way. It does this by creating a series of binary oppositions, some of which have implications for our study of the language of the news media. There are four main binary oppositions, opposing poles, which can help us understand how meaning is created by contrasts and complements within any system of communication. These binaries can be represented in tabular fashion thus:

Structure/Speech
Synchronic/Diachronic
Paradigmatic/Syntagmatic
Denotation/Connotation

Semiology encourages us, first, to explore the difference between the underlying system that organizes the signs, which can be compared to the grammar of a language – how it is organized and ought to operate – and the everyday use of those signs in practice. We might call these 'structure' and 'speech'. Second, it stresses the difference between contemporary analysis of meaning and analysis of meaning across time, referred to here as 'synchronic' and 'diachronic'. Third, it highlights the selection from 'paradigms' – lists – or from 'syntagms' – chains – as options, and fourth, the difference between denotation – the literal meaning of language – and connotation, the more figurative associations which words gather over time, generating new implications and even entirely new meanings.

Although such distinctions are useful when considering any process of meaning production such as news, distancing the reader as they do from the familiarity of the language and the mechanisms which are taken for granted because of their daily routine, there are problems when applying these binaries to the language of the news which, as we will see, is an extremely fluid and reflexive medium. The 'structure' or established grammar of signs in operation corresponds to the patterns of news value and priority whereas the everyday examples of news corresponds to the more flexible variations of 'speech'. Yet the underlying patterns of the news are themselves highly flexible and can accommodate the patterns of contemporary speech and practice. Hierarchies of news value can be varied to allow unfamiliar and even contentious voices to be heard as long as they do not destabilize longer-term patterns of meaning. For instance, a dissenting Iraqi voice or opinion may be heard on the front pages of the newspaper but this will not become the longer-term view of the newspaper. An African victim of famine may be interviewed on the news on an isolated occasion but this does not detract from the overall silence of these people or fundamentally alter the statistical fact of their merely occasional intrusion into the news.

With regard to the distinctions between the synchronic (of the moment) and diachronic (over time), it is almost always the case that the historical, longer-term aspect of news, although relegated to a position of less prominence, is still present in the contemporary reporting of events. This is how perspective is maintained, and a relatively stable worldview retains coherence for an audience. In other parts of this book we will see how the analysis of contemporary news language can only take place in a way which explores the historical rooting of that language as an essential part of its context. An obvious example would be the way that the anniversaries of war are commemorated where the past is the central point of the contemporary story, or even a more mundane story where a concise reference to the past is embedded in the present and the reader is expected to make the connection for themselves from within the accepted cultural framework of the newspaper's language. In this next example, a football manager's reference to Winston Churchill is drawn out and emphasized, and through this emphasis it is thereby continuing to contribute to the resonance of the war-time leader in vernacular culture. In a pre-match talk, football manager Ian Holloway is reported in the *Daily Mirror* (10 May 2004) to have said: 'I gave the players a bit of Winnie – 'we'll fight them on the beaches' and all that type of stuff.' The report itself highlighted this by using the headline 'BULLDOG SPIRIT' and stressing that he had taken 'a leaf out of Sir Winston Churchill's book'.

For our purposes, denotation refers to the literal meanings of language in the news. This is the prime function of news language to provide a literal account of the events in the contemporary world. However, once the context of a particular news story is established and the newspaper is confident that the reader will understand the reference, it is often able to vary the language and even to provide an indication of its position on a particular topic by using more connotative language such as metaphor or an intertextual reference which can reinforce its relationship with the ideal reader. For instance, a story about Cherie Blair's payments for celebrity lectures may be headlined denotatively:

Cherie's lectures under threat as Number 10 is urged to rein her in

(*Independent*, 11 June 2005)

Yet it may later be referred to as 'Cheriegate' in an allusion to the political scandal which became known as Watergate and would resonate as such by connotation with informed readers. It is also connotation which allows the Deputy Prime Minister, John Prescott, to be referred to as 'Two gaffes' in an article in the *Daily Mail* (27 May 2004) in an oblique reference to his other nickname in the popular press, 'Two Jags' as he is the owner of two luxury Jaguar cars.

In terms of selecting language in order to shape a story in the news and to give it coherence within the overall patterns of the newspaper, two processes are at work. One is a selection from a series of possible syntagmatic chains. These are familiar storylines which fit into the preferred news values of a newspaper.

The second pattern of selection is more at the level of chosen vocabulary, where adjectives, nouns and verbs can be varied once the pattern of the story is in place. This form of selection is referred to as paradigmatic.

It is sometimes better to visualize these patterns. The vertical one, like a shopping list that we read down or up, is the paradigmatic, and the horizontal one, from side to side, like a chain of communication, is the syntagmatic. Both paradigms and syntagms provide choice to a writer or speaker and can be used to convey political preference, colloquial intimacy with audience, and cultural expectations, among many other choices. Consider what the selection from the following paradigmatic choices might indicate:

Two Jags
John Prescott
Prezza
The Deputy Prime Minister

Then consider how the range of paradigmatic choice available to the newswriter among the following can radically alter the potential implications of the syntagmatic selection of the story 'Politician does "x" to his staff':

'Two jags' axes department
Prezza sacks staff
Deputy Prime Minister reshuffles team
John Prescott reorganizes his front line

Syntagms are also indicative of the identity of particular news media. Campaigns, political allegiances, tone of address are all enmeshed within the recurring patterns of news stories within particular newspapers or broadcast news institutions. The war on terror, insurgency in Iraq, paedophile threat, moral panics, social concerns, pro or anti EU bias can all provide examples of how news appears to wait for certain patterns to present to its audience.

The election victory of Hamas in January 2006 is clearly a news event which would fit with most news organizations' set of priorities. The syntagmatic chain of meaning is one where the party has won the election. However, within that rather obvious sequence there is scope for particular newspapers to put an interpretation on the event by their selection of different vocabulary from a potential vertical list of paradigmatic options. The party is either referred to by its organizational name 'Hamas' or it is referred to by reference to its militant past, 'Islamic bombers'. The choice of vocabulary to describe the party in the headline is clearly a significant element in determining the framework which the newspaper intends the reader to interpret the piece within, and fits with longer narratives of interpreting news from the Middle East on these two papers:

Hamas scores stunning win

(*Independent*, 27 January 2006)

Islamic bombers triumph at ballot

(*Times*, 27 January 2006)

Activity 5.1 🔑

Find examples of the syntagmatic and paradigmatic choices made within newspapers by comparing accounts of the same event.

For all the shortcomings of the binary extremes of semiology, analysis based on its insights into the process of language as a system of meaning has implications which are of enormous relevance for the study of the language of the news. It assists in understanding, for instance, how our language organizes the world and how this is often what we come to term reality. It can be used to demonstrate how, in terms of the language of the news, this reality is structured differently depending on its socio-cultural and national context. It enables a certain denaturalizing of meaning and gives access to what may be considered as covert. One drawback of this is that it implies hidden texts which are more real than surface texts, although this study will insist that there is nothing hidden that cannot be considered on careful and consistent reading of the language of the news. This final point is quite important, as it goes against the grain of how news is intended to be read. It amounts to reading news out of its proper context. News is intended to be consumed in a hurry, on the move or as an accompaniment to other professional or domestic chores. Newspaper reading, radio listening, television viewing are all transitory patterns of reception and the texts are not designed to be revisited. This is why when one does start to revisit them, compare them and contrast different generic output one can begin to see things which were not apparent on first consumption. This however does not mean that they were not there the first time round or even hidden.

French critic Roland Barthes (1974) developed an influential model of semiological analysis which is divided into three orders of signification. It is useful in the way that it sets out a developmental relationship within meaning from lower to more complex levels of association within language. The first level is the iconic level. Meaning at this level is self-contained. It can be seen in the photographs of world leaders, celebrities or infamous criminals in our news media as well as in the use of the names of those people. These are unequivocal and instantly recognizable to global audiences. From George W Bush to Saddam Hussein, from Madonna to Nelson Mandela.

The second order consists of the ways in which society values signs and puts them to use by attributing meaning to them in political and cultural ways. This is where we see signs deployed as connotation and as part of longer narratives which fit with the cultural and political preferences of particular sections of society.

Paras off to expel Taliban

Almost 5,000 heavily armed British troops were dispatched yesterday to blast Al-Qaeda from Afghanistan for good.
Around 3,300 of those were ordered to the lawless southern badlands of Helmand province.

(*Sun*, 27 January 2006)

5,000 Brits face Taliban

More than five thousand British troops are to wage war against the Taliban and Al-Qaeda in Afghanistan, the Government said yesterday.
Specially trained Paras will lead the £1 billion two-year operation in response to a resurgence of Taliban and terrorist militancy in the lawless Helmand Province.
The past year has been the deadliest in Afghanistan since US-led forces ousted the Taliban government in 2001. Ninety-two US personnel died in the country last year alone.

(*Daily Mirror*, 27 January 2006)

Although the *Daily Mirror* and the *Sun* take divergent views of Britain's role in this overseas conflict, one thing which unites them is a strong sense of patriotic support for the soldiers on active service overseas on behalf of the British Government. The selected words, 'paras' and 'Brits' are abbreviations directed at a readership that appreciates the connotations of this colloquial style, designed to give an impression of communal understanding of the place of these particular troops in the British national imagination. The words are selected from a paradigmatic list which at its most denotative and value-free might have the word 'soldier'. The syntagmatic chain of the headlines emphasizes the active role of the soldiers while the verbs chosen, 'blast', the nominalization 'insurgency' and the adjectives used to categorize the enemy and reduce them to passive victims of the operation are all notable stylistic features which indicate the processes through which a story about British military involvement overseas is articulated very much within the social and political framework of its targeted readership. This view of the military being on the side of a public which can be relied upon as being patriotic and identifying itself with the military is not necessarily a universal feature of social attitudes to the military in all countries but one very much implicitly associated with the special place of the military within the British political memory, and it is one which is actively reinforced by news media coverage which foregrounds the loyalty and bravery of troops over political questioning of their role. Another significant feature of the coverage is the way in which the only spokespeople are British military and political personnel. It is rare in stories involving the army for an overseas politician or even a rebel fighter to be approached for a quotation, indicating that even in their use of sources, newspapers restrict themselves to a categorization of respondents which fits into these broader cultural significations.

These narratives which foreground preferred readings of history and society have been referred to as myths by writers such as Roland Barthes. His use of the word 'myth' is a particular one which needs some attention. The use of the word myth does not indicate that the narratives are not true, as in some contemporary uses of the word. What it emphasizes is the way in which myths, old and new, form combinations of narratives which tell us about deeply held aspirations and anxieties of particular societies at particular moments in their history. The notion that semiological analysis can enable us to begin to unravel the complex ways in which the narratives which form a core part of our social and political understandings of our cultures has made a rich and varied contribution to critical writing informed by semiology. The French anthropologist, Claude Lévi-Strauss explored belief systems in terms of the mythemes, the small constituent parts of larger myths which chart human, cultural values. Russian writer Vladimir Propp considered the ways in which the structure of Russian folk tales could be analysed according to their morphological patterns. Each story was made up of certain recognizable and often interchangeable characters and plots. Building on this, Roland Barthes provided in his work *Mythologies* (1974) a selection of readings of mid-twentieth century France as a postcolonial, consumer society using advertisements, magazines and other popular cultural activities as his sources.

The third order of signification, combining with the first two, is the most complex stage at which signs take on meaning within a cultural context. This is when the particular connotations and myths involved in the process of developing social meaning in language become embedded as common sense within social representation and the point at which they generate power and become associated with the dominant belief patterns of the time. This is particularly relevant to the language of the news, as this must fit into established patterns of expectation and consumption which it shares with its target audience.

 Activity 5.2 o-r

Can you identify any common characters or plots which are constantly featured and reformulated in the news? Do you consider that these familiar features determine the shape and nature of the daily news?

Social semiotic

It has been argued that semiology downplays the complexity of textual activity. Meanings in language are negotiated in a variety of ways between users of the system and its social contexts. This is why it is important to view language as both a social and therefore ideological system of meanings.

The linguist Michael Halliday (1978) is often referred to in contemporary accounts of the language of the news media. This is because he developed an application of the ideas of de Saussure which were more informed by the specifics of social and even political implications than some of the more arid analyses of semiology implied were possible. He also concentrated on the particular challenges of how language generated social significance as its prime aim. This form of socially centred linguistic analysis has been termed social semiotics. Social semiotics stresses that meanings in language are negotiated between users of the system and its social contexts.

This approach stresses that the meaning of language is therefore constructed socially. It develops as an interaction between the producer and the audience. It is not simply present in the signs of language in a simplified version of semiology. Social semiosis is the process through which language expresses the cultural and ideological location of the producers and consumers of the news. It also provides a critical reader with evidence of the ways in which the structures and power relations of everyday social existence and expectation are structured. The language of the news can be described as a social semiotic since it encodes/contains meanings which are structured on the basis of social location and identification. The text of the news media is a linguistic form of social interaction. The social aspect lies chiefly in the fact that the writer can always select from a range of options which always have different levels of significance, and these choices tell us as much about the writer's cultural and institutional location and ideological orientation as they do about the idealized audience. Newspapers in particular spend a great deal of effort maintaining a particular address to their readers. This can be described as an idiom, a style of presentation in a language which is directed towards a socially located sense of identification.

This chapter will explore how the language of different newspapers appeals to particular readerships and how these audiences are to an extent already there, structured in the text. From a commercial perspective this makes sense as it shows how these news media are targeted to those who they expect are reading, and as a consequence this audience can be presented to the partners in news production, the advertisers.

According to the social linguistics of Halliday, grammar is connected to the social and personal needs which language fulfils. In order to achieve this, he argues that there are three identifiable functions to language, the ideational; the interpersonal and the textual. The ideational function corresponds to the way in which language structures experience, how it represents the world, how it constitutes our reality. The interpersonal function demonstrates how language creates identities and relationships. These might include the identities offered to politicians, celebrities or other protagonists featured or the relationships represented between reporter–audience–experts. The way in which a newspaper's language is selectively targeted at a particular audience by its preference for particular vocabulary or language structure also forms part of this interpersonal function. Thus the interpersonal function assists in the construction of social relations. The textual function corresponds to how language is given coherence and cohesion by its surface features as well as by its relationship with other texts within the news or from any other area of our culture featured in the news. It produces complex interconnections with other texts through the variety of choices in the language used. The textual function is demonstrated in the way in which the story depends upon interviews, press releases or even wider social and cultural information which have to be selectively deployed to give it overall cohesion with the lived experience of contemporary readers. It is also important to remember that language performs all three of these social and textual functions simultaneously.

Ideology

Ideology is a highly controversial term and the processes which it refers to are even more controversial than the term itself. Yet it had a remarkably simple beginning. It was coined in the late eighteenth century to designate the history of ideas. It has subsequently travelled a long way to become a highly contested critical term in our vocabulary, particularly within the study of the language of the news media. One meaning of ideology which is of little use to us in this study is that which defines the word as a rigid set of political ideals which are imposed upon an oppressed population by a ruling establishment and which must be believed without questioning under pain of punishment or death. Ideology has become a much more subtle and integral part of our daily lives than this definition would have us believe. Ideology can be used as a much more sophisticated tool of analysis for our purposes, to explore the complexities of how power is represented in the mediation of everyday life. We could go so far as to say that it lies within that which we take for granted as self-evident or obvious. In order to begin discussing ideology, it may be useful to return to a summary of certain important points about semiotics. Semiotics encourages us to see that the linguistic sign is of an arbitrary nature at the start – any word can represent any object or concept – but by the process of signification, it takes on connotations and is inserted into a wider system of coherent narratives. Such a socially attuned system of meaning is structured within the dominant belief systems within our culture. This means that signs can be deployed flexibly to work within political and cultural contexts within our news media. Words have traditional associations but they can be steered towards fresh implications by skilful practitioners. In stressing the social nature of language, semiotics insists that signification can only take place within the consensual understanding of a community of language users and their collective understanding of the norms of their society and the relationship of those norms to established patterns of association between those in power and those outside those positions. Therefore any attempt to alter the meaning or the use of words must be brokered against the backdrop of these socially shared sets of meanings in order to continue to make sense to the broader community. It is worth bearing in mind that a change in language does not necessarily entail a change in social practice, so the shift for instance, from referring to 'chairperson' or 'chair' instead of 'chairman' as the generic form does not immediately banish sexism from the boardroom just as attempts to make the use of racist epithets illegal does not by itself banish racism from our societies. However both are examples of practices which help to highlight the linkage between language and discrimination, not a bad thing in itself and probably as good a place as any to start.

The insights which semiotics bring to the critical reader can assist in understanding how ideology operates through language deployed for particular ends by powerful groups in society, including the media, but only if they gain the understanding and approval of the majority of a language community. Look at the book *New Labour, New Language?* by Norman Fairclough (2000) to see how the political project of 'New' Labour was negotiated ideologically and linguistically at the same time. It is an excellent illustration of how political language is, even when we are taking it for granted. Semiotics is useful in exploring ideology precisely because it de-naturalizes meaning and emphasizes its social and ultimately political nature. For our purposes, relating to the language of the news media, we can define ideology as the structuring of beliefs from a particular perspective. This perspective is a complex combination of the viewpoints of media institutions, powerful sectors of society and audience, and presented in such a way as to convince its audience that it is natural and unchanging. For instance, the national emphasis of most of our news media is a profoundly ideological phenomenon. It seems inconceivable that a newspaper would not organize itself around a projected national audience. This means that the political and economic assumptions needed for us to accept the world from the perspective of an individual nation go without comment. Newspapers also characteristically target specific social groups based on the reach and ambition of their advertising, and within this they often assume a predominantly male audience in the emphasis of much of their content and the privileging of items such as sport.

The first thing to bear in mind when considering the term 'ideology' with regard to the language of the news is that it should not be interpreted as meaning that ideology is simply a distortion of communication. All forms of communication carry with them the social markers of preference and choice. This is particularly so of complex forms of communication such as news. So to a large extent the idea of a form of communication which was not distorted to some degree by the preferences of its producers or consumers is an impossibility. The choice and preference which the producer of the language has access to and the system of preferences which the receiver chooses to consume are made from a series of socially structured options rather than distortions of some pre-existing ideal and untarnished truth. Ideology can be better explained as the process of producing meaning and value for particular audiences and how this process enables such meanings and values to find a coherent place within dominant social and political frameworks.

News media act ideologically when they create and maintain social coherence. They do this as a parallel function to their communicative and economic roles. Their priorities are first to produce something identifiable as news, distinguishable for example from fiction, advertising copy, an instruction manual or poetry, and second to sell that news to a market which corresponds to the advertisers' view of their ideal consumer. In performing these two tasks the news media must maintain a consistent enough set of views and interpretations of the world in order to appeal to a relatively stable audience. The news media produce this sort of consistency in their selection, classification and organization of point of view and the most obvious way in which these tasks are effected is in the range and register of language. Classification and the structuring of viewpoint create micro-specific versions of the world for particular audiences. This is especially true of attitudes towards the nation-state, celebrity culture, issues of gender or the representation of outsiders to the host community whether these are ethnically, culturally or socially significant. Within the language of the news media we can therefore expect to find evidence of how meanings and values are produced which reflect and construct the dominant social and political frameworks of the media institutions themselves and the wider society to which they belong.

Ideological critique stresses the social and political nature of consensual values and therefore allows a critical reader to be able to act as an active witness to the structuring of frameworks of belief. Using ideology as an analytical tool enables an active and critical reader to deploy a practical consciousness and to engage in independent critical analysis of mainstream media representation. This approach enables a much more open and optimistic engagement with the prevailing power within society than in viewing ideology as a totalitarian straitjacket which constricts our ability to engage with the real world. It allows a set of contestations during which the apparent consensus so carefully constructed by the news media for their own particular socially and nationally located consumers can always be negotiated as a form of both social and textual interaction.

Activity 5.3

In the following set of binary distinctions, it would be as naive to agree wholeheartedly with the left-hand column as it would be cynical to regard the right-hand column as articulating the whole truth about the news media. A more considered view might be located somewhere between these spaces, closer to one or the other extreme to varying degrees depending on the respondent's experience or perception. It is instructive when faced with categorizations like this to take time to consider how the news media function in your view. In order to make a strong justification of your argument you will need to gather material and give examples to support your viewpoint and to persuade somebody else why you hold the views you do on the role and function of journalism in the contemporary world.

Does the language of the news provide

Facts about the world	*or*	A constructed point of view?
Reflect the world	*or*	Make the world what it is?
Represent the consumer	*or*	Construct the consumer?

Find examples to support your argument.

Eagleton has written widely on the phenomenon of ideology and its varying and contested definitions. The following list of potential definitions has been drawn up using his work. Relating these definitions to the preceding debate, you can begin to consider which combination of definitions can be applied to the language of the news.

(a) The process of production of meaning, signs and values in social life;
(b) A body of ideas characteristic of a particular social group or class;
(c) Ideas which help legitimate a dominant political power;
(d) Systematically distorted communication;
(e) The conjuncture of discourse and power;
(f) The medium in which conscious social actors make sense of the world;
(g) The indispensable medium in which individuals live out their relations to a social structure;
(h) The process whereby social life is converted to a natural reality.

(Eagleton, 1992)

Activity 5.4 ⚷

Use the list above of the sometimes conflicting ideas of how ideology can be defined to generate your own version of how ideology operates within the news media, using your own examples. This will assist you in developing an understanding of how your own views on the nature of the language of the news media fit into wider discussions.

Ideology, semiotics and audience

From an ideological perspective, the manufacturing of the audience is also significant as it predetermines how the newspaper will attempt to maintain its coherence on certain issues and the idiom with which it 'talks' to its audience. Each newspaper presents a particular worldview and through the register and style of its reporting and the selection of its news values it identifies its readership in terms of social classification. The news media, most obviously the press, use language to frame events already selected as fitting within a carefully considered range of significance and they use it to establish a sense of social solidarity. They use mnemonic hooks to recall and maintain that sense of solidarity. These are words or phrases which enable a reader to easily locate a protagonist or an event within the expected values of the news medium. The use of 'Our boys' to refer to British soldiers on active service fits these protagonists immediately within a tabloid discourse of patriotism. The use of comparisons of Maxine Carr with Myra Hindley in recent years is a strong indicator of how the newspapers which use this comparison wish the readers to interpret Carr, despite the fact that she is not a convicted murderer. All the time, use of language is designed to reinforce the sense of shared values between reader and news medium as in a pact of solidarity. This pact is renegotiated from a general template of news values and semantic and syntactic categorizations on a daily basis and is part and parcel of the process of ideology. The language of the news media provides one of the essential channels through which conscious social actors make sense of their place within the dominant power relations at a particular time and place. Each news medium has a slightly different take on contemporary power relations and will therefore place itself as a particular articulation of the social grouping or class. The social semiotic of the language of the news is therefore shot through by ideological considerations in the ways in which it invites solidarity or reflects shifts within dominant ways of thinking. One of the main achievements of the press is its ability to present a relatively stable worldview for its readership throughout its pages. This representation of a stable and conventional community to its readers has profound ideological implications since it assists the construction of a consensus through the social process of reading a newspaper. Thus the newspaper is the repository of many of the vital ideological debates of the day. This chapter will examine in particular how the 'public idiom' of particular newspapers assists in the creation of a conventional community of readers, politically and culturally, and how this constitutes an ideological activity. Each newspaper uses a set of devices to project the voice of its ideal reader in a form of textual ventriloquism and even flattery. This is amplified by the advertisers who sell products through the paper to the readership identified in the editorial. The construction of a stable and distinctive public idiom is one of the chief strategies which enables the newspaper to create links to an audience and act as a conduit for the sort of social communication expressed by Barthes (1974) in his third order of signification. It does this through its language and the way in which that language represents an ideal audience. It can be done through the explicit cries of the popular tabloids or the more subtle discourse of the elite press or even of public service broadcasting.

We can integrate discussion of the concept of ideology with the functions of headlines as discussed in the previous chapter as they orientate an ideal readership towards the values and interests of a particular newspaper. Even in the narrowing gap between elite and popular press, the headlines still tend to distinguish the differing agendas of the two main sorts of newspaper. Humour can identify the specific sense of readership of a newspaper by attempting to connect with the assumed knowledge of a readership. An understanding of the latest twists and turns of a reality television show might be assumed of a popular audience whereas a quality newspaper might be more at ease flattering the assumed elite cultural knowledge of its readers.

In the following extract, we can see how this voice is directed towards readers. Slang, popular television and song references are all used intertextually to connect readers' knowledge of popular representations of the police and car salesmen with the latest news on a robbery. The intended audience is inscribed through these features into the story and such recognition forms part of the identification and also part of the entertainment within such stories.

£53M HEIST SENSATION

Hello, John, got a new motor?

COPS RAID DODGY CAR DEALER'S FARM

THIS is the 'Arthur Daley' crook whose home was swooped on yesterday in the hunt for the £53million Security blaggers.

(*Sun*, 1 March 2006)

Headlines reduce the complexity of an event for purposes of summary and display but they also perform that process of summary in order to reduce the meaning of an event to fit within the already existing parameters of the newspaper's worldview. Headlines also function in this way but more subtly within the discourses of television, online and radio news. They do not break news as such, they integrate events into pre-existing frames of understanding. The patriotism implicit in the following extract is based on both the patriotism of identification through the possessive adjective 'our' but also the political revulsion towards 'Blair' referred to without the familiarity and levity often conveyed when using his first name in the news. By its concentration on the contradictions in the chain of events, the syntagm, the newspaper endorses its opposition to the war at the same time as it endorses the bravery of the soldiers involved.

Our 100th soldier is killed for a lie

So what does Blair do? Send more troops.

(*Daily Express*, 1 February 2006)

Ideally a headline reduces the complexity of an event to the news medium's and the ideal audience's viewpoint, thus performing an absolutely essential part in the ideological framing of events in the world. This assumed, shared perspective is very much a part of the ideological compact of news.

In any successful news performance in any medium the values of the news institution whether it be newspaper or radio, television or online, must become the values of the audience. The two must be seen as interchangeable as the primary function of news is not simply presenting what is new in the world but more significantly enabling a regular audience to make sense of what is new in the world in terms of what they already understand about that world through the medium of that news provider. News is therefore a fundamentally conservative force, rooting the new in established patterns of understanding and leaving the investigation of eccentric ways of reinterpreting the world to other areas of media production. This not only narrows down the view of the world for the audience, it narrows down the view of the audience being generated by the news medium. Both processes are conservative and have the effect of reinforcing a stable view of the world from the perspective of dominant social perspectives because the institutions of the news media are themselves incorporated within such perspectives and function to make a profit out of the preservation of most aspects of the political and economic status quo. Both processes serve to create the impression of a coherent and unified social and even political audience. Yet they can also contest dominant views and make this very much part of the identity of the newspaper by fitting into what is perceived to be the viewpoint of its readership, as when the *Independent* chose to highlight what it interpreted as the folly of Government plans to revisit plans for Britain's nuclear industry, highlighting its views by printing the headline on its front page in glowing phosphorescent yellow and by emphasizing that the criticism came from the government's own advisor:

WARNING

NUCLEAR POWER IS DANGEROUS, EXPENSIVE AND UNWANTED

(AND THAT'S THE VERDICT OF TONY BLAIR'S OWN ADVISORS)

(*Independent*, 7 March 2006)

A similar oppositional stance is paraded, confident of its readers' views, when the *Independent* chooses to highlight the plight of women internationally:

THIS IS YOUR LIFE

(if you're a woman)

International Women's Day Special Edition

(*Independent*, 8 March 2006)

The voice which is sometimes used in the headlines is also a useful point through which to explore what sort of ideologies are embedded within the language of the news. This is predominantly something observed within newspapers although occasionally it can be seen in other news media. The main questions to be asked are who is speaking, and the secondary question, on whose behalf are they claiming to speak? There is a complex relationship in the competing and often complementary voices of the news headlines between the newspaper, the reader and the protagonist within the news story. One of the ways in which this is fore-grounded, particularly within the newspaper, is through the varying use of titles, names, first names and even nicknames. The voice represented allows a dominant perspective to be created, inscribing a position for readers/audience within the text of the news.

In the next editorial we might wish to consider who is speaking on behalf of the collective possessive objective 'our'. It clearly establishes at the start of the piece a rhetorical identification between newspaper and reader and at the same time it distances both of these from 'Leaders' who are noticeably deprived of any possessive adjective, implying in contrast to 'our' worries that they do not belong to 'us'. The piece continues with a declarative, with capitalization of the first two words to add typographical emphasis: 'AT LAST the truth is out'. The Home Office has 'admitted' – a verb which comes with an implication that it has been hiding this truth for some time and a truth which has been known, according to the newspaper by 'millions of people'. The number here is significant: 'millions' is an open-ended, rhetorical figure which serves to emphasize the credibility gap between popular knowledge and strong implications of official obfuscation. The alleged anxieties of the ordinary people are encapsulated in a strong rhetorical triple flourish, finishing with the most emotionally charged and least quantifiable: 'jobs, public services and their way of life'.

The second paragraph begins once again with a declarative and is reinforced by its cross-party appeal and by its use of the modal verb of obligation 'should'. It continues to build up a picture of a country divided between ordinary people who value 'traditional British virtues' and a 'fashionable metropolitan elite' who are posited as the enemies of ordinary people. The changing tides of fashion are thus counterposed to the traditions of British life.

By the third paragraph, 'worries over immigration' and 'the pace of immigration' have been ratcheted up to the presupposition of 'uncontrolled immigration' which is not only a rhetorical leap but assists in reinforcing the negative stereotypes of migrants in the sentence it is used. The impersonal verbal expression, 'has been associated' means that the piece does not use any direct relational verb to link migrants with negative activity but it places a more subtle version of this accusation into the argument for the consideration of the reader. The piece ends with a repetition of 'perhaps' to underline that its hope that politicians will now comply with the newspaper's own agenda on this matter is only a faint one and reinforces the idea that it is possible that the politicians will remain out of touch with 'millions of people'.

Leaders must reflect our worries over immigration

AT LAST the truth is out. The Home Office has finally admitted what millions of people have been saying for years: the pace of immigration into this country under Labour has left communities acutely anxious about the impact on jobs, public services and their way of life.

Leaders of all political parties should take note. It really isn't racist for people who value traditional British virtues to worry about the impact of large numbers of newcomers, many from countries with no tradition of democracy, free speech or civic order.

It would be a boon to democratic debate if our fashionable metropolitan elite would now end its smear campaign against anybody voicing sceptical views about large-scale migration.

Migrants can bring both good and bad things. On the plus side can be a capacity for hard work, an enriching of the host culture and a particular patriotic pride at being accepted in a new land. But there are downsides, too. In Britain's case uncontrolled immigration has been associated with an upsurge in tuberculosis, HIV, dangerous driving, knife and gun crime, curbs on free speech, the supply of illegal drugs and pressure on social housing. And of course, terrorism.

> **Perhaps Labour and Liberal Democrat politicians will now apologise to Michael Howard for placing emphasis on immigration as an issue during last year's general election campaign.**
> **And perhaps Mr Howard's successor, David Cameron, will now find the courage to start once again putting ministers on the spot over their failings in this area.**

(*Daily Express*, Editorial, 8 March 2006)

News is not an isolated communication channel but forms part of a wider set of power relationships within society. By its structuring of language, news places itself in relation to those power relationships, thus throughout this book embedding of power within language is referred to as discourse.

Semiotics can also help us understand further the social relationship between news product and consumer. News is not of course a unified product. It differs depending on which country it is produced in, inflected as it is by national interests. It is also differentiated by social considerations. Categorization displays an ideological orientation of news towards its intended audience. Certain news is designed to be consumed by the more politically aware, or those with more highbrow cultural tastes, other formats are designed for those with a greater interest in entertainment culture, and some attempt to provide a combination of both. Other news can be directed towards people according to their age range or lifestyle. The clipped headlines of 'Drive Time' news on the radio or text alerts are good examples of the latter, directed to people on the move and, in the case of text alerts, at the generally younger people who are happiest with mobile technologies.

Audiences can be called upon explicitly to fit into the long-running scripts which form part of a newspaper's identity. Such scripts can be placed within identifiable positions which are familiar to readers as well as appearing to embody the core beliefs of the readers. This sort of call to the readers is made 'mythical' by its elliptical expectation that the substance of the particular story is a fundamental aspect of how the lowest common denominator of the readership is connected to a wider set of social meanings and therefore how the newspaper's identity makes sense in general cultural terms. In the next two examples we can see the contrast between the expectation in the first that the readers of the *Independent* will approve of and support liberal electoral reform by signing a petition, while in the second the *Daily Express* reveals that a story it had reported prominently the day before had drawn a furious response from readers and it generates a mnemonic declarative slogan to signal that the newspaper is keeping open the option to continue with this story as an ongoing campaign which fits in with its traditionalist Christian values.

32,000 readers sign up for change

More than 32,000 readers of the *Independent* have joined the campaign for Democracy since it began 13 days ago.

(Independent, 2 June 2005)

thousands of Daily Express readers contacted us to say they felt insulted that a crucifix had been removed from a hospital chapel.

KEEP THE CRUCIFIXES

(Daily Express, 6 June 2005)

The semiotics of style

Style as well as content has a significance in the overall meaning of particular news media. Whether a newspaper chooses to employ colloquial language in its hard news reporting and how such colloquial language is used in opinion pieces or in lifestyle pieces within the elite press indicates how they perceive a sprinkling of contemporary resonance to be a productive part of their relationship with their own readers. It is a good example of the cultural convergence between the elite and popular press. Sometimes the grotesque consequences of combining the banal and the tragic can be uncomfortably exposed, as on the front page of an elite newspaper, the *Independent* of 1 August 2005, where the murder of Anthony Walker and haircuts are both awkwardly and prominently displayed on the front page.

The ten worst haircuts

From Mullets to Mohicans, Susannah Frankel cuts through a poll of tonsorial crimes
[with photos of Kylie Minogue and David Beckham]

(Independent, 1 August 2005)

Cameron (1996) has observed the ideological implications of style within the language of the news, as well as the commonsense explanations for why the institutions themselves often claim that it is of little consequence:

> style politics . . . are ideological themselves. Though they are framed as purely functional or aesthetic judgements, and the commonest criteria offered are 'apolitical' ones such as clarity, brevity, consistency, liveliness and vigour, . . . it turns out that these stylistic values are not timeless and neutral, but have a history and a politics. They play a role in constructing a relationship with a specific imagined audience, and also in sustaining a particular ideology of news reporting.
>
> (Cameron, 1996: 315)

We may return here to Bell's observations on audience design. Clearly the style of a news medium is of importance in how it attracts and retains an audience. This is not simply an economic aspect but also an ideological one as it involves the construction of a viewpoint which maintains an appeal to a specific form of audience and its spectrum of worldview. Channel Five's language and format have been characterized by an appeal to a more specifically youth-oriented market. The *Daily Telegraph*'s recent announcement of its innovative text news service is an acknowledgement of the need of the newspaper to move with the times technologically while maintaining an overall politically conservative worldview.

 Activity 5.5 o—ᴛ

Draw up a list of stylistic features which different newspapers and different broadcast news programmes use to attract specific readers from differentiated audiences.

Jointly produced consensus

Critical linguistics or discourse analysis can show how dominant patterns within the representation of our society can become legitimized not through a process of brainwashing but by a process which has been called hegemony. This means that subordinate groups of people, in this case consumers of the news media, are drawn into a consensus on the workings of that world because they are shown a consistent and favourable view of how they themselves fit into that world. The public idiom of each news medium is absolutely central to the negotiation of the norms and conventions of the ideal audience and is therefore an example of how hegemony is negotiated through language. As we have seen, the audience is inscribed first and most obviously in the headlines of the news-papers, which are drawn from the dominant news values constructed as the values of the community, and these are amplified and reinforced throughout the whole of the newspaper to provide in various ways an impression of conversation between newspaper and reader and ultimately of a consensual view of the world. Campaigns generated by the newspaper and scripts and narratives familiar to the readers in their tone and style of address are evidence of the coherence of the newspapers' approach to maintenance of audience identity. Outsiders to the views of the world constructed on behalf of this audience are either routinely ignored or categorized as marginal and held up to ridicule or they are categorized as a threat to society as a whole. The news media play a significant part in this process of dividing the public world into the binary divide of 'them' and 'us'.

This consensus is inscribed throughout the news by implicit calls to readers. These can be explicit, as in declarative calls to the readers to participate in letter writing, or displaying stickers or posters distributed by a newspaper. The character of campaigns has to fit within the identity which newspaper and readership share. The news values of particular news media are more subtle markers of this consensus, as too are the register and style of language targeted at a particular audience and what Matthew Engel (*Guardian*, 3 October 1996) has called the 'unity of tone' which can be seen threaded through newspapers. This unity of tone corresponds to the ideological wrap which Van Leeuwen writes of:

> fragmentation of newspapers in separate, separately unrelated sections and articles is only apparent, and that 'news stories' can on a deeper level, be related to those feature articles in which 'helpful advice' is given to readers.
>
> (Van Leeuwen, 1987: 208)

He goes on to consider how even the style of differing narrative techniques in popular and serious newspapers form part of this process of audience construction and therefore the construction of political expectation:

> stories are for those who, because of their social status and education, are denied the power of exposition, while exposition is for those who have been given the right to participate in the debates that may change society.
>
> (Van Leeuwen, 1987: 199)

These features which position an audience also at the same time are part of the political positioning of news media. The hegemony enacted in producing an identifiable style, tone and politics within a particular news medium enables the impression to be formed that the consensus has been negotiated jointly between the news media and the consumers although in practice it is much more producer-led:

- The communication flow of the news is from an organizational top to a viewing/listening/reading base.
- The audience/readership is often reified by producers of news as the reader/viewer/listener, or in the massified data of opinion polls, viewing figures or the Audit Bureau of Circulation figures.
- In terms of ideology this means that the views of the hierarchy are well and truly embedded in the news values of these operations.
- It is part of the sophistication of their language that they can embody these values while selling themselves to consumers as if they embodied these consumers' views of the world, in a language which appeals to them.

Discourse

Discussions of semiology and ideology within language bring us to discussion of how these aspects of meaning, belief and politics come together. The process of combining power, language and knowledge is often referred to as discourse. The word 'discourse' has been used for a longer period to refer more straight-forwardly to extended stretches of speech or text. In terms of text analysis it formed part of a concerted attempt to get beyond the study of individual words or sentences to an extended and socially integrated view of text. In terms of literature, it was an opportunity to open debate on the work of a particular author and to integrate it within the patterns of social and political culture which relate to the place of their work historically and in the contemporary world.

For the purposes of understanding how the language of the news fits into questions of institutional and social power, discourses could be defined as systematically organized sets of statements and traditions which give expression to the meanings and values of an institution. They act to constantly and flexibly describe and limit what it is possible to say within the context of that institution (Kress, 1985: 6–7).

To complement these definitions, Edward Said can be quoted as an illustra-tion of how the social power of the author fits into wider discussions of language and power. His insight takes us back to considerations of how writers of the news are working not simply as individual agents but far more extensively within the constraints of institutional and social expectations which have the power to shape our very understanding of reality:

> writing is no private exercise of a free scriptive will but rather the activation of an immensely complex tissue of forces for which a text is a place among other places where the strategies of control in society are conducted.
>
> (Said, 1978b: 673)

Discourse analysis

Carrying on from the general definitions of discourse, we come to the appro-priation of the term as a tool to explore the language of the news media. For the purposes of the news media, discourse can be explained as how systems of knowledge and power are expressed through language. All communicative action takes place within the systems of discourse. The question to be asked is whether it reproduces the shape of dominant discourses or does it challenge or attempt to restructure it? This is particularly important with regard to the language of the news. Formalist analysis of language, including the language of the news, provides an account of how news is structured, what vocabulary it uses, and how various parts of the news is differentiated from headline to opinion piece. Discursive approaches to language study such as those used in this book draw language into a wider set of references to social, cultural and political areas. They stress the ways in which language functions as a text among other texts; where those other texts may include the political economy, national location, and political and social opinions. The language of the news media works in terms of these socio-cultural contexts. Discursive language analysis attempts to locate the language of the news within as wide a set of contexts as possible in order to explore how it fits with dominant everyday patterns of belief and power. Therefore, discourse analysis as part of critical linguistics is an investigation of the strategies which legitimate or naturalize the social order. It explores the ways in which the language of the news contributes to discourse production at an institutional level and to discourse reception at the level of the assumed reader. The professional practice of journalism is embedded in the assumptions of the user.

Discourse analysis can demonstrate how the language of the news media constructs social knowledge which allows its audience to locate itself socially, politically and culturally. Since it looks at how the language of the news simultaneously acts upon the social world and is shaped by that world, discourse analysis is a form of speech act analysis. News media implicitly allow access to socially valued resources such as information, opinion, and institutional authority. Discourse analysis encourages us to look against the grain of the transitory flow of the news for longer narratives of meaning such as 'scripts' and to consider the political implications in the particular selection and structuring of the flow of information and authority, especially in the networks and individuals whose voices are given priority by the news and the language which frames these. Discourse analysis can help a critical reader chart the explicit relations between public and private representations and in charting the relations between social groups. The critical interpretation of that process of social cognition allows us to analyse socially shared representations of hierarchies and therefore the power relationships they enact.

Summary

The main analytical points of this chapter lie in the definitions of ideology and semiotics. The chapter clarifies how these terms can be applied to enable a better understanding of the social complexities of the texts and the implicit audiences of news media. This chapter has moved the discussion on to consider the ways in which the language of the news media communicates not just information but also a sense of the power relations and social identities which form part of our contemporary world. It does that through the creation of a consensus around what a particular news medium and a targeted ideal audience expect from that world and the news attempts to find a language and a set of editorial strategies to match. Style as well as content can illustrate how the language of our news media communicates a great deal about the political realities of our everyday world.

Suggestions for further reading

Bell, A. and Garrett P. (eds) (1998) *Approaches to Media Discourse*. Oxford: Blackwell.

Chandler, D. (2006) *Semiotics: The Basics*. London: Routledge.

Eagleton, T. (1992) *An Introduction to Ideology*. London: Verso.

Halliday, M.A.K. (1978) *Language as Social Semiotic: The Social Interpretation of Language and Meaning*. London: Arnold.

Simpson, P. (1993) *Language, Ideology and Point of View*. London: Routledge.

Wodak, R. (2003) 'What CDA is about – a summary of its history, important concepts and its developments'. In Wodak and Meyer (eds) *Methods of Critical Discourse Analysis*. London: Sage.

6 Gender

Introduction

This chapter will build on the analytical tools of the opening chapters, and begins a series of chapters which look at particular themes across the language of the news. The first theme will be the representation of women. It will apply the previous discussion on critical linguistics and discourse to question how language acts to construct and contest gender roles in the news media. It incorporates this into general discussions of a range of perspectives described as a feminist critique of language. It will explore how the representation of women demonstrates the continuing marginalization of women in society whether it is in the low incidence of news involving women in the elite news media or their sexualization in the popular tabloids. The question of when women become news will be central to these discussions as will analysis of both the vocabulary and syntax used when they do break into the news.

Language and gender

Some might claim that the news media, in reflecting an already existing world, are gender-neutral and succeed in representing the world in as objective a fashion as possible. They might also claim that any imbalance in the reporting of women in the news is simply a function of pre-existing imbalances in the social world and that journalism does not seek by itself to make any alterations in those imbalances as its role is one of reporting not attempting to change the world. Such commentators may also have a profound suspicion of anything claiming to be explicitly feminist and see their own perspective as natural or objective. Rebecca West had an opinion on feminism which preceded much debate later in the twentieth century and which highlighted the sensitivities and ideologies which the term aroused in critics when she wrote:

> I myself have never been able to find out precisely what feminism is: I only know that people call me a feminist whenever I express sentiments that differentiate me from a doormat or a prostitute.
>
> (Rebecca West, 1913)

Broadly, we could claim that there are three perspectives on the role of language in the representation of gender in journalism. First, there is a determinist view which sees language as creating sexism through its structures and ideologies. In the 1930s American anthropologists/linguists Sapir and Whorf developed the hypothesis that the language that we use ultimately determines the world we inhabit; different language, different world. They concluded this on observing the very different syntactic and semantic categories that certain native American languages employed to describe their world. This world they concluded was radically different to the world which the English language described. It is considered to be an extremely deterministic view of language. It was developed by Dale Spender (1980) to a position which proposed that in a world ruled by men, the language was also fundamentally shaped by them in order to maintain social and cultural control. Thus she argues we communicate through a 'man made language'. For most, although a provocative polemic supported by some exceptional evidence, Spender's views do not really encompass the subtlety of how gender is expressed within language and therefore have little to offer in challenging sexist practice (Black and Coward, 1998, and Simpson, 1993). Any form of linguistic determinism has difficulty in explaining how things happen to change the society in which language is such an overwhelmingly dominant force.

Second, there is a more socially oriented view that language does not cause sexism but that it acts as a reinforcement to attitudes and behaviour already prevalent in society and which exist independent of language. This approach considers language to be part of a process which naturalizes sexist divisions within society. The third view is that language is of no importance to the operation of sexism in society. Supporters of this viewpoint may also typically claim that sexism does not exist, has never existed or has been removed from society by feminist pressure over the last few decades and may suggest that we are now living in a post-feminist era of equality of rights and opportunities. In fact, certain commentators such as news anchor and journalist Michael Buerk have publicly claimed that such pressure has even made the world into a place which has begun to systematically discriminate against men and that this is having a marked and pejorative effect on society as a whole as it shifts to a set of more feminized values.

Certain cynical sections of both the public and the news industry consider that the bottom line is whether owners are able to make a profit, no matter what the content. They wonder why they should take the issue of gender representation seriously. In some parts of the news media there is a strong feeling that feminism is outdated, irrelevant and restrictive in a world which has already delivered equality for women. This view can be condensed into the term 'post-feminism', and a symptom of this trend is the new masculinism which has seen the rise of the Lad Mags such as *FHM, Nuts* and *Zoo* which reinforce this tendency as well as giving rise to a corresponding abrasiveness in the young female magazine market. Often the content and language of these magazines, which also filter over into mainstream newspaper journalism, are little more than a return to old essentialist and restrictive views of the predetermined roles of men and women.

I'm a feminist but these bints have gone too far

(Norman Johnson, *Guardian*, 4 February 2006)

> It's been a tough old week for Ruth Kelly. Once regarded as a safe pair
> of hands, despite catching criticism for her membership of Opus Dei
> and for having a remarkably deep voice for a woman, she has found
> herself facing very tough questions on sex offenders in schools.

(Pendennis, *Observer*, 15 January 2006)

The idea conveyed by this language that we have a gender-specific set of roles
is of course highly restrictive and conservative, and limits the ways in which we
are able to imagine ourselves outside the narrow confines of normality. Many
areas of the news media have an important part to play in both establishing and
challenging social and cultural norms of behaviour for men and women. The new
essentialism of the language of much of our news media has been a profoundly
reactionary force within journalism. In characteristic fashion the *Daily Mail*
represented a best-selling account by a woman, identified in the article as a
'lesbian', as having shaken 'the feminist movement' and the 'militant feminist
movement':

THE BEST-SELLER BERATING WOMEN
(BY A LESBIAN DISGUISED FOR 18 MONTHS)

How she became 'he' and shook the feminist movement

WHEN Nora Vincent decided to analyse the battle of the sexes, she
wanted to see both sides of the story.
  So she called herself Ned, cut her hair, wore male clothes, added a
stone in weight by exercising to increase the muscles in her arms and
shoulders and put on a sports bra to flatten her breasts. . . .
  And what she discovered in her secret life has shocked the militant
feminist movement. Instead of producing the anti-male diatribe that
was expected, she has published a best-selling study that is highly
sympathetic to men and berates women for not being understanding
enough.

(*Daily Mail*, 13 January 2006)

The sort of story which follows is often used to endorse the idea that discrimination is now something which works against men and to deflate the argument
that sexist divisions still affect society predominantly to the disadvantage of
women. It presupposes agreement, in a newspaper popular with women readers,
that sexism was something which existed 'in the past' but generates its own
version of the discourse of post-feminism when it highlights claims which argue
that the situation has been reversed in some professions:

Squeezed out, the male job seeker

IN the past, the victims of sex discrimination at work have been over-whelmingly women.
  But a controversial study has revealed that in certain professions male job applications are much more likely to be discriminated against than women.

(*Daily Mail*, 23 January 2006)

This third view, in all its variations, tends to trivialize the whole issue of the relationship between language and gender. As often is the case, the best way to construct a perspective is to engage in a consideration of these perspectives and use them to test how the language of the news actually operates in practice and how this language fits into the broader questions of gender and society. If the language of the news tends to reinforce practices of discrimination present in broader society, this does not mean that we are unable to reflect upon this situation and ultimately to change it. There are many good examples of how women journalists challenge the dominant practices of the news media both in their critical approaches to the language of journalism and in their challenge to patriarchal attitudes by their pre-eminence in the traditionally male dominated areas in which they work. Yet despite these examples of progressive practice on a more abstract level, at a more abstract level the language of journalism continues to organize our world into categories which are arranged as convenient for dominant ideologies of gender where the male is the norm. It is most often organized towards perspectives which construct and perpetuate male dominance as if it was natural and eternal. Clearly, this has ideological implications. For instance, the language of journalism can act as a functionalist encoding of such assumptions. This means that the language functions to provide the views and opinions of gender which conform to dominant and consensual patterns as socially accepted norms. However, it does not follow that they cannot be challenged through critical reading and through practice which contests them. If we can observe patterns of discrimination towards women in the language of the news media then we can consider them, in the light of these observations, not merely as descriptive but also of manifestations of the practice of discrimination. Language therefore takes on a material force in the representation of women in the news. And so, from a more optimistic stance, does resistance to it.

Activity 6.1 o—r

Find examples of women writing in the news who challenge what you consider to be gender stereotypes.

News as androcentric discourse

We may like to consider the view that the language and values of news are structured according to a male-oriented or 'androcentric' set of rules, meaning that very often news values are to a large degree simply male values. Questions of agency are paramount in examining gender representation in journalism. Who is reported? Who does what? Which respondents are selected? Who is news-worthy? Who is the reporter? All these are important questions which reveal as much about consensual social values with regard to women as they do about the values of particular news media institutions. Ultimately we need to ask when does female become news and how is it reported? To these two questions we may add a third which has less to do directly with the language of the news and more with the ways in which it is mediated: what is the role of women journalists?

There is a lower incidence of news about women as they are generally regarded as less newsworthy as social actors. This conforms to their relative under-representation in society as a whole as figures of social or political importance. This lower level of coverage, far from merely reflecting the status quo, can be seen as actively contributing to the continuing lower status of women in society. It has three very distinct consequences, depending on the sort of journalism being studied. The first is the quality press which despite not being actively involved in the direct denigration of women still manages to system-atically ignore them for most of their coverage and provide a form of 'symbolic annihilation' (Tuchman, 1981). The second consequence is that when they do become news it tends to be because they have departed from the normal expectations of male-dominated society or can be seen as fitting within the stereotypes of women as sexualized objects. The popular tabloids provide ade-quate illustration of this trend:

THESE BOOBS ARE MADE FOR GAWPING

(*Sun*, 27 January 2006)

When women become news in the elite press it is often when a story which fits them neatly within cultural expectations of the traditional roles of women are to the fore, such as in the following story:

> ### Fertility kit offers women a glance at biological clock
>
> WOMEN who fear that they will miss out on the chance of motherhood if they decide to delay having children may now have their concerns assuaged with a high street fertility test.

(*Times*, 26 January 2006)

 Activity 6.2 o━ㅜ

When do women become news? Find examples of women as news from a range of different newspapers. What conclusions can you draw?

Interestingly the *Daily Mail*, so much targeted towards a middle-brow female readership, is quick and corrosive on any threat to its own claims to speak for women. The language of the next piece is all the more vitriolic for it being directed against a renowned 'feminist champion' although the paper is quick to qualify the title with the participle 'posing'. It carries on immediately to contrast her 'posing as a feminist champion' to the mirror opposite of 'doing women down' not just on occasions but throughout 'her whole career'. The hyperbole not only undermines the claims to feminist heroic status but construes her as a career women-hater. What follows employs alleged deficiencies in her argument, aspersions against her grasp of reality and gratuitous comments about her appearance to undermine her point of view. Clearly, when it comes to repre-senting the views of women nothing will be allowed to stand in the way of the *Daily Mail*'s perspective.

> ### Why DOES Janet Street-Porter hate women?
>
> She'll be back on TV this weekend, posing as a feminist champion. In fact, she has spent her whole career doing women down.
>
>   THIS SATURDAY evening Janet Street-Porter makes the latest in a long line of comebacks with a programme in which she examines the role of women today. . . .

In the subsequent hotchpotch of the speculative, the old and the simply mistaken, she claims that, although women have made advances, 'The fact is that we're more miserable than ever.'

No evidence is offered for this assertion, but on Planet Janet facts must never be allowed to get in the way of a good rant.

Then with the bit between those famous teeth, she's off: apparently there are rotters out there who feed us images of perfection that we cannot live up to, a phenomenon which is 'at the heart of the problem for women today'.

(Femail Opinion, *Daily Mail*, 26 January 2006)

THEY BLAME BREAK-UPS FOR SOARING CRIME RATES AND YOBBISH BEHAVIOUR

The career women who are saying NO to divorce

FREEDOM from marriage was once cherished by the liberal female elite as one of the most important acts of women's emancipation.

But now well-educated women are turning against divorce in their droves, say researchers.

Divorce is becoming the preserve of the poor and ill-educated as career women shun the 'easy way out' or marriage, a [University of Maryland] study says.

(*Daily Mail*, 23 January 2006)

The third consequence of this gendered demarcation with the language of the news comes in magazines, and the increasingly voluminous magazine sections of newspapers, where a certain version of the female is celebrated commercially for a range of audiences from the pre-teen to the mature female readership. This concentration on an idealized female readership has been in evidence since women were first identified as a specific commercial market in the eighteenth and nineteenth centuries. Indeed women were written for as an audience by men as soon as their commercial potential became clear in *The Ladies' Mercury* from 1693, edited by John Dunton, before the mid-Victorian *Englishwomen's Domestic Magazine* began to consolidate the view that the female could be constructed almost uniquely around the areas of domesticity, a subtle and suppressed sexuality and a much more overt consumption. Traditionally, menial copy writing was produced by female 'penny-a-liners' and such was the low prestige of women journalists that some, such as Harriet Martineau in the mid-nineteenth century, chose to adopt a male persona; 'writing in drag' as Easley (2000: 154) has put it.

Accusations of stereotypical female roles in the contemporary news media reinforce the pervasiveness of androcentrism across journalism. Women journalists have increased in number and in status since the days of the 'penny-a-liners' but the increase in women journalists has however been mainly in the 'velvet ghetto' (Creedon, 1989) area of lifestyle-led magazine journalism, and this has been amplified by the increased inclusion of this sort of journalism in newspapers from the founding of the *Daily Mail* in 1896. Women are also more in evidence in television, particularly as news readers, leading some – such as prominent television news reporter Kate Adie – to complain about 'bimbo journalism' being used to boost viewing figures. A recent example shows how women news anchors can still be perceived as 'news candy' – pleasing on the eye even in the opinion pages of elite newspapers, demonstrating that this is not necessarily a phenomenon restricted to popular newspapers:

> **Don't be dotty, go for totty**
>
> If Natasha Kaplinsky can bring the bleary-eyed public to the television at 7am then that is surely a good thing. In craning for a view of her legs, the viewer may absorb something of the state of the world which is surely better than none. She delivers added value, is a hot property and her salary reflects the fact . . . telly totty.

(*Times*, 7 June 2005)

The piece above courts the colloquial appeal of 'totty' and rhymes it with 'dotty' to present the debate about the relative worth of attractive news presenters to one which is reduced to the physical appearance of the news presenter in question. It also claims that the audience, equally stereotypically represented as 'bleary-eyed' males are 'craning for a view of her legs'. The humour of the article does nothing to deflect the implicit acceptance of the realpolitik of television news being more about the attractiveness of the female presenters than the intrinsic worth of the news or intelligence of the audience. Here, a woman news anchor becomes news because of her physical appearance. Intriguingly, the reports of these spats within the community of journalists themselves are conducted in language which indicates the sets of assumptions and therefore discrimination at work in the area of gender:

Natasha hits at no brain slur

Kaplinsky, 33 . . . John Humphrys and Andrew Marr . . .

(*Daily Mirror*, 7 June 2005)

The headline refers to Natasha Kaplinsky by her first name only, an indicator of her reduced status compared to her male counterparts who are referred to by both first and surnames, while in the main body of the article she is referred to with her age, unlike her male counterparts whose age does not seem to be significant for the emphasis of the story.

Newspapers and magazines incorporate sets of linguistic conventions with regard to many aspects of their ideal audience, including their gender. These provide sometimes complex patterns of representation. Consider for instance the article, 'The Page 3 Girl Speaks to Women Too' by Patricia Holland (1983) which speculates on the attractions of aspects of a sexualized representation of women in the 1980s. The *Sun* sought and succeeded in making a sexualized and 'liberated' lifestyle attractive to a young female readership on the basis that it offered women a representation of having fun in their lives. Despite their reputation, even the popular tabloids are rarely offensively sexist, preferring to mask any chauvinism behind claims of playfulness, pleasure or irony. It is more interesting to observe how the different forms of representation converge in different ways but around familiar themes. News media construct gender-specific profiles to add to the other assumptions of the ideal reader's social location, consumer habits and political preferences. Therefore the issue of a celebrity trying hard to maintain physical and aesthetic health for the sake of her media image is criticized in no uncertain terms, combining ageism with sexism, as close-up photographs of the star Madonna are commented upon as the main story on the front page of the *Daily Mirror* and also on the same day in its leading article. The language, punning, critical of the fading physical attributes of the singer emphasizes specifics of her appearance, age, parental status and diet in ways which male celebrities are not generally exposed to. Among the exhaustive details of her daily regime the compressed noun phrases are particularly characteristic of the tendency of such news about women to squeeze them into restrictive categories: 'The 47-year-old', 'The mum-of-two':

SADONNA

Is the Queen of Pop's quest for eternal youth taking its toll?

SHE'S wowed the world for two decades – but even a fashion icon can have an off day.
  And when Madonna arrived in Paris yesterday looking decidedly less than glamorous, fears were raised that her relentless fitness regime may be taking its toll on her looks. The 47-year-old's skin was stretched across razor-sharp cheekbones and her chin was puckered as she turned up for a Gaultier fashion show. . . . The mum-of-two exercises at least three hours a day, sometimes runs 10 miles, and eats mainly wholegrains and vegetables.

(*Daily Mirror*, front page, 26 January 2006)

On pages 18 and 19 her photo is scrutinized and compared to all sorts of unappealing aspects of other celebrities' appearance, using an intertextual reference to a popular song to reinforce all the cultural stereotypes of an older woman trying to maintain her looks and based on the explicit presuppositions of universal claims for 'any fortysomething'.

The Mad years

AS Tammy Wynette once sang, sometimes it's hard to be a woman.
 And Madonna is clearly finding holding back the years tougher and tougher.
 She is the envy of any fortysomething, but perhaps now she is trying too hard.

(Voice of the Daily Mirror, *Daily Mirror*, 26 January 2006)

The elite press is not immune from this sort of humorous flagging of stories involving women, especially when we recall the Tuchman perspective on how women are routinely marginalized within the discourses of elite news. This changes when a story which allows a humorous headline about an argument from the world of opera can be woven into its news sections:

Opera world splits along the cleavage line

When two opera singers have a difference of opinion, a genteel spat over the interpretation of a Puccini aria or suitability for a role in La Bohème, might once have been expected.
 But in the lucrative and crowded world of 'light classical' it seems that cleavage is the burning issue for stars vying for top-spots in the easy-listening charts.
 The latest front in the opera wars was opened yesterday when Maina Laslo, a Russian singer whose rendition of *Ave Maria* has made her one of Classic FM's most played artists, objected to a record company executive's suggestion that she needed to 'sex up' her image.

(*Independent*, 26 January 2006)

The patterns of discrimination

The representation of women in the news media fits into culturally organized categories which reinforce common preconceptions of women in society. These representations have an influence in maintaining and reinforcing the marginalization of women as a form of functionalist coding. The language has an actual material force in cementing these assumptions. Christine Gledhill has argued the importance of media representations in creating such normative views:

> Media forms and representations constitute major sites for conflict and negotiation, a central goal of which is the definition of what is taken as 'real', and the struggle to name and win support for certain kinds of cultural value and identity over others.
>
> (Gledhill, 1997: 348)

In the next example there is much linguistic evidence of how the 'real' is defined for women readers with regard to fashion and physical appearance. Even within the discourse of fashion writing, the emphasis on body shape, dress sense and social judgement provides a strong accentuation of the norms for young women celebrities to adhere to:

So who did you come as Sharleen . . . a Scottish widow? Or Morticia [from Adams Family] Or Marilyn [rock singer]

STAR'S BURNS NIGHT FRIGHT

POP star Sharleen Spiteri looks more like a leftover from Halloween as she arrives for a Burns Night supper.

The Texas singer's frocky horror show sent jaws dropping when she turned up at a trendy London restaurant dressed all in black.

Glasgow-born Sharleen, 38, made a complete haggis of it in a dowdy outfit that could have come straight from the TV advert for Scottish Widows. The chart-busting mum-of-one normally has her finger firmly on the fashion pulse with her unique and quirky style.

But sadly this time she ended up looking like a cross between Morticia Addams and Marilyn Manson in her vintage Stella McCartney gown.

The floor-length black satin number did little to flatter her sexy figure – clinging in all the most unforgiving places like some kind of Gothic nightmare. And Sharleen's slicked down black curls didn't exactly improve the image.

You'd have thought that as a one-time hairdresser she would have known better.

We can only assume she was going for a pale and interesting look. But without the killer dress it just didn't work.

(Fashion editor, *Daily Mirror*, 27 January 2006)

Characteristics of writing about women in the news include assumptions of male gender in pronoun choice, marked over-representation of women in deviant roles, reference to women as a part of family or as dependent on a relationship to a man, more frequent reference to the age, hair colour (sometimes reduction to this alone, metonymically) and dress or bust size in tabloids, diminutives (girl), informality of address compared to male equivalents, titles and forms of address differentially employed, over-lexicalization and most offensive terms, and scripts which compress social expectations of women in certain roles, employed to ideo-logically frame women into expectations of social norms.

 Activity 6.3 o—ᴛ

Look at the following examples and analyse how their language use fits into the patterns of representation outlined above:

Cilla's tycoon boyfriend dates blonde half his age. . . . Madejeski has been spotted on dates with a beautiful blonde not even half his age.

(*Daily Express*, 30 May 2005)

Sharapova . . . the Russian babe.

(*Sun*, 1 June 2005)

Give up the cash, Cherie.

(*Daily Express*, 6 June 2005)

Cheating wife who abandoned son in pub

(*Times*, 7 June 2005)

Money-mad Cherie . . . Shopaholic Colleen

(*Daily Mirror*, 7 June 2005)

Modified, compressed noun phrases allow for very compact summaries of well-established female roles and stereotypes. In the following examples it is not simply a case of compressing information to fit into the restricted space available

in the newspaper. It is more significantly compressing information and prior-
itizing aspects of that information which fit with views of women which are in
themselves restrictive of their social roles:

Wife who cried rape
Mum gave her hubby the slip
Mother is jailed for a year
Mother-of-two, Davinia
A cheating wife
A mini-skirted brunette

 Activity 6.4

Can you find further examples of these sorts of noun phrase?

As Patricia Holland has argued (1998), popular tabloids, in particular the
market-leading *Sun,* have sexualized popular culture in their treatment of women
in their pages. This can reduce women to being motivated uniquely by a desire
to be attractive to men. Aliteration frames the opening of the description of the
plight of 'fat and frumpy' Kathryn Thomas as she is located within an abbreviated
pattern of popular romance as if it constituted the only route to happiness and
fulfilment for a woman, 'she would never find true love'. Having lost weight and
jettisoning her former attire for stereotypical 'mini skirts and string bikinis' she
can now be described as the female norm for this paper as a 'slim hottie':

> **Fat and frumpy Kathryn Thomas thought she would never find true
> love. But after shedding 5st 6lb and swapping her elasticated trousers
> for mini skirts and string bikinis she is making up for lost time in the
> hunt for Mr Right. . . . NOW . . . Kathryn is a slim hottie.**

(*Sun,* 6 June 2005)

Even the highly contentious issue of teenage pregnancy can become abbreviated,
as in 'teen mums' or 'gymslip mums' (*Daily Express,* 6 June 2005).

Such language sexualizing everyday culture is not restricted to women,
although it takes them as its chief focus. There are also times when the sexual
activities of men, especially when it is regarded as deviating from the projected
heterosexual norms of the readership come into play:

A SECOND LIMP-DEM MP CONFESSES:

I'M GAY TOO

(*Sun*, 26 January 2006)

GAY HUGHES: I'VE NOT PAID FOR SEX

Lib-Dem challenger denies using rent boys

GAY MP Simon Hughes denied last night that he had romped with male prostitutes.

(*Sun*, 27 January 2006)

Here the whole argument is one based on negatives while emphasizing the abnormality of his behaviour; 'not paid for sex', 'denies using rent boys', 'denied last night' while liberally sprinkling the story with the titillating vocabulary of sexual scandal 'paid for sex', 'using rent boys' and 'romped with male prostitutes'. It is interesting to contrast how a different newspaper featured the same story:

Hughes admits he denied gay affairs

In an exclusive interview with the *Times*, Simon Hughes, one of the Liberal Democrat leadership contenders, at first denied being gay. But, 12 hours later, he admitted having both homosexual and heterosexual relationships, and defended his earlier decision as a judgement dating from his political baptism in the 1980s.

(*Times*, 27 January 2006)

The language used to create a prurient and discriminatory emphasis in the reporting of the case in the *Sun* was picked upon by editors of gay newspapers and magazines in an article in the *Press Gazette*:

Gay press slams 'schoolboy' humour

Editors criticize 'Limp Dem' and 'another one bites the pillow' jokes in Hughes coverage. . . . 'insidious homophobia'. . . . *Sun* managing editor, Graham Dudman . . . 'It wasn't homophobic, it wasn't nasty, it wasn't offensive, it was funny. . . . They're both jokes, plays on words. If people haven't got the sense of humour to be able to see that, then I suggest that they ought to lighten up a bit.'

(*Press Gazette*, 3 March 2006)

Activity 6.5 o━┳

Select an elite newspaper and a popular tabloid and compare the selection of words – the lexical map – which creates a cultural image of contemporary women across the two newspapers. Then compare your findings with a fellow student.

As well as lexical maps of the vocabulary of representations of women in the news we can also look at the ways in which transitivity can be observed playing a part in the cultural patterning of such representation. This means that we can look at the ways that verbs are used. Do women act or are they the recipients of the actions of others? Kate Clark (1998) has alerted us to such patterns in her study of the language in coverage of domestic violence in the Sun where even though it is the women who are victims, there are strong linguistic patterns which suggest that these same women are in part to blame themselves.

Popular tabloids may be the most obvious and easiest targets for accusations of discriminatory language in representations of women but the quality press is not exempt from criticism. Criticism of the representations of women in the elite press comes from two directions. First, women are symbolically annihilated, according to Tuchman, in so far as the qualities' news agenda is very much informed by the male values of the institutions which dominate their pages: hard news, politics, business, sport. Second, when women do become news it is often because they happen to fit into the cultural patterns which inform most of the tabloids' news agenda.

Single women fuel craze for 'female friendly' flats in Japan

Japan's single women were once best known for their love of shoes and handbags. Now the country's *Bridget Jones* generation is snapping up special female-friendly flats as well. . . . The relative property boom also reflects the fact that many Japanese women today have more in common with the heroines of the New York television series *Sex and the City* than with their mothers.

(*Daily Telegraph*, 3 June 2005)

In the example above, women, and even more unusually Japanese women, are the subject of a story in the elite *Daily Telegraph*. It starts with a stereotypical summary of young Japanese women 'best known for their love of shoes and handbags'. It then moves on to make an intertextual connection with the character of Bridget Jones to reinforce the Hollywood image of the global young woman. It then proceeds to locate the women further in this media consumerist vein by reference to the influence of an American television series *Sex and the City* as being more significant than the role of their mothers. Other possible explanations are ignored such as economic pragmatism, or developing cultural independence (unless on an American model).

In the next example, the wife of Tony Blair is taken to task for seeming to cash in on her husband's celebrity. This however is not the whole story. She is criticized as much for wanting her professional independence as for her alleged desire to exploit her dependence on his name and status. Her status is emphasized by the repetition of 'husband' with relation to 'position' and 'Government', further personalizing the relationship by the use of a possessive adjective, and the piece finishes off with the hint of a remark about her attractiveness, 'not a pretty sight'. The piece seems to suggest on one level that she can't have her cake and eat it but closer inspection reveals that it means that she cannot have any cake and must go hungry.

> **Buy your tickets here for Mrs Blair's show. It seems that the Prime Minister's wife cannot resist the temptation to cash in on her husband's position. . . . In the past she has made it clear that she was entitled to pursue her own career as a lawyer, even if that meant opposing her husband's Government. Cherie Booth, QC. . . . She does . . . look like someone cashing in on being married to the Prime Minister. It is not a pretty sight.**

(*Times*, 3 June 2005)

Newspapers often feature women when they can easily fit into the role of 'mother', especially when bravery in domestic situations can be highlighted. The woman in the story below can be referred to as 'Wonder woman', and as a 'cancer mum'. This reinforces the idea that women's first role is as mother and further categorizes women by its casual repetition:

> **WONDER WOMAN**
>
> **Clear of cancer . . . mum who forced the Government to hand out miracle drug**
>
> THE mum who fought to make a wonder drug available to all breast cancer sufferers has beaten the disease.

(*Daily Mirror*, 27 January 2006)

The next extract shows that even when the woman in question has another role which defines her, for instance, in terms of her employment, the newspaper can choose to foreground her as 'Mum' and to then shift quickly to referring to her solely by her first name, while the male policeman is referred to by his complete professional title:

> **Mum butchered in street by stalker**
>
> A KNIFEMAN stabbed a woman to death in the street yesterday after lying in wait for her. . . . Linda Hewitt [thereafter Linda]. . . . Twice-married Linda. . . . Det Supt Harry Stephenson. . . . Linda worked for HM Customs in Newcastle.

(*Sun*, 27 January 2006)

There are times when the magazine style of a newspaper such as the *Daily Mail* can be deployed when writing about the Mark Oaten affair to provide a contemporary guide to middle-class morality and pragmatic marriage guidance. It assumes that the Oaten affair is a story with relevance for 'everywoman' and places the main focus on the traditional expectation of the woman as the fulcrum of stability in the marriage, particularly with regards to responsibilities for the children.

> **Femail Forum**
>
> Tess Stimson, 38, is a novelist and author of *The Adultery Club*. She is divorced and lives in Florida with her second husband and three children aged three, eight and 11.

FOR MOST of us, the lurid stories this week involving Liberal Democrat MP Mark Oaten and his kiss 'n' tell rent boys are no more than unsavoury – and fleeting – tabloid headlines.

Some may celebrate his downfall. Others regret the loss of a promising career. But this is first and foremost a *personal* catastrophe; not for Oaten, who deserves his misfortune, but for his wife, Belinda, so publicly humiliated, and their two daughters.

The only question now on the Oatens' minds must surely be whether their marriage has a future.

No doubt there is a chorus of voices telling Mrs Oaten to change the locks and leave his suitcase on the doorstep. But no woman with small children walks out of a marriage without a backward glance, however angry she may be.

We know too well the price our youngsters pay for divorce: poor achievement at school, low self-esteem, problems forming lasting relationships. Never mind the practical issues – a reduced standard of living, often a move to a new home. . . .

But staying with a man who has looked you in the eye and then lied through his teeth isn't an easy choice either. . . .

There comes a time when the only thing to do is face the truth and acknowledge that a relationship is over.

Then, and only then, can you start to build something new. And Mrs Oaten, you *will* find someone who is able to truly love you.

I should know. Two days before Christmas, I married my second chance, the man who restored my trust and belief in love, and I have never been happier.

(*Daily Mail*, 26 January 2006)

Women journalists

Having considered the language used to represent women in the news, we can complete this assessment by looking at the way in which women journalists are employed within the presentation of news. This raises some interesting questions which we may briefly flag here. What range of styles are available to women writers, in particular columnists, and does their increasing presence in the news media alter the shape of contemporary news? When do women present broadcast news – genre and discourse? What do they report? How do they look? Are they merely used as a telegenic opportunity to present traditional androcentric news? Are they confined to specific reporting functions?

Summary

In this chapter we began with an overview of how language can be said to incorporate certain attitudes towards women. The language of news is a powerful medium for the reinforcement of views of the world which are dominated by a male perspective. We have seen how the patterns of language reinforce views of women as predominantly sexualized and juvenalized in much of the popular press and absent from the world of action and important political and economic affairs in the elite press. The issue of how women journalists themselves are employed and represented is also discussed.

Suggestions for further reading

Black, M. and Coward, R. (1998) 'Linguistics, Social and Sexual Relations: a Review of Dale Spender's "Man Made Language"'. In D. Cameron (ed.) *The Feminist Critique of Language*. London: Routledge.

Clark, K. (1998) 'The Linguistics of Blame'. In D. Cameron (ed.) *The Feminist Critique of Language*. London: Routledge.

Holland, P. (1983) 'The Page 3 Girl Speaks to Women Too', *Screen* 24 (3): 102.

Holland, P. (1998) 'The Politics of the Smile: "Soft News" and the Sexualization of the Popular Press'. In C. Carter, G. Branston and S. Allen (eds) *News, Gender and Power*. London: Routledge.

Page, R.E. (2003) 'Cherie: lawyer, wife, mum: contradictory patterns of representation in media reports of Cherie Booth/Blair', *Discourse & Society* 14(5): 559–579.

Romaine, S. (1999) *Communicating Gender*. Mahwah, NJ: Lawrence Erlbaum.

Simpson, P. (1993) 'Gender, Ideology and Point of View'. In *Language, Ideology and Point of View*. London: Routledge.

Van Zoonen, L. (1994) *Feminist Media Studies*. London: Sage.

7 News, narrative and the nation

Introduction

Narrative is an essential component of how our news media select and structure information. This chapter will explore the ideological work involved in the narrative conventions which are specific to news and the cultural importance of the language involved in the process. Narrative is a key to community values, shared assumptions and reference points: it is a set of stories told in terms of other stories. This means that narrative is political in the way that it maps onto pre-existing explanations of how the world operates or deliberately sets out to contest those versions. Narrative can be conservative or radical but within the institutional and generic confines of the news it tends to conform more often than not to consensual and conservative patterns. These include, most significantly, the narrative shape and vocabulary of the nation.

Narratives operate so as to narrow the differences between potentially contradictory, paradoxical or incongruous facts in order to establish closure around the expectations of the targeted audience. In general terms news does not deal with open-endedness. It is driven by solutions, no matter how temporary or provisional. To illustrate these concerns in a tangible form, this chapter will look at how the nation is narrated, particularly in the press, and the core vocabulary used to maintain a cohesion around the nation. In the symbolic representation of the nation, ideology and narrative coincide.

Narrative

Narrative, according to Hayden White (1984), is the transformation of knowing into telling. Our news media consist predominantly of stories, not of facts. These stories fit, in the spirit of White's observation, to a set of patterns which in many ways precede the events which they tell. This chapter and the next will explore the implications of this observation in terms of social power and language in the news: whose stories are told and in what terms? These chapters are connected through their shared interest in these stories; the first from the point of view of how an insider perspective is developed; the second based on how outsiders are represented to that insider audience. The stories have to make sense in terms of where they are located in longer cultural memories and how they relate to the institutional patterns and preferred narratives of particular news organizations before they can be considered suitable for inclusion in the news.

Narrative is a universal social phenomenon which occurs across history in all parts of the world. We need to place events into narratives in order for them to make sense. They contribute to our understanding of archetypes within human experience which also appear to form part of a shared human legacy. We may think of folk tales such as Little Red Riding Hood or the legend of King Arthur and the Holy Grail or the older epic poems of Homer. They all share important information about Western culture and are of great interest to readers even today, not least for the continuities in narrative form which they display. Yet narratives are always specific to particular cultures and are valued in terms of what they reveal about the concerns of contemporary society and can tell a reader much about the values and beliefs of that culture from their structure and content.

Narrative is always bound by the relationships between power and language in any given society. Its characterizations and vocabulary can either act on the world in order to legitimate these dominant power relationships or they can be used to develop alternative or radical appraisals of the social. This is implicitly referred to in a commonplace – 'the sides of a story' – which implies that any narrative begs an interpretation, asking the audience which side they are on. Most narratives and indeed their interpretations are opportunities for the playing out of competing versions of social and political reality. Most conventional narratives, including the narratives of most news have been clearly marked by the patterns of the status quo in terms of a preferred reading. It is because of this power contained within a narrative to support or contest hierarchies of social authority that they are referred to as 'speech acts' by linguists. Stories are positioned or interpreted as part of a social activity. They are never solely performed for the sake of entertainment or even information. They provide positions for their audiences.

In his seminal contribution to the theorizing of narrative, Vladimir Propp (1968) in *The Morphology of the Russian Folk Tale* writes about the types of story and the types of character which in combination form the bulk of most European folk stories. He is keen to demonstrate how these elements are combined to provide stories with strong patterns of expectation about what would happen next and strong moral conclusions which are used to legitimate social norms. His analysis identifies certain types who occur in various guises across a range of folk tales. These include 'hero', 'villain', 'outsider', 'helper' and 'foolish victim', and they are placed within micro-narratives which may include 'leaving home', 'encounter with helper', 'encounter with villain', 'hero acquires a magical agent', 'the hero returns' or 'hero receives a reward'. The folk stories tend to be structured around broader themes of normality, disruption, loss, and return to normality, with community values at their core. Significantly, these cycles of disruption and return to normal can easily fit within the narrative conventions of the nation, and the news media contribute fully to this pattern. The societies constructed and reinforced in the stories reveal a great deal of themselves and their attitudes to those considered as outsiders to them. The happy ending may be indicative of a society in which social norms can be confidently reinforced. The moral at the end of many folk tales has a similar didactic function. A sceptical society may prefer its narratives to foreground incongruity and unreliability in their endings.

Activity 7.1 o—r

Look at the 'Father Flash' story in Chapter 2 (page 45). What does it tell us of the role of types and plots in news stories in terms of Propp's theory of narrative? Can you find other stories which might fit into the patterns of this sort of traditional tale?

Looking at narratives in general from the perspective of linguistics we may observe some similarities with the deep generative grammar which Chomsky has postulated. Chomsky claims to have demonstrated that humans, whatever language they speak, have an inbuilt, genetically programmed set of rules which allows them to make sense of and to learn any language which they are exposed to as their native language. This is because all languages, according to this view, whatever their superficial distinctions, share a deep grammar which is applicable to all languages as a common set of building blocks. He claims that all humans are born with a Language Acquisition Device which enables them to learn language and that this ability is a fundamental part of what makes us human. The transposability of narratives across different societies through history makes us aware of the possibility that there is also a deep structure which enables us as humans to understand how our societies encode information which allows us to appreciate what is important to understand about the culture of that society and its values. This sort of insight gives sense to the vitality of the seemingly enigmatic statement of the narrator of Jeanette Winterson's *The Passion* when she writes: 'I'm telling you stories. Trust me' (1988: 160). Any stories, such as novels or those in the news, draw on deep understandings of the beliefs and fears of our society, and they can also be places where alternatives to dominant readings of society are rehearsed.

We may apply certain of Propp's insights to the language of the news. News has developed historically and within particular institutional and generic frameworks to become something which can to a large extent be predicted in terms of its general content, structure and characterizations. Smith (1978) has argued that there was a shift in news values by the end of the nineteenth century from a relating of information about the world in terms of facts to a concentration on the story as the basic unit of the news. This came as newspapers were becoming more geared to the demands of mass readerships and as the demands of advertisers to make the content of the newspapers more attractive in terms of entertainment became more pronounced. This concentration on stories means that news is often not always, strictly speaking, looking to relate something new but rather something which, although novel in terms of the event covered, still fits into already existing frameworks in terms of politics, personalities, opinion and belief. To a certain extent, therefore, we might suggest that all news is in fact old news, or at least based on established narrative patterns which place events in the world within the norms and value-structures of contemporary society.

Hayden White (1984) has asked provocatively for our purposes, 'Could we ever narrativize without moralizing?' If we apply this insight to the language of news narratives this would imply that in the selection within and between news stories there is a process of preferencing and relativizing taking place which tells us as much about the moral values of a particular society as it does about any intrinsic news value of the stories themselves. The news values therefore are part of the overall moral expectations of contemporary society.

From a different perspective, the social and cultural patterns of the news are so deeply engrained in the expectations of the audience that in many ways there is little that is new about news. It is more like a constant process of reconfiguration within certain types of story and characters. Pressures to produce to deadline also mean that once a news medium has placed a breaking story within the appropriate pattern, it must wait to see whether initial reports and assumptions are accurate. In the context of this imperative for news to match pre-existing patterns of understanding, Toolan (1998: 238) has written, 'Newspapers . . . often do not know what they're talking about'. This is especially true of rolling news, which has so little time to reflect upon the wider implications of the news as it breaks, since the speed of delivery to match the technology available becomes increasingly more important than the substance and more subtle nuances of the events themselves. It seems the closer to immediacy that reporting news becomes the less able it is to break free from predetermined narrative frameworks of understanding. Toolan claims that in this immediacy, contemporary news has no other way to look but backwards as it has no way of knowing how events will unfold, and all attempts at closure position it in terms of what has happened before and how this in turn was reported. Occasionally, to provide a little variety, news programmes and newspapers may revisit a story to review progress or perspective but this is very much the exception.

Two variants of narrative pattern have been highlighted by Gripsrud (1992) and Langer (1998) as being key components of news today. They are referred to as 'melodrama' and the 'other news'. Briefly, melodrama is a sort of narrative that highlights severe differences between good and evil which are presented with a variety of characters and situations that are strong on shock, disgrace and morality. Clearly these are stories of perennial interest to the news. A typical scenario for the melodrama is the sexual scandal involving a prominent politician. The following example of Liberal Democrat MP Mark Oaten highlights the fall from office of a man characterized in melodramatic terms as somebody afflicted with a fatal flaw. His fall is portrayed as domestic as well as political; and professional. The *Daily Mail* features three headlines over two pages on the

Oaten story. Actional verbs highlight the reckless and driven nature of his conduct and this in turn is emphasized by the stark contrast between the two dramatically opposed and irreconcilable aspects of his personality, 'devoted father' and '£80 an hour rent boy'.

How could he do this to his family?

The moth that flew straight to the flame

Devoted father and the £80 an hour rent boy

(*Daily Mail*, 23 January 2006)

The *Times* also emphasizes the story in similar terms:

Fall of man who would be leader

In addition, it chooses to highlight in a stand-out quote a statement from one of the prostitutes he had been involved with which stresses the binary divisions of this saga:

"Oaten was a regular punter. He's a troubled man living a very dangerous double life."

(*Times*, 23 January 2006)

In yet another account, compressed noun phrases are used to focus on the actions which have defined the man in news terms:

Sex scandal Oaten flees to save marriage

Disgraced Mark Oaten . . .

(*Daily Mirror*, 23 January 2006)

Others choose to use the scandal story to maintain a continuity in political scandal which fits well within the traditions of the British news media and which are melodramatic food and drink to them. One example of this coverage provides an instant history lesson in summarizing a list of prominent politicians involved in such scandals from 1800s to the present day, under the headline 'SEX, LOVERS, RENT BOYS AND MONEY'.

In the next example, we see the melodrama stripped back in the headline to simple characters who could be straight out of any Proppian analysis; the father and the son. The archetypal nature of the story is emphasized by the fact that the main protagonists are not named until the third paragraph. Until then they are referred to by their status in the melodramatic narrative; 'dad' and 'son'. Added to the characters is this simple formulaic plot which is elaborated in terms of the tragedy, which is reported as the father has died defending his son from an attack by an unknown assailant. It is further suited to the melodramatic mode by the simple division between a 'mild-mannered, lovely bloke' and an 'abusive' man.

THE HERO DAD KILLED PROTECTING HIS SON

Stabbed as he raced to stop attack

A DAD was knifed to death as he ran to help his son who had been stabbed outside their home.

Lawrence Steel, 44, raced out of his local pub after receiving a phone call to say that Craig, 23, was being attacked.
    As the lorry driver sprinted up an alleyway, he came face to face with the attacker and was knifed twice in the heart. . . .
    Friends said the 'quiet, peaceful' family have been devastated by the attacks.
    Lawrence was described as a 'mild-mannered, lovely bloke'. . . . The 'abusive' man is said to have turned on Lawrence. . . .
    A 22-year-old man from Newcastle has been arrested in connection with the attacks.

(*Daily Mirror*, 23 January 2006)

 Activity 7.2 o—ᴛ

Can you find examples of melodramatic stories in the news? How does the language used accentuate the melodramatic elements of the story?

Langer (1998), on the other hand, while considering the news format of what he calls, 'Tabloid Television' has observed a pattern of 'existential anarchy' where bad things happen in the world to ordinary people, without explanation or justification, and where victims of random violence and injustice in the world simply have their suffering reported. Both are depressing perspectives in that they represent a world devoid of any rationality or any historical or political framework of analysis for these events. People are represented simply as victims of irrational and depoliticized forces. Such narratives act to de-historicize processes within the social world. Their proliferation means that there is less of a tendency for news to want to deal with causes or to analyse events, as it seeks more and more to report, narrate and move on to the next.

One common form of the 'other news' drawn from the lives of ordinary people is that of the plucky survivor; the heart-warming story of somebody surviving an accident and illness through their own good fortune. These are most valued within the language of the news when they can be tagged with a catchy, mnemonic rhyme which summarizes this micro-narrative, such as that used below:

ANNELIECE BEAT TUMOURS AT THREE TO BECOME A BALLERINA

Cancer to dancer

(*Sun*, 23 January 2006)

Below are a couple of other examples of stories of the unusual, the bizarre, the randomly violent which are increasingly used to map onto readers' expectations of news narratives and which are used because of their reliance on the clichés and familiar patterns of their narratives.

MUM 'FINDS' TSUNAMI GIRL ON HER LOST FILM

Sad trip retraces daughter's steps

A GRIEVING mum has retraced the final steps of her tsunami victim daughter – from camera film lost for nearly a year.

(*Sun*, 23 January 2006)

NO CONVICTION: HEN NIGHT WENT HORRIBLY WRONG

Lion tamer's bride free

(*The Advertiser*, 25 January 2006)

MOWER KILLS IVF PIONEER

(*The Advertiser*, 27 January 2006)

HEDGED OUT

**Couple lose bid to axe neighbour's leylandii . . .
Because it's 10ft short**

THE first couple to use new laws to try to cut down a neighbour's
leylandii hedge have lost their case.
   Bill and Heather Hannan were told the 30ft foliage looming over the
bottom of their garden will not be a problem . . . until it grows another
TEN FEET.

(*Daily Mirror*, 24 January 2006)

A FAMILY ONCE MORE

**How a private eye's hunt for relatives inspired an incredible
reunion for 10 brothers and sisters torn apart 50 years ago.**

IN her job as a private investigator, Ann Archer tracked down stalkers,
fugitives and killers.
   Yet tracing her family tree has turned out to be more gripping than
any of her criminal cases . . .

(*Daily Mirror*, 23 January 2006)

A woolly dog not to be sneezed at

HERE'S the perfect pooch for anyone allergic to dog hair: the
Jackadoodle.
   The tiny hound, a cross between a Jack Russell and a toy poodle, has
an unusual coat like fluffy wool that doesn't trigger sneezing among
people who can't cope with canines.

(*Daily Mirror*, 23 January 2006)

Activity 7.3 o—r

Find further examples of the 'other news' and see how they develop familiar patterns in their characters and plots which make them recognizable to readers.

Nation, narrative and news

Both melodrama and the 'other news' are successful because they build upon the conventional expectations of a range of human interest stories. Readers recognize the recurring protagonists and plotlines. Yet the most influential narrative in the news does not concern the micro-narratives of human interest. It is the macro-narrative of the nation. The development of news and the nation have been inextricably entwined since the introduction of printing to Western Europe from the fifteenth century. The narratives of the news are nothing if not communicators of political closure, most often around a stable idea of the national community and its political complement, the nation-state. It was the growth of the flow of information about the world in the languages of the everyday people, the vernacular, which enabled the inhabitants of these countries to become increasingly aware of their common national interests, their national identity. The formation of nation-states begins from this period onwards, developing momentum at the same pace as the dissemination of news binds them into a community which bases its understanding of itself on the imagined community of the nation (Anderson, 1986). These communities depended very much more on the style in which they imagined themselves rather than any material facts, and therefore it became essential how the printed communications of the era began to weave narratives of national endeavour with a vocabulary and symbolism which would endorse the national project. This made good commercial sense as well as good political sense. Readerships could be gathered and maintained if they felt that they were part of a community, represented consistently as being associated with attractive and even virtuous characteristics and attributes of the nation.

The nation as a cultural and political form of identification has become a global phenomenon, spreading to practically all corners of the world. Some see it as a regressive phenomenon which hinders harmony and understanding between people, as well as giving them irrational grounds to go to war to protect the distinctiveness of one nation over another. Others view it as an inevitable part of modern life that allows forms of belonging and social cohesion which

are characteristic human imperatives to find expression in a form extended
to a wider community than family or immediate friends. Indeed it is impossible
to imagine modern political life without the existence of the nation-state.
Nationalism certainly has two faces, one benign, all face-painting and national
anthems, the other malignant, characterized by hatred of outsiders to the
national community and a narrow-minded certainty that one nation is superior
to all others. The nation then as a phenomenon is a distinctly Jekyll and Hyde
affair. Some have identified this as being one of the essential dynamics of
nationalism; the relationship between its banal, everyday manifestation and its
vigorous, extreme outbursts.

National narratives provide coherence and fixity rather than dialogue and
problematization. These provide cultural stability as a backdrop for politics
and economics which ensure the cohesion of power elites. The stabilities of the
narratives of nation mask the radicalism of social change and present a world
explained in terms of the way it used to be, and it is a narrative often declaimed
from the summit of national achievement in the past rather than any contemporary location of excellence or future projections.

Narrative conventions of the news

The news media narrate a particular form of the national interest in both their
structure and their style. Structurally, national news tends to relegate the
concerns of other countries to a lower priority, whether that be down the running order of a broadcast or away from the opening pages of a newspaper. This
process of grouping national news away from international news has been
referred to by Michael Billig as 'news apartheid' (1995). It is a process which
suggests that international news can be sectioned away from national news or
marginalized or even ignored if national priorities demand it. These conventions
depend as much on the institutional demands of the industry, which needs to
sell to people who consume their news predominantly at a national level, and
also on the cultural expectations of consumers still involved in the discourse of
nationalism. This nationalist function can be subtly woven into the sequencing
of a newspaper or it can be explicitly flagged, as in the *Australian*. Here, home
news is entitled 'THE NATION' and the newspaper itself has as its strapline
'KEEPING THE NATION INFORMED'.

The nation, because of its long-established history as a form of political and
cultural identification, provides a bridge between private experience and public.
It acts as a form of security and stability in a changing world. However, because
of its restrictive nature, it provides that security for particular, privileged insiders
to the national group. Paul Gilroy is referring to this downside in the title of his
book *There Ain't No Black in the Union Jack*, and in it he explains the wide-
ranging appeal of the narrative of the nation to maintain the privilege of those
insiders to the nation on a variety of grounds:

Its [the nation's] novelty lies in the capacity to link discourses of patriotism, nationalism, xenophobia, Englishness, Britishness, militarism and gender difference into a complex system which gives 'race' its contemporary meaning.

(Gilroy, 1987: 43)

In terms of the narratives of news, this means that the overall dominant framework of the nation provides a template for the ways in which insiders and outsiders to this master narrative are depicted. One of the main characteristics of any news is the way in which it follows a predetermined set of preferences according to where the potential news of the day fits into national priorities. In terms of narrative and news values some stories are worth more than other stories and this is particularly the case when dealing with stories of a national character or which deal with an issue of direct concern to the perceived insider community of the nation. In the next extract, which reports on the pending vote on the EU constitution in the Netherlands, the vote is first framed in terms ('D-Day') redolent of the history of Britain as victorious in war. Opposition to British political preferences are personalized in the character of de Villepin. The relational verb 'is' provides a strong claim that he can be reliably identified as a 'nationalist', and a 'staunch' one at that. In contrast there is no reference, relational or otherwise, to the British as being 'nationalist', weak or strong, and the word is here used to imply a fundamental and defining distinction between the British and the French. De Villepin's political identity is further categorized by mentioning his heroes, stereotypically anti-British figures from history, Napoleon and de Gaulle. Actional verbs later on in the extract, 'he fought' and 'he champions', set him up further as a man actively opposed to British interests and also the interests of an elite national ally of Britain's, the US.

D-Day for Europe as Dutch vote

M de Villepin, whose heroes are Napoleon and Charles de Gaulle, is a staunch nationalist whose views are mostly anathema to Britain.
    As Foreign Minister, he fought passionately to stop Britain and the US going to war in Iraq. He champions the state-led French social model over 'Anglo-Saxon' economics.

(*Times*, 1 June 2005)

In the context of all of this implicit narrative of national history bolstered by subtle allusions to wars involving Britain and France, it is no surprise to see, in another piece that week, a repeated metaphor which suggests that Blair and the French president Chirac will be doing 'battle' over the future of Europe.

Battle for the heart of Europe

Tony Blair is preparing to battle with President Chirac of France over Europe's political direction for the coming decades . . .

(*Times*, 31 May 2005)

Despite the emotional appeal of the nation as a familiar narrative within the news, there is also a sound business explanation for the prioritization of national stories, as these are what nationally based consumers of news have become used to expect. The cultural and political norms of the nation have been associated with the news for so long that it has become an expectation for news audiences. The political economy of national news is inscribed in the audience – the national 'we'. This national pride is asserted below to contrast Britain unfavourably with Ireland in economic terms, using a humorous pun on tigers and tabbies to emphasize the difference, as well as depicting Ireland in even this short piece by reference to three clichés with which an English readership is supposed to relate.

Irish economy surges ahead of UK

We need some paddy power [illustrated by a picture of a pint of Guinness]

NO wonder Irish eyes are smiling – their economy is beating Britain's hands down.
  No wonder Ireland's economy is called the Celtic Tiger.
  Britain's by comparison, is a neutered tabby.

(*Sun*, 25 January 2006)

On occasions, that economic imperative to highlight the national also stretches to its opposite, the denigration of that which opposes the national interest. At this point, the negative symbolism and connotation that articulate the outsider which acts as the reverse to national identification are given expression.

In an era of increasing technological change, which has seen the rise of international travel, the exponential acceleration in the speed of information flow and an increased awareness of the diversity of people and places, we might be tempted to believe that there would be less need for such restrictive categories as national identities and that our news media might reflect that. However, these intensifications have led paradoxically to an increased search for ethnic and national identification, possibly exacerbated by the national imperatives which structure our understandings of the world through our news media and by cultural insecurities when faced with such an unstable world. This can sometimes be explicitly articulated as part of the specific appeal of newspapers to their readers as national and ethnic subjects, as in the next extract. The 'traditions' are in danger of being killed not by identifiable people but by a de-personalized, de-contextualized process: 'PC madness'. This in itself contains the presupposition that 'PC' is a material process and one which can kill traditions, identified by the possessive adjective 'our' as integral to a British way of life. The next sentence is an inversion of the usual word order. The MPs and Muslim groups would as subjects usually be placed at the head of this sentence but the inversion is a characteristic of newspaper language which allows the focus to be shifted from the subjects of the sentence to the potential victims, which are closer to the perceived interests of the readership: 'British traditions'. The convention here also allows the positions of both MPs and Muslim groups to be elided, as if forming a seamless consensus without need of any further clarification. 'Politicians' and 'community leaders' are claimed to be united in responding to the proactive decision of the *Daily Express* to 'preserve our national heritage'. This is emphasized with the rhetorical addition of 'Thousands of Daily Express readers', in order to quantify a tangible sense of community in the concerns the newspaper insists it is representing. When the readers are said to have 'backed a call', the role of the newspaper is highlighted as a literal 'speech act' in prompting such a voluminous response to what are being represented as widespread anxieties about the preservation of traditions. It is also interesting the way that the newspaper seems to suggest, as is common in much media reporting of ethnic issues, that the indigenous British have 'politicians' to represent their views whereas the ethnic minorities merely have 'community leaders', in a binary expression of unequal access to political representation. The piece finishes by inserting this event in what it claims is a long list of similar connected narratives, which reinforces the assertion for the readership that such a process as 'PC' is having an incremental impact on the minutiae of British life, and that implicitly without the activity and awareness of this newspaper it would go unremarked, and consequently the identifiable qualities of British life would be inexorably eroded.

Plea to halt PC madness killing our traditions

British traditions are being killed off by political correctness that offends all cultures, MPs and Muslim groups warned yesterday.

Politicians and community leaders backed a call from the Daily Express and thousands of readers to preserve our national heritage while still keeping Britain multi-cultural. . . .

Thousands of Daily Express readers have swamped our phoneline to register their disgust.

> It is the latest in a long line of controversial decisions – from flying the flag of St George to stopping parents from filming their children in school plays.
> Last year a Women's Institute in Essex was banned from supplying cakes to a hospital because kitchens could not be checked.

(Daily Express, 7 June 2005)

The views of this piece are amplified in the argumentation of the leading article that day (see below). There is a series of imperatives – 'preserve', 'face', 'leave' – which are directed at nobody specific but are articulated from within a voice that speaks from the position of 'Britain's heritage' and which draws this community together using the familiar possessive adjective in 'our heritage' which is repeated twice in the same piece. The imperatives are amplified by the use of modals 'must' and 'will'. The blame is shifted from 'the people who practise other religions' to the 'officious Left-wing panjandrums', a term which conflates two criticisms into one from the point of view of this newspaper: one that such decisions are in themselves 'Left-wing' and the second that they are 'officious'. The world here is demarcated between this tolerant but potentially volatile community and those depicted as zealots who will, if they are not stopped, bring anger down on the heads of those outsiders to the community. Yet Britain is depicted here as a religious society, despite the overwhelmingly secular nature of contemporary Britain, and one in which continuous heritage is the norm. It is a good example of that attempt within nationalist discourse to fix identity within nationalism and to oppose it to ethnic and political outsiders.

> ### Preserve our heritage or face a terrible backlash
>
> Britain's heritage must not be allowed to be destroyed. . . . The real culprits here are not the people who practise other religions but officious Left-wing panjandrums, who want to pander to ethnic minorities at the expense of the rest of us.
> They must not be allowed to get away with it. What these people do not seem to understand is that if they continue trying to deny and suppress Britain's traditions, there will eventually be a terrible backlash. . . . Leave our heritage intact.

(Daily Express, 7 June 2005)

There are broad political implications which emerge from studying the narrative patterns in news. They provide closure around certain structures and solutions which act to reinforce the stability of the social and political systems that the newspapers support, and all national news media conform to a specifically national set of priorities on behalf of audiences that are constructed very much in these terms. Think of either the *Sun* newspaper or the *Times*, both owned by an international media conglomerate but both emphatically British (even English) in their orientation, for the sake of the political economy of their location in the British market, despite their ownership.

The pioneering work of Galtung and Ruge (1973), which explored the composition of news values, is an extremely important contribution to the study of the narratives of news. It analyses selection, characters, themes, and the construction of communities of insiders and outsiders, as well as narrative closure around the readings preferred by the news media institutions themselves. This work has recently been extended by a study by Harcup and O'Neill (2001) which updates the framework developed by Galtung and Ruge for the twenty-first century. Categories such as threshold, unambiguity, meaningfulness, consonance, reference to elite nations, and reference to elite individuals all function best within the news when they are linked to national narratives.

'Threshold' refers partly to the size or importance of an event, but more specifically to the importance of an event to a particular audience within a national setting. This explains the preference for coverage of events which have prominent British protagonists involved or which clearly impact upon interests that are defined by the news as British interests. The accidental deaths of British tourists, British involvement in natural disasters abroad, the involvement of a celebrity in an otherwise unremarkable event, such as a conviction for a speeding offence or a trip to a brothel, can all become part of this nationalized narrative of news value.

In the following example it is the plight of 'expats' which creates the news value of a story on the sufferings of British people who have relocated to warmer climates. It fits into the threshold expectations of this particular newspaper in particular, as it forms part of the middle-aged, middle-class readership, a significant part of which aspires to overseas property ownership. It is a readership profile which it manages to embody so successfully and therefore the story has a strong resonance with this ideal community and thus finds space in the paper.

> **Raped . . . kidnapped . . . gassed in their beds and burgled . . . how horrifying violence is driving thousands of expats to think again about new lives in the sun.**
> **Death of a dream.**

(*Daily Mail*, 2 June 2005)

'Unambiguity' refers to the need for news to be straightforward in both its meaning and its intended audience. Both of these features complement national interest. News is not the place for complexity of meaning. It functions to reduce the potential complexity of the world by eroding multiple or confused meanings down to clear and unmistakable meanings. An audience is addressed in the assumption that it is located within a common range of national sentiment and belonging. Although the audience is free to impose different interpretations on the nationalized unambiguities of news which might be supported by their different experience of life in Britain, the news items themselves do little to encourage such diversity and are more usually suited to close around national preferences for understanding and interpretation. In the next extract, an emotive plea is made for cross-generational understanding of national pride which draws heavily on the assumed knowledge of the importance of the Second World War generation for definitions of contemporary Britishness.

> **One generation grew to manhood with a dignity and pride that lasted them a lifetime, and was an inspiration to the children they brought into the world.**
>
> **And the other generation, although they can wave their white-and-red flags until Wayne Rooney collects his free bus pass, believe in nothing, stand for nothing and contribute nothing of value to the country they profess to love so dearly.**
>
> **Sixty years of peace have ruined the British male. He is now a soft, pampered bully, self-mutilated with crap tattoos, his self-esteem so fragile that he – with his mates – is ready to kick your head in for any insult, real or imagined.**
>
> **They might be proud of their country. But what have they ever done to make their country proud of them?**

(Tony Parsons, *Daily Mirror*, 21 June 2005)

'Meaningfulness' is also defined to a large extent by how expectations of what a particular audience expects from its news media affect what is covered in a news medium. The proximity of a news story to the interests of its target group will determine its newsworthiness. Social, economic, cultural and most importantly national factors all play a part in ascertaining whether a story has meaningfulness, and this meaningfulness is always filtered through the perceived interests of the audience. Below we can see a rich and indicative twin set of paradigms from which stereotypes of British social classes can be drawn:

> **Who will win the hearts of the nation when sporting cultures collide?**
>
> **HENMANIA V ROOMANIA**
>
> **THE TWO faces of modern Britain will stare back and forth at each other between Lisbon and London SW19. . . .**
>   This is a clash of cultures to beat them all. It's the Gladwys Street End versus Centre Court. It's a pint of lager versus a glass of Pimms, a burger versus strawberries and cream.
>   It's chewing gum versus sipping an energy drink. It's a wife called Lucy and a daughter called Rosy versus a childhood sweetheart called Colleen. It's a lad called Wayne and a dad called Wayne Senior.
>   And at its most basic, it's the inner city versus the countryside, working class versus middle class, football versus tennis, privilege versus under-privilege.
>   Something to divide us, but this week and maybe next week too, something to bring us together.
>
> **Oliver Holt**
> **Chief Sports Writer**

(*Daily Mirror*, 31 May 2005)

Consonance and elite nations

'Consonance' has relevance to the national narrative at the heart of newsworthiness. It refers to the predictability of events. Within a national context, some stories become news because they fit with what an audience expects at particular times of the year. To this end, media diaries are drawn up well in advance of events which will have a nationally public importance. It is a very astute economic strategy, combining forward planning with resource management. The diaries thus constructed tell us a great deal about the cultural core of British life as imagined by the news media and their audience. How the news media stays in harmony with that core as it shifts in emphasis over the years is a crucial calculation which, when managed adroitly, enables the news to keep in step with the national mood by reinforcing the dominant patterns to its rhythms. As if to shape this consonance still further, newspapers can conduct their own polls of their own readers to take a highly selective reading of national sentiments and report them back to that same readership. The results of the poll are filled out with a further set of characteristics, a series of paradigm choices from long-running contemporary scripts.

> ## ANXIOUS POLL FOR THE SUN . . .
>
> ## ANXIOUS BRITAIN
>
> **Internet porn, chatroom perverts and the hoodie menace top modern fears**
>
> MODERN living is causing a culture of fear in Britain today, a shock new poll of Sun readers reveals.
>   You worry more about CRIME, HEALTH and MONEY than you did 15 years ago.
>   But it is the horrors of porn on the INTERNET, chatroom PERVS, VIOLENCE against children and the hoodie YOB CULTURE which cause you the most anxiety. . . .
>   There is overwhelming support across the board for The Sun's campaign for prison ships to solve the crisis of overcrowded jails. . . .
>
> [last two paragraphs]
> A reassuring 87 per cent of Sun readers are happy with life at the moment, compared with 79 per cent of the public in 1991.
>   And you rate British newspapers, especially your No 1 Sun, as the best in the world.

(*Sun*, 23 January 2006)

Newspapers can involve themselves in activities to exploit popular sentiment and fold it within longer claims to represent the feelings of the nation as a whole. This is effected through astute selection of events but just as importantly through skilful deployment of language which draws the newspaper and the national interest together. The actional verbs which the *Sun* triggers in the next example are central to placing the newspaper as the catalyst for this campaign. 'Launches', 'teamed up' and 'urging' are all used to generate support for the apparently trivial aim of saving the bones of the whale that drowned in the Thames to be displayed in the National History Museum. This act is portrayed as saving the bones 'for the nation'. The link with the readers is not only expressed through the emotional contingency of the story but also directly through the appeal to 'our generous readers'.

> **Memorial to Wally**
>
> THE Sun today launches a £10,000 appeal to save Wally the Whales's bones for the nation.
>   We have teamed up with experts and conservationists to help preserve the skeleton for crucial scientific research. . . .
>   The Sun is urging our generous readers to help meet the £10,000 bill with an appeal for cash. . . .
>   The skeleton could then go on display at the Natural History Museum in London.
>   The museum's curator Richard Sabin said: 'We desperately want to save these bones for scientific research. I can't thank The Sun enough.'

(*Sun*, 21 January 2006)

One recent example of the articulation of the nation in the news came in response to the announcement that the BBC was going to drop its long-standing early morning musical medley, the 'UK Theme'. When it was announced, there was a wide-ranging expression of outrage that such a British institution should be dispensed with. The *Times* personifies Britain as actively coming together in opposition, although the real extent of the opposition was in fact a mere twelve thousand.

Britain unites in campaign to save radio theme tune

(*Times*, 27 January 2006)

Two days earlier the same newspaper had featured columnist Libby Purves on its opinion pages to argue that the tune constituted nothing short of 'a five-minute masterclass in national identity'.

In the *Daily Mail*, normally no friend of Gordon Brown, the Chancellor is referred to, to bolster the argument that the medley should be retained – once he has made it clear that one of the reasons chimes well with the agenda of the traditionalist newspaper:

> He cited the 'Britishness' of the medley composed by a refugee from the Nazis as a key reason for keeping the 30-year-old tradition going. . . . A fortnight ago, he called for the establishment of an annual British Day to celebrate national values. . . . Mr Brown believes the BBC should keep on a medley composed by a refugee that celebrates music considered an integral part of national cultural history.

(*Daily Mail*, 26 January 2006)

A commentary on the affair by Andrew Roberts sums up in its headline much of the flavour of the *Daily Mail*'s position on British cultural matters when he asks: 'Can't they simply leave well alone?'

He fits it within a well-worn lexicon of British signifiers, 'understated, inoffensive and as British as toast and marmalade, eggs and bacon' and, fitting in with another well-rehearsed script of the *Daily Mail*, he ponders whether the reason is that the tune 'simply isn't European enough for the politically correct apparatchiks of the BBC'. And he claims that tradition always loses out, as if counterposing the traditions which support the survival of national identity with the march of modernity:

> **There is a terrible tendency in Britain to destroy things for the sake of it. And it always seems to be the traditional, customary and inevitably, much loved institutions that disappear.**

(*Daily Mail*, 26 January 2006)

Reference to elite nations is a category of central importance to the news values of any national media. The nation is the home nation. News is composed along the lines of what Michael Billig, as we have seen before, has termed 'news apartheid'. It is corralled into separate spaces and arranged in a hierarchy with the home nation prioritized as of more importance than the foreign. Even the foreign is then sub-divided into the foreign which aligns with the perceived dominant values of the priority nation, having preference over other nations, such as the USA and Canada.

> **4,000 troops to be sent to troubled Afghan province**
>
> Since the new year there has been a spate of suicide attacks, with one bomber killing at least 20 people in Spin Buldak on January 16. The day before another bomber killed three in Khandahar, including a Canadian diplomat . . .

(*Times*, 25 January 2006)

> ## Death of an American dream
>
> **Briton goes missing after his wife and daughter are found shot dead in bed at home**
>
> FOR Neil and Rachel Entwistle, their personal website was proof that they were living the great American dream.

(*Times*, 25 January 2006)

Elite nations for Australia are, in addition to its Western allies, clearly outlined in *The Advertiser*'s Asia–Pacific section which regularly highlights the geographical and economic importance of countries such as Taiwan, Japan, Malaysia and Indonesia to the Australian national interest.

At the other end of that elite spectrum, we have nations which are considered so low in this set of preferences as to be grouped into continental or sub-continental lumps such as 'Africa', 'sub-Saharan Africa' or so-called 'Eastern Europe'. The elite nation can also be contrasted with specific nations which, because of history or their contemporary importance to the elite nation, take on a special form of negative newsworthiness. These nations in terms of Britain, for instance, tend to include Germany and Argentina, because of military and sporting rivalries, and Iraq and Iran because of contemporary issues, in particular the fact that they feature so heavily in the foreign policy objectives of Britain's ultimate elite nation and ally, the USA.

Elite individuals are also quite clearly mapped onto particular national expectations of the audience. Politicians, sports people and celebrities are all flagged upon the basis of their location within the longer narratives of nationally based television or film culture or the national political scene, and are hardly recognizable once they are observed from outside that national orbit of influence. The global dominance of Hollywood is an exception to this trend and is an example of how a certain sort of parochial West Coast American culture has, through the political economy of film, become recognizable as part of a national–global news agenda. Yet looking at the popular press in Britain is to be reminded of how nationally oriented these media are in their coverage of popular media culture, despite claims that we are living in a global media era. The American variant is an exception not a rule as elite media individuals usually remain well within the boundaries of exclusively national interest.

Elite individuals can also be drawn from history. Churchill, St George, John Bull – real and fictitious – the resonances are greater when they connect with the longer narratives of nation for a nationalized audience. These features of news value do not function in isolation but in combination with each other and within the general framework of national interest. A story which can combine as many of these features as possible is more likely to become news than one which can claim a more limited spread of relevance.

 Activity 7.4 o━┳

Find a news story and analyse it in terms of these different categories, and see how they link with each other to develop as rich a national news narrative as possible.

The critical implications of an analysis of news stories from the perspective of national interests are clear. News functions to close down the possibility of synchronic contestation. This means that it prefers to provide instant comprehension to an audience rooted in parochial, nationally based explanations of the world. You will recall from discussions on semiology that synchronic analysis refers to analysis which concentrates on the present. Yet this synchronic aspect is always informed by an implicit understanding of the longer narrative of the news in terms of its national context, and the way in which this nation is constructed at the same time by an understanding of its diachronic nature, its cohesion over time, across history. In its structural and thematic organization of narratives, news functions to discourage dispute about its message and its meaning or channels such disputes into areas of the news package such as letters pages, e-mails or Readers' Editors where it can be dealt with in ways which do not compromise the ideological and institutional identity and consistency of the news medium itself. The rationale for closure and stereotyping is that news is not equipped to deal with the complexities of social and political processes without channelling them into the national narratives described here. However, this is not the same as explaining why news has evolved in such a way as to actively eradicate such complexity.

The political economy of the news media favours the institutional and political status quo because the media depend on this status quo for the continuation of profit and market stability of their identity. They therefore prefer forms of textual condensation around macro stories which provide underlying continuity to audiences within a limited range of variety in subject matter. Despite this, press narratives share with fictional narratives an ability to shift over time. These shifts are referred to as diachronic shifts. Good examples of this, where news shifts its political perspective over time, are how narratives on race, the British nation and foreign allies/enemies have shifted as social and political contingencies have shifted. Consider, for example, how Nelson Mandela shifted from ostracized communist agitator to universally respected hero within the news media, and how South Africa in general has undergone a shift in representation. It was once considered by most in the sports media that discussion of apartheid in relation to South African sport was an example of mixing sport and politics and to be discouraged if at all possible. This too was often the case in the reporting of the experiences of black footballers in England when confronting racism on the terraces. Both of these news narratives have undergone radical shifts in recent years.

 Activity 7.5 o━┳

Choose a special day in the national calendar. It might be a day which you know about in advance such as St George's Day, an international sports event or a Royal occasion, or it might be something which occurs quite spontaneously. Chart the vocabulary, iconography, style of stories and metaphors which all combine to present a vigorous portrait of the nation in the news.

Non-elite nations

The other side of the coin is the way in which news coverage of non-elite nations reinforces the centrality of the national narratives of the news. In part it does this by continuing the normative assumptions that most news is national news or at least has a direct and immediate national interest. Yet it also performs this task in the way that such news, when it does emerge, is covered, and what the main news values concerning non-elite nations are. The following set of ironic instructions to journalists and authors is a good indicator of how mainstream media deal with the non-elite nations of Africa:

How to write about Africa in five easy steps.

1. Always treat Africa as if it were one country. Don't get bogged down with precise descriptions. Africa is big: fifty-four countries, nine hundred million people who are too busy starving and dying and warring and emigrating to read your book.
2. Adopt a sad, I-expected-so-much tone. Establish early on that your liberalism is impeccable, and how much you love Africa. Africa is to be pitied, worshipped or dominated. Whichever angle you take, be sure to

leave the strong impression that without your intervention and your important book, Africa is doomed.

3.   Always include a Starving African, who wanders the refugee camp nearly naked, and waits for the benevolence of the West. She must never say anything about herself in the dialogue except to speak of her (unspeakable) suffering. Moans are good.

(Binyavanga Wainaina, 'The View from Africa', *Granta* 92, 15 January 2006)

When Africa does become news it is likely to be part of the dominant pattern of representation of a continent characterized as corrupt, diseased and chaotic. On occasions, in contrast, journalists can provide direct commentary on the mechanics of assumed news values, including the limitations of most news media when it comes to news about Africa. The following two extracts provide eloquent pleas for news editors to think more ambitiously and even more generously about the real interests of their readers, rather than settling for outdated and comfortable assumptions to err on the side of conservatism. They both understand the systematic nature of news values but don't think that it necessarily reflects the nature of national interest nor the imperatives for good reporting.

Don't let disaster get in the way of a real story

. . . Brendan Cox, emergency specialist at Oxfam [says] 'News editors have quite a crude idea that the public is not interested in black people dying [in a country] far away. So it's hard for us to get past these gatekeepers. The media shouldn't be the arbiter of humanitarian intervention.' . . .

Possible reasons for this are the difficulty of access and the dangers of reporting. Other emergencies may go under-reported when stories are deemed too complex or when there's difficulty getting a human angle. Disasters with a 'home connection' – like areas popular with holidaying Brits – may get more attention.

(Ben Flanagan, *Observer*, 18 December 2005)

Foreign news a distant memory

. . . I fear the press has its bearings wrong. It thinks all Britons have the same world outlook as the overwhelmingly white Anglo-Saxon people it employs. In the wake of the attacks on the capital, the papers keep telling us in a self-congratulatory way, that London is one of the most cosmopolitan cities. But you would never know it from the papers' own content.

(Peter Wilby, *Guardian*, 25 July 2005)

Sporting examples

It is indubitably the popular tabloids who lead the field when it comes to chauvinistic appeals to national identity during sporting contests. The 2004 European Football Championships provided fine examples of the inventiveness and variety which these papers draw upon, in order to build upon old clichés of national identities and stereotypes of other national groups and manage to invest them with contemporary resonance for a new generation of sports national fans. Among the strategies were a host of mock invasions of the capital cities of rival countries to highlight the stereotype of the opponents, the alleged virtues of the English and the specific role of the newspaper in leading such a daring stunt. In describing the 'invasion' of a square in Lisbon and the display of the 'world's biggest flag' the *Sun* (24 June 2004) is headlined 'FOR ENGLAND AND ST GEORGE' with nationalist reference to the English patron saint and an allusion to the words of Shakespearian hero Henry V.

In addition, the newspaper provides a direct quotation from a poem by First World War poet Rupert Brooke, making explicit the connections between sport, resonant patriotic war poetry and contemporary nationalism: 'If I should die, think only this of me: That there's some corner of a foreign field that is forever England'. The resonance of this allusion in terms of national memories of war can be seen carried over in the metaphor used in the *Sunday Mirror* (13 June 2004) to refer to the stadium in Portugal, where the action will take place 'in the Lisbon trenches'.

The combination of puns, popular media celebrities called upon for their views of the match, and confirmation of the linkage between virility and sporting prowess are all used as paradigm selections to fit into the syntagm of mock invasion once again in the case of Paris:

WE WIN, ONE GAUL TO NIL

SUN'S MARK DE TRIOMPHE

<u>Our flag on Paris arch</u>

On the back page there is a picture of David Beckham holding the national flag aloft and the headline: 'Balls v Gauls . . . and ours are bigger than theirs says Becks' (*Sun,* 12 June 2004).

Reference to a contemporary hero, Wayne Rooney, is reinforced by direct reference to more traditional Greek myth when readers of the *Daily Star* are told in declarative fashion to:

RUB HIS GOLDEN EARS FOR LUCK

. . . When he and the rest of the England team line up for the national anthem tonight, rub the 18-year-old's golden ears and think: "Wayne's a winner!"

We reckon the flow of positive energy will give Wayne and the lads an extra boost to carry them into the semi-finals. Then you can stick this page in your window to show we're behind the boys.

(*Daily Star*, 24 June 2004)

The binary distinctions which allegedly divide nations are stripped down to their essentials in the *Daily Mail*:

Unleash our iron men to combat French flair

Ericsson's priority here is to enhance the warrior reputation of his adopted footballers.

(*Daily Mail*, 12 June 2004)

The tradition of associating Britain with the manly metaphors of metal against the dubious qualities of the French as possessed of 'flair' contributes to a hierarchy of virility which has moral as well as martial overtones. This has been identified in longer term studies of national characters such as John Bull from as far back as the Napoleonic Wars.

The use of the word 'warrior' to describe the footballers representing England adds to the militaristic lexical field upon which the championship is presented.

In the next extract, the agentless passive 'is being billed' adds a spurious yet anonymous air of authority to something which is only happening in the pages of the popular tabloids. The piece makes full use of the register of historical enmity between the nations as military rivals by using Wellington and Napoleon as markers in the debate:

SVEN GORAN ERIKSSON believes he has won the hearts and minds of the nation – but knows the events of the next three weeks will decide whether he remains an honorary Englishman. . . . It is an intriguing sub-plot to a game that is being billed as the biggest battle of wills between the English and the French since Wellington used the flanks to beat Napoleon.

(*Daily Mail*, 12 June 2005)

Unthinking, chauvinistic fervour is traditionally contrasted with the more measured approach of politicians during these international competitions. In the
next extract, the *Daily Star* positions itself and its readers on the side of the
British envoy in Lisbon who is contrasted with the more cautious, even reluctant
approach of Tony Blair. The newspaper creates its own maelstrom of outrage.
Actional verbs predominate – 'hoisted', 'snubbed', 'jammed' – to set up the dis-
agreement between the 'angry' fans showing their 'fury' and Tony Blair:

Envoy: I will fly flag for England

. . . to show his support for our football heroes . . . Patriotic envoy David
Bough has proudly hoisted the St George's Cross over the British
Embassy in Lisbon. . . . proud Bough. . . . But Tony Blair was still refusing
to fly the England flag last night – despite the fury of Daily Star readers.
  Angry fans jammed the Daily Star's phonelines after we revealed the
PM had snubbed calls to display the red and white flag over govern-
ment buildings. . . . 95 per cent of readers . . . Union Flag.

(*Daily Star*, 17 June 2004)

It is also characteristic on these occasions for full use to be made of the narrative
of national decline as a contrast to the sudden outpouring of patriotic fervour.
The *Sun* bemoans the inability of some to honour the 'legacy of our war heroes'
and shifts the blame from football and the hooligans themselves to 'decades of
liberal hogwash' which it lays squarely at the door of the Government and the
decision, which the paper clearly opposes, to sanction 24-hour drinking.

THE SUN SAYS

English disease

WHY can't some Englishmen behave themselves abroad?

For the same reason they can't behave in towns up and down the
nation every Saturday night: **DRINK.**
  We have allowed a culture to grow in which mindless yobbery is seen
as manly by some sad individuals. . . .
  They are an embarrassment to the legacy of our war heroes.
  What's happening in Portugal can't be blamed on soccer. We are
paying for decades of liberal hogwash, when self-discipline vanished.
  Now the Government fuels this volcano with all day drinking.
  It makes decent people weep.

(*Sun*, 17 June 2005)

Nation under threat

One aspect of the nation itself is that its discourse survives only to the extent that it is perceived to be under threat. It is at this point that enemies, real and imaginary, need to be marshalled in order to remind the insiders of the national group what exactly is at stake. The integrity of the national community, its borders and its traditions can all be threatened in ways which appear capable within this discourse of eroding or even dissolving the nation. In the next story, a hospital in Leicester has been reported as removing bibles from hospital wards in case this offends ethnic minorities. The selection of the story as newsworthy tells us of the news values of the *Daily Express*, as it was not covered across the news media. It is also used to leap hyperbolically to a rhetorical question, in imitation one supposes of an idealized reader responding to the story, which suggests that the country has finally been taken over by madness.

> **Banning Bibles from our hospitals is just insane**
>
> Have the last vestiges of common sense been drained out of this country? Leicester NHS Trust's proposal to remove the Bible from hospital wards in case it offends ethnic minorities is as ludicrous as it is misguided.

(*Daily Express*, 3 June 2005)

A second piece shows that it is not just the beliefs and traditions of a nation which may be claimed as being under threat but the physical borders of the country. The following extract posits a country which has 'gaps' and 'gaping holes' in its borders, leaving it 'wide open to terror attacks'. The headline belongs to a recognizable newspaper syntagm which starts with 'The scandal of' and is completed by whatever fits the newspaper's agenda for sensation. The following sentence is, again in newspaper style, inverted, so that 'a report has warned' is relegated below the 'gaping holes in Britain's border defences' which takes the prominent and more influential position at the head of the sentence. There is a presupposition that security lapses have left the country open to a particular form of threat – 'terror attacks'. The piece then goes on to state more of the provocative claims before returning to the report itself. The extract finishes by reference to a stunt carried out by the newspaper during which fake bombs were smuggled into the country to expose breaches in security. There is a rhetorical twinning of the inadequacies of Britain's security to emphasize the point made by the newspaper on the back of the report: 'inadequate at most . . . non-existent at others' which assists in fixing the argument in the readers' minds. Clearly the newspaper had a prior interest in this issue, which prompted it to put it to the test in a way which it could feed back into its concerns about security. The fabric of the nation seems here to be threadbare and exposed, let down by inadequate controls and resources to combat terrorism. It fits perfectly within the narrative of the nation under threat, and begs a strong security solution which would presumably police and patrol these borders so that the integrity of the nation can be maintained.

The scandal of Britain's wide-open defence line

Gaping holes in Britain's border defences have left the country wide open to terror attacks, a report has warned.

Security is inadequate at most ports, and non-existent at others. Police, who should be spotting terror suspects, waste their time ferrying petty crooks back from France – offenders who then get bail.

The report, by Lord Carlile, independent reviewer of the Terrorism Act, comes three months after the Daily Express exposed terrifying gaps in security, by smuggling in fake bombs.

(*Daily Express*, 1 June 2005)

Threats to the nation are articulated not only in terms of cultural threats but also economic threats and they are not restricted to newspapers at the more traditionalist, conservative end of the political spectrum – they are as likely to appear in the *Daily Mirror* as in the *Daily Express*. In the next example we see the argument of one columnist pivoting on the assertion that there is a particular antithesis between the interests of the 'people' and the politicians of the EU, who are referred to as a 'governing caste' in order to highlight the alleged distance between these politicians and the European electorate. The string of qualifiers which precedes the nominal 'governing caste' acts as a summary of all of the negative features of these politicians, and serves to endorse the view of them from the perspective of both columnist and newspaper: 'self-anointed, unaccountable, hand-in-the-till'. Verbally, the modal of the headline 'must' is a strong indicator of the preferred course of action, and the 'we' is inclusive of both newspaper and people associated as constituting the nation. In addition the repetition of the relational verb 'is' goes to reinforce the clarity and certainty of the situation.

> **We must get back to the basics of EU trade now the French have said Non**
>
> . . . The Euro-elite, the self-anointed, unaccountable, hand-in-the-till governing caste of the New Europe, is well aware of the people's exhausted patience, and terrified of it. . . . There is an unbreakable freemasonry that unites all who worship power and wish the electorate would just shut up and do what it is told.

(Max Hastings, *Daily Express*, 1 June 2005)

A similar style of language is used in the next extract for the more abstract process of outsourcing Government jobs. The jobs are described in terms of the possessive adjective 'our' and India is said to be answering for 'our' firms as these jobs are outsourced. The economic processes of contemporary capitalism are not clarified by the agentless headline and nor is the metaphor of 'shipping' jobs abroad. The only solution is expressed in the simple declarative, 'Keep our jobs here' and the ministers involved criticized in the harshest terms of comparison with lunatics.

> **20,000 GOVERNMENT JOBS TO GO ABROAD**
>
> **SECRET plans to ship up to 20,000 Government jobs overseas are being worked on by ministers.**
>
> **INDIA ANSWERS FOR OUR FIRMS**
>
> **Keep our jobs here**
>
> SHIPPING jobs overseas when unemployment is rising is the economics of the madhouse.
>   When such a plan is being hatched in the Whitehall ministry responsible for dole queues, it seems the lunatics have taken over the asylum.

(*Daily Mirror*, 23 January 2006)

Direct narratives of nation

On occasions, however, nations are narrated in the news not obliquely and not through reference to figures or events from the past but by bold and direct statements of the central narrative, as we can see in some of the pieces which seem to be part of a deliberate editorial policy to inject a reinvigorated form of explicit and didactic nationalism into the celebration of Australia's national celebration, Australia Day:

Come let us rejoice

Celebrating Australia Day is back in fashion, so grab your flag and start waving, writes Stuart Rintoul

THERE was a time when Australians, if they were at all good-hearted, were obliged to agonise on Australia Day.

If we had to celebrate a national birthday, the argument went, then we ought at least to reflect, however briefly, on the cost of establishing the nation as well as its achievements. We should be conscious that Aboriginal people regard January 26 as Invasion Day and reflect on the illogicality of a nation founded by a British governor and still tied to Britain's monarchic apron strings. It was, all in all, a troubling kind of celebration.

Sick to death of this politically correct introspection, Australians elected John Howard and almost 10 years later are again blithely celebrating the simple joys of being Australian, according to some of the nation's most savvy market researchers. As a result, flag makers are reporting bumper business.

(*The Australian*, 26 January 2006)

Prime Minister John Howard's Australia Day speech on the teaching of history

A history we should all understand

Any worthwhile educational curriculum should ensure that children learn to read and write, gain a basic grasp of mathematics, and a fundamental understanding of their historical beginnings.

Prime Minister John Howard argues, and not without justification, that history is not being appropriately taught in Australian schools.

Mr Howard says history is too often neglected and, in many schools, it actually repudiates or questions the nation's development and achievements. . . .

History [if properly taught] will help young people appreciate the value – and the advantages – of being Australian.

It is a wonderful story which is not being properly told.

(*The Advertiser*, 27 January 2006)

In both of these examples there is a clear strategy which includes a preliminary discussion of the previous anxieties and reservations about wholeheartedly embracing Australia Day. The first argues that it was the result in the past of over-sensitivity to a political correctness. The second, endorsing the opinions of the Prime Minister, claims that it was because of inaccuracies in assessing Australia's history. The first exhorts the readers as an embodiment of the nation to enjoy the day; the second calls on Australia to teach its own history in a way which celebrates the positive aspects of Australia's past. Neither has any time for positions which question or seek to qualify the success of the contemporary nation. Both are very positivist narratives which seek to place past concerns within a category which can be considered as beyond debate. In the first it is stated that 'Australians' voted for Mr Howard as if his success was endorsed by the whole country and as if his only policy was to reinforce a straightforward and uncritical celebration of the nation and the readers are exhorted to relish 'the simple joys of being Australian'.

Summary

This chapter considers the structure of narrative and how this plays a central role in the shape and content of news. The fact that narrative builds upon expectations of and contributes to the maintenance of conventional ways of interpreting and categorizing events in the world make it very much a part of the ideological operation of news. It achieves this predominantly by creating accounts which are related in terms of insiders and outsiders to a national community. This aspect of the narratives of news makes sense commercially as well as culturally, as news is most often consumed within the imaginary communities of the nation. National narratives within the news often draw upon longer historical memories and are at their most assertive when history and nation can be combined in the language of sports reporting.

Suggestions for further reading

Anderson, B. (1986) *Imagined Communities*. London: Verso.
Bhabha, H. (1990) 'Introduction: Narrating the Nation'. In H. Bhabha (ed.) *Nation and Narration*. London: Routledge.
Billig, M. (1995) *Banal Nationalism*. London: Sage.
Bishop, H. and Jaworski, A. (2003) '"We beat 'em": nationalism and the hegemony of homogeneity in the British press reportage of Germany versus England during Euro 2000', *Discourse and Society*, 14(3): 243–271.
Brookes, R. (1999) 'Newspapers and national identity: the BSE/CJD crisis and the British press', *Media, Culture and Society* 21 (3): 247–263.
Conboy, M. (2004) 'Heroes and demons as historical bookmarks in the English popular press'. In R. Phillips and H. Brocklehurst (eds) *History, Nationhood and the Question of Britain*. Basingstoke: Palgrave.
Edensor, T. (2002) *National Identity, Popular Culture and Everyday Life*. Oxford: Berg.
Gilroy, P. (1987) *There Ain't No Black in the Union Jack: The Cultural Politics of Nation*. London: Hutchinson.

Kumar, K. (2003) *The Making of English National Identity*. Cambridge: Cambridge University Press.

Spencer, P. and Wollman, H. (2003) *Nationalism: A Critical Introduction*. London: Sage.

8 Narratives of exclusion

- Introduction
- Classification of outsiders
- Africa and the Middle East
- Lexical maps
- Metaphor
- Strategies of argumentation
- Insiders as outsiders
- Summary
- Suggestions for further reading

Introduction

Just as the normative influences of the news can reinforce feelings of belonging to a community they can also contribute symmetrically to the exclusion of certain characters from the mainstream. This is a fundamental part of the function of the newspaper in constructing its sense of community. Without outsiders there could be no core audience. The news, in its selection of those groups which are categorized as outside the parameters of the national community and in its use of language to present them, is a powerful influence in moulding the social expectations of the groups which we perceive as welcome or acceptable within our society.

One important way of identifying outsiders is not in the direct reporting of the facts of a case but in the metaphorical cluster of words used to generate an implicit picture of the groups described. This belongs to the area of connotation discussed in Chapter 5. This is an area well worth examining, for it indicates that the press in particular needs to involve itself in the symbolic realm of metaphor if it is to make a group stand out from the everyday. It is often used to represent outsider groups in language and this enables the popular press in particular to sensationalize coverage of them. This chapter will concentrate on the language used to report issues such as asylum seekers, Islamophobia and other forms of more general social exclusion. Moreover, as Richardson (2004) and Van Dijk (1991) have demonstrated, this prejudice is also present in a different way in the elite press which uses what they refer to as 'elite discourse' to systematically marginalize outsiders by other means than direct hostility or pejorative sensationalism.

This latter mode of more discursive exclusion from the mainstream includes a wide range of linguistic elements which we have already considered in broad terms: strategies of argumentation, rhetoric and lexis either figuratively or literally, narratives which contrast to narratives of inclusion of the social semiotic of the national news media, the selection of spokespeople and the elevation of community leaders.

Classification of outsiders

Before the specific language of a news story is determined, the classification of particular groups of people as newsworthy – and whether that newsworthiness is predicated upon positive or negative aspects – already provides an important structuring principle for those represented as outsiders to the national community.

In order to clarify our thinking on these matters it is necessary perhaps to distinguish different forms of negativity towards outsiders. Even within a nation there will be rivalries and stereotypical views of people from other regions or cities. This sort of negativity is best categorized as parochialism, an inability to understand the world outside one's narrow local community of experience.

Nationalism and patriotism are often used to express attachment to a particular country and, on the face of it, do not in themselves imply any hostility towards other groups whether they be national, regional or ethnic. Both are irrational, not based on any intellectually defensible grounds and always in danger of edging into chauvinism. Chauvinism is when people allow feelings of attachment to one community, usually a national one, to become infused with perceptions of the superiority of that community and a corresponding negativity towards outside communities. Some claim that nationalism and patriotism already have the potential for chauvinism within their structures. That potential has been eloquently drawn to our attention:

> Patriotism has an inherent flaw. By preferring one segment of humanity over the rest, the citizen transgresses the fundamental principle of morality, that of universality; without saying so openly, he acknowledges that men are not equal.
>
> (Todorov, 1993: 183)

Racism takes these irrational divisions one step further and attempts to categorize people on the basis of the alleged superiority or inferiority of identifiably different ethnic or religious groups. It is reductionist in the extreme, dealing most often with crude stereotypes of groups outside the everyday experience of insider groups. Given the traditional role of the news media in representing that world outside our everyday experience, their coverage of ethnically or religiously different groups is of crucial importance. Thankfully, examples of overt racism are rare in our news media but this does not mean that other, more structural and sometimes seditious manifestations are totally excluded. A recent claim by the Metropolitan Police Commissioner, Sir Ian Blair, that the news media were guilty of institutional racism and the furious backlash it provoked in the media was testimony to how sensitive a subject this is.

So Plod's PC – but are we?

... We're not ticking bureaucracy's boxes here, devoting equal resources to every crime scene. We're picking and choosing – and remembering the readers we have, the people who've paid money up front. Is that suitably fair and balanced? Not always. Institutional racism? Sometimes, perhaps, in its assumptions about our society of readers and viewers. But understandable, commissioner, with a slight change of mind-set? Absolutely.

(Peter Preston, *Observer*, 29 January 2006)

Throughout history there have been many varieties of characterization for those represented as different to insider communities and as constituting a threat to the stability of the home community, but the pattern of these representations has remained quite familiar. Often the trigger for hostility is religion but often it has simply been the fact that someone came from outside that made them a perceived threat. Before recorded history there were folk narratives about the dangers of outsiders arriving in communities, such as that which became popularized in the German tale of the Pied Piper of Hamelin. Until modern times, only the wealthy, and those professionally employed to travel such as soldiers and sailors , statesmen and tradespeople ever travelled more than a dozen miles from the town or village where they had been born. This created a set of very parochial views of the world outside local communities.

The irrational mistrust or hatred of the outsider or foreigner is referred to as xenophobia. This is very different from the more specific and sustained prejudices against specific groups that we refer to as racism. Anti-Semitism has the longest history as a specific form of racism over the whole of the European continent, and was the first example of the systematic exclusion of a distinct ethnic group from mainstream culture. This form of racism has of course had catastrophic effects on the Jewish population of Europe through the Holocaust, and the media representations of the Jews in Nazi Germany in the 1930s and 1940s certainly helped to create conditions in which the extermination of Jews could take place.

What we might call Islamophobia also has roots long back in the history of relations between the Christian West and the Muslim East and has its first manifestation in the series of wars and occupations known as the Crusades. A perfect example of the ways in which such hostility can be drawn upon to denigrate and vilify a whole section of humanity can be found in the way that in the Old French poem, *La Chanson de Roland,* the dark-skinned Moors are described as possessed by, and sometimes as indistinguishable from, the Devil. The tendency to see other peoples as inferior, particularly those with identifiably different features to those of indigenous Western Europeans, was magnified by the expansion of colonial trade from the fifteenth century onwards, and was formalized into a style of scientific racism in the nineteenth century as a justification for exploitation by the rival European powers. It was clearly easier to exploit foreign people if the colonial power could claim a superiority over subjects, is justified in terms of a technological, religious, cultural or even biological rationale.

Since British culture has such a long association with imperialism and colonialism dating back to the sixteenth century, it is unsurprising that many elements of such 'superiority thinking' towards peoples who are identifiably different from the historical type of the white British have survived and indeed flourished. The British news media, and not just the popular media, are economically and culturally bound within those historical patterns of prejudice and stereotype and are part of the communicative apparatus which reproduces an inferential form of racism in institutional ways on a daily basis. This contributes to 'elite racism' in practice, as Van Dijk (1993) has termed it. To explore this we need to identify patterns of representation within news agendas and word selection when the news deals with information about those construed as ethnic or national outsiders. One of the ways in which our news media routinely artic- ulates covert or hidden forms of xenophobia or racism is through the narratives and forms of argumentation which are used to privilege white British institutions and characters at the expense of others.

At the structural level of employment practice, Peter Cole's report for the Society of Editors (2004) on the exclusion of black journalists from local newspapers in areas of Britain which are predominantly populated by ethnic minorities is a disturbing testimony to the entrenched patterns within British society, and particularly in professional access to channels of public commu- nication.

This form of patterning, as with other forms of discriminatory practice in our culture, encourages stereotypes, especially among people who know no better because of a lack of contact with minority groups and who rely on the discourses of the media for their information about those categorized as outsiders to a version of a British way of life which is represented as mainstream. Over time the uniformity of this discourse closes down the news media variety of repre- sentation so as to confirm that despite the occasional good story, the prevailing treatment of those identifiably different from the white British mainstream is maintained as inferior, problematic or worse. Ian Law (2002) has conducted detailed content analysis of the representation of ethnic minorities in the British media.

While there is little or no overt expression of or sympathy for racist views which would of course be illegal under current legislation, and despite the fact that any suggestions that Britain is a racist society are categorically denied and any examples of racism are vehemently condemned, Law still found that approximately one third of popular tabloid stories and one half of the elite press's coverage were negative. He found that old scripts were often used as framing devices for stories, as if white audiences needed this sort of orientation to under- stand why news about black people was in the frame. The news therefore drew on a narrow range of images of ethnic minorities, images which often conformed to a limiting and negative set of stereotypes. On the other hand, the issue of institutional racism was low on the agenda, even though it was widely acknowl- edged as forming a big part of the problem of how news media represent ethnic British minorities.

Minority groups were consistently represented as a social problem not as a national asset, and the issues facing specific minority groups were character- istically low on news agendas. In the light of these observations it is hardly surprising that news about ethnic minorities only becomes a part of the mainstream media once a problem specific to that grouping emerges. Since news is not in general terms very good at providing longer contexts to stories, in waiting for something of short-term significance to emerge from the ethnic minorities it is almost predetermined that these will fit longer and negative scripts that will resonate with the white readership's cultural understanding. This reinforces the impression that ethnic news is bad news. Van Dijk found in one study of the Dutch press (Dijk, 1999: 12) that of 1,500 headlines relating to ethnic issues, not a single one was positive when it involved minorities as active responsible agents.

As mentioned above, there is a historical context for this as the contemporary discourse has evolved over time and not from a vacuum. In fact, many of the patterns of racist thought processes were established before transatlantic colonialism and imperialism became common. It was the treatment by the English of their Irish neighbours which first gave coherence to their particular patterning of representations of outsiders. Liz Curtis in her book *Nothing but the Same Old Story*, traces the continuities of representation from Irish to Black African as the English and then the British state sought legitimacy for their treatment of peoples overseas as inferior. Many of the examples in her work are drawn from the periodical press, with nineteenth-century magazines being particularly prominent in their construction of discourses of racism with regard to both Africans and Irish. Her book includes examples of how the imagery used to describe and belittle the Irish was informed by stereotypes of Africans, how the descriptions were complemented by allegedly scientific proof of the inherent inferiority of these groups of humans and how similar discourses are drawn upon in the contemporary world to justify differential treatment of outsiders, particularly in the language and illustrations of the press.

Africa and the Middle East

Many studies focus on the ways in which our media represent the political/ geographical area of the Middle East and the continent of Africa. Heather Jean Brookes (1995) is particularly interesting on this topic, as she has examined the language of elite newspaper coverage of Africa and traced the dominant metaphors of 'darkness', 'savagery' and 'corruption' and the dominant themes of news reports which make the pages of these newspapers, and found that both combine to produce an overall picture of Africa not dissimilar to accounts from the colonial days of the nineteenth century. The conclusions of her work are reinforced by many a correspondent, such as journalist John Ryle when he claims: 'The African continent may look as if it is an incomprehensible nightmare. . . . But that's because westerners don't understand the politics and can't even speak the languages' (*Guardian*, 22 November 1997). This is of particular significance because it illustrates how an individual journalist can contribute to the debate in critical terms, but overall the patterning of news on Africa remains locked into the same prejudicial shapes. Much of Edward Said's work, particularly *Orientalism* (1978a) and *Culture and Imperialism* (1993), has relevance to the news media's representation of the Islamic outsider. He is at his most penetrating when he writes that Orientalism is, 'the positional superiority which puts the Westerner in a whole series of possible relationships with the Orient, without ever losing him the upper hand'. The importance of this to analyses of the representation of Islam in the Western media is difficult to overestimate, as we witness fresh waves of Islamophobia which allow discursive shifts to accommodate the West's strategic changes in foreign policy but keep at their core the identification of the Orient as implacably hostile and inferior to the West. This was noticeable in the shift of enmity from Iran to Iraq and now back to Iran as the realpolitik was followed by the discourse of the news. Such narrative shifts give credence to Toolan's (1998) view of the political structure of news stories over time, or diachronically, to use the semiological term.

Indigenous racism is fostered as a specific, structural element of Western societies; 'There Ain't No Black in the Union Jack', as Paul Gilroy summarized it. It has developed out of the histories which have formed these societies and their relationships to outsiders. These histories still have a structural role in common sense, ideological assumptions which form to a large extent these societies' understanding of their place in the world and their relationships with those who come from outside their geographical and cultural borders. We do not expect to see examples of overt racism in our news media, yet Chris Searle's book *Your Daily Dose: Racism in the Sun* is a reminder of just how virulent a form of racism was available for daily popular consumption, a relatively short while ago in the mid-1980s. For one thing, such expressions would contravene the laws of the land. However, this does not prevent a more insidious form of racism remaining very much part of our news media landscape. Stuart Hall (1981) has termed this 'inferential racism' and the elite racism mentioned above, as defined by Van Dijk, is another permutation of this. The latter exists as an ethnic white ideology in which white beliefs are transferred across institutions as commonsense, unexplored practices which serve to maintain white supremacy in cultural and economic terms. Such preconceptions also discriminate against stories which may be more interesting or more informative from minority groups but which are excluded because they do not fit the white-dominated news values of the mainstream media.

It may seem at first sight strange that in a globalized economy there are still the same patterns of mistrust or hatred of those who do not share our lifestyle, religion or nationality. This patterning of xenophobia within parts of our news media has been able to persist through to an age of media globalization. Barber (1995) has been able to shed light on part of this perplexing dynamic. He points out that there is a large degree of resistance within both excluded and dominant groups to the process called globalization. He sees it not as a flattening, unidirectional flow of influences but as one which meets and needs to incorporate or at least engage with resistance on the way, as part of the process. This phenomenon of globalization which had been until recently represented, particularly in Western news media, as a homogenizing process conducted on behalf of the interests of the dominant Western economies, has drawn hostile resistance from those excluded from this hegemonic process. Barber describes the to-and-fro of influence as being 'Jihad/McWorld' wherever Western interests clash with those of indigenous peoples in poorer parts of the world. He does not consider that the outcome is a foregone conclusion. In addition, the process of rediscovering national and ethnic roots is not one which is monopolized by the poorer, economically exploited nations. It is driven by a strand of resistance to more generalized global forces of homogeneity in the West with the rediscovery of the 'ethnic' insider, and the heritage and genealogy of its core members.

We need to be able to analyse how interethnic strife is reported and, more generally, answer the question: When does 'race' or ethnicity become news? We can, following Van Dijk, look at the structure and content of headlines, the topics covered, the social actors and most importantly the spokespeople who are called upon to represent and articulate the views of minority groups, the style of such stories and the ideologies inscribed within them. The 'scripts' – the assumption of a common framework of knowledge and narratives on ethnic news and ethnic affairs – are crucial in establishing the ideological perspectives of various news media on these topics.

 Activity 8.1 o—x

Identify examples of when 'ethnic issues' become news. Do they form a negative pattern?

Lexical maps

Often, national or ethnic outsiders to a white British mainstream are represented by absence from news agendas. They do not fit easily with consonance with the idealized British nation and are therefore not seen as routinely relevant to the interests of that audience. Furthermore, given the nationally inflected news values of most media institutions, it is hardly surprising that those marginalized from the mainstream are not represented proportionate to their presence in and impact on this country. When they *are* represented, then the language used to describe them is of even more significance, as too are the occasions which make them newsworthy. How often do asylum seekers become news in terms of cheating, overwhelming Britain's system of benefits or depriving local people of their livelihoods? If these are the only times they are referred to, it is is hardly surprising that they tend to be viewed eventually as being the problem rather than running away from problems in their own countries of origin. 'Asylum cheats', 'benefits tourists' are common scripts in the popular press, and Muslims in particular are routinely referred to as 'mad fanatics', 'fundamentalists' and 'Asian perverts', resulting in an overwhelmingly negative portrayal of Islam. This can become a crescendo of vehemence when dealing with a particularly newsworthy example of Islamic extremism:

> **'EVIL HOOKY', 'evil Hamza', 'mad mullah', 'EVIL hook-handed terror preacher', 'The preacher of hate', 'Islamic fanatic', 'Muslim fanatic', 'disgusting stain on this country'.**

(*Daily Star*, 6 May 2004)

Even when defending itself against accusations of racism from the Home Secretary, the *Sun* newspaper (28 May 2004) relies upon the same discourse to present the alleged threat to its readers from asylum seekers:

> And he also agreed it is not 'racist' to feel alarmed that thousands of asylum cheats flood into this country.
> Yet 'racist' is the word Home Secretary David Blunkett used to describe the Sun's cautious coverage of this crisis.

The *Sun* continues in repeating the characteristic accusations against them: 'abuse of free handouts', 'clampdown on asylum cheats', 'benefits tourists', 'to milk the system'.

In the news media the relevance of this language needs to be constantly scrutinized. Racist practice is not static but demonstrates that the concept of progress in human affairs cannot be regarded as a simple teleology, moving us forward to a better, more liberal world. Even the liberal institutions within the news media do little to provide a rectifying balance to this state of affairs. Their proposition is not an explicitly anti-racist one, more one based on a passive following of public consensus which is, as we have seen, a predominantly white consensus.

Metaphor

As we have seen, metaphor can act as a bridge between symbolic representation of the world and the reality of the world presented to the audience in the language of the news media. Once a set of lexical patterns have been established which allow us to place stories about ethnic and religious minorities within certain expectations, the politics of association around that language can be powerfully reinforced by metaphorical clusters. In terms of style, metaphor is integral to, not an accessory after, the fact of representation of ethnic outsiders, as it is in the representation of all groups within society. The constructing of one event in terms of another has a definite ideological impact. The word 'swamping' when referring to the arrival of immigrants or asylum seekers is an ideal illustration of both script and ideology, both woven within a metaphor. The 'macropropositions' written about and analysed by Brookes (1995) identify the dominant stories as a framework within which individual tales from Africa are embedded. Another set of factors is associated with the participants who are selected for interviewing, and which of them is allowed to have credible quotations reinforced and, conversely, when discrediting devices are used to detract from the reliability of an informant from outside the conventional media-centric mainstream.

Having established a metaphorical pattern, it can then be embellished to make the imagery more provocative and more effective as below in the development of the metaphor of the 'wave' crashing onto British shores and the reference to other countries having 'water-tight laws' to prevent this happening to them:

Tony can't turn the tide

A tidal wave of economic migrants is moving across Europe and is about to crash onto our shores.
  Why?
  Countries such as France and Germany have set up water-tight laws to ensure their welfare handouts cannot be creamed off by foreign freeloaders . . .

(*Sun*, 3 May 2004)

Strategies of argumentation

Individual words and phrases fit into longer patterns of narrative expected by the audience within a particular national context. These narratives of inclusion and exclusion include scripts which predispose an audience to certain longer-term frames of reference with regard to those represented as hostile to the indigenous community. Building upon the vocabulary of outsiders, we can see how certain language devices can amplify these outsider 'scripts'.

In the next extract, the declarative of 'WELCOME TO THE ASYLUM' with its pun, playing on two meanings of the word 'asylum' presupposes the madness of government policy and seeks to play on the assumption that the investigation is merely confirming the presuppositions of the readers:

> **Welcome to the asylum**
>
> A Mail reporter spent a week in our asylum courts. What he found there was stupefying inefficiency, profligacy, incompetence and deceit on a massive scale. A truly despairing picture of a system on the point of total breakdown. And, guess what, you're paying for it.

(*Daily Mail*, 29 May 2005)

In a front page piece in *The Australian* about Australia day (below) there is a tacit acceptance of the argumentative logic of the Prime Minister that there is a set of values which are 'core Australian values' which can be elevated above multiculturalism as well as serving to reject racism. The abbreviation of these values to 'old Brit values' in the headline is a cosy closure around what many might perceive to be core-white values in an essentially multi-ethnic contemporary Australia. The report implies through its headline and its unproblematized reporting of the views of the Prime Minister that racism can be rejected at the same time as multiculturalism:

> **Howard puts emphasis on old Brit values**
>
> John Howard has outlined his vision of a tolerant nation that rejects racism while placing core Australian values ahead of multiculturalism
> . . .

(*The Australian*, 26 January 2006)

Immigration is only represented as problematic: 'The issue of immigration is still explosive' (*Times*, 2 June 2005). Spokespeople from ethnic communities are only called upon to adjudicate on issues on which a newspaper had a preconceived position:

> **Fury over Bible ban**
>
> Ian Mair (Gideons International executive director in the UK): 'The only thing that I can think of is that this is motivated by political correctness gone mad'. . . .
>   Resham Singh Sandu, Sikh chairman of the Council of Faith, poured scorn on the trust's claim that the Bible could offend ethnic groups. He said: 'I don't think many ethnic minority patients would object to the Bible in a locker.'

(*Daily Express*, 3 June 2005)

Alliteration in familiar patterns is also an abbreviated argumentative strategy that allows a newspaper to condense a position which it represents to its readers as the expression of a consensual view. Put simply, alliteration bypasses argument in the following case, as it allows an easy recall of association between madness and mullahs. This is reinforced later in the short extract by the emphasis on 'fanatical Muslim fundamentalists'. With such regular representations of Muslims in such pejorative terms, it is hardly surprising that the whole religion begins to take on a negative perspective in the mainstream British media, so that any mention of Muslim or Islam has a tendency to be associated with these negative attributes.

The murderous Mullahs

Few Western reporters are allowed to visit Iran. In this powerful dispatch Ann Leslie paints a horrifying picture of a violent and corrupt dictatorship run by fanatical Muslim fundamentalists.

(*Daily Mail*, 22 May 2005)

In the following brief example a modal verb, 'must', expressing compulsion, is entirely paraphrased by the headline writer from the actual words of the judge.

Britain must deport more failed asylum-seekers, says top judge

(*Times*, 25 January 2006)

On occasions, the use of inflammatory and discriminatory vocabulary can come to be commented upon by other news media, and even the police may become involved:

'Asian perverts' show axed in race riot fear

. . . pulled by Channel 4 from last night's schedule after police warned it could spark race riots.
  Edge of the City claims to show how Asian men are targeting white girls as young as 11 for sex and drug abuse in the West Yorkshire city blighted by disorder in 2001. . . . young Asian men . . . bricks, bottles, petrol bombs . . . some of the worst disturbances in Britain for 20 years. . . . BNP . . . banned from marching in Bradford.

(*Daily Mirror*, 21 May 2004)

The following day the *Guardian* reported the police response to the *Daily Mirror*'s story which was particularly critical of their use of 'Asian Perverts' in the headline.

> Colin Gramphorn the head of West Yorkshire police said, 'A Daily Mirror headline, "Asian perverts show axed in race riots fear", was false and incendiary. I think it gets very close to the criminal standard of inciting public disorder. What basis is there for the word "Asian Perverts"? The investigation we have done has arrested both Asian and white men.'

(*Guardian*, 22 May 2004)

 Activity 8.2 o—

What strategies of argumentation, vocabulary and metaphor are used in the news media to reinforce the status of ethnic minorities as outsiders to the British nation?

Insiders as outsiders

There are other ways in which social outsiders can be drawn in similar ways to those excluded on grounds of religion, ethnicity or skin colour. What is interesting is that the linguistic patterns of exclusion remain similar, despite being aimed at different targets. The cycle of exclusion is reinforced by the amplification of vocabulary, metaphor and transitivity patterns. The working class is no longer represented as a threat to the political and economic status quo, apart from isolated cases where a trade union is portrayed with all the old venom of yesteryear when threatening to take industrial action. Times have changed – organized labour is not the challenge that it once was. This does not mean that representations of the working class are any more positive. They are represented as a cultural threat, as for instance in the moneyed stereotype with no manners and no taste, the latest media construction of the working class: the chav. On the news that footballer Wayne Rooney and his partner Colleen McLoughlin have spent £50,000 on Christmas lights for their house, described as a 'chav paradise', the *Sun* uses the headline 'CHAV A MERRY XMAS!' (14 December 2005).

The occasional emergence of the working class into the news only goes to show what a routinely middle-class institution the news media is. This is of particular importance when we observe how the blue-collar British are most often dealt with in the popular tabloids that target them most often as readers. They are rarely the subjects of the news except in stereotypical and negative ways. They are more often the intended audience and despite the fact that they are regularly addressed in a language which imitates a working-class vernacular, when unemployed, impoverished, blue-collar people are articulated as the subjects of a distinct news item, it is often in the crassest terms, aimed at excluding them from the more wholesome if idealized working-class readers. The dynamic of insiders and outsiders works at this level too.

Across the press there is a whole range of paradigm choices for sensational stories which may include any of the following, who are often explicitly differentiated from either the right-minded readers of particular newspapers or the nation as a whole, or on some occasions both, as readership and nation coincide:

> A hoody-wearing yob
> Monsters in the making
> neo-crims in hooded tops
> unruly pupils
> Hoodies
> feral youths
> Binge drinkers
> THE SAVAGES
> paedo
> **PERVERT**
> **TEENAGE** thug
> rootless deadbeats
> TAGGED CONS
> VIDEO NUT
> UGLY THUG
> Lotto lout

Popular tabloid newspapers expend time in investigating cases of social security fraud which appears to reinforce the division of the country into the honest and hard-working and an idle underclass which they do their best to expose. Using hyperbole to arouse alarm in readers, suggesting that such fraud is endemic and ignored by central government, the *Sun* uses the emotive term 'nation' to underline the threat this underclass poses to the British community as well as helping to suggest that the scale of the problem is national and that benefit fraud is demeaning and enslaving the people of this country; all achieved with an economy of reference: **'Scandal of a nation enslaved to benefits'** (*Sun*, 27 January 2006).

In its in-depth report, the newspaper again indicates that it is a national problem rather than a regional or local issue by referring to 'idle Britain'. It draws in the local community by the use of stills from a neighbour's video to demonstrate three cases of disability benefit fraud, and the perpetrators are castigated as 'skiver', 'cheat', 'fiddling dad', 'benefit cheat', 'work-shy scrounger'. The compressed noun phrases in particular allow a reduction of the personal circumstances of the cases to be abbreviated into scripts which antagonize a readership which is already alerted to the stereotype of social security fraud. The impression of indigence among this section of the working class is reinforced in one story where a man is said to be living with a woman, Tina, 'and her brood'. Implying that this is a widespread problem by referencing the nation so prominently is easier to deal with in the sensationalized news values of the popular press in particular than, for instance, the issue of the millions of pounds of unclaimed benefits and tax rebates.

It is interesting to see how a category such as 'chav' can be alluded to in the headline of a newspaper (below), orienting the reader towards a certain perspective on the details of the story which follows, despite the fact that the word is not actually used by any of the participants in the story. It is a very good example of semantic categorization ordering the story in terms of contemporary stereotypes. The newspaper is effectively drawing social conclusions for the readership in terms of preconceived labels:

Has my chav sister killed mum?

(*Daily Mirror*, 8 November 2005)

In effect, the newspaper is providing a portrait of a 'chav'. The word not used anywhere but in the headline and is not attributed to any informants in the story. It seems it is the newspaper's category for the suspected killer, and the category is filled out by the detail in the report: 'the drug user. . . . lots of swearing. . . . Sara and Thomas were privately educated but she went to a comprehensive and left school at 16. . . . fell in with the wrong crowd'.

'Chavs', 'benefit cheats' and a whole host of other categories can be placed in narratives of outsiders to the assumed insider community of law-abiding *Sun* readers.

In the following, the newspaper politicizes the script, by referring to the rhetoric of Labour as it was on the point of achieving power in 1997. It echoes back to that political rhetoric with its own demotic, typographically enhanced slogans, opening with a strong declarative, 'Remember these?' It draws the outsiders into a wider circle of what it claims is a series of political and social failures by the Government which the collective of nation and readers – 'we' – must pay the price for:

Double failure

<u>REMEMBER these?</u> 'Education, education, education.' 'Tough on crime tough on the causes of crime.'
   Two key planks of Government policy since 1997. Yet new figures show they have failed on BOTH.
   School standards are DOWN. Violent crime is UP.
   One leads to the other. Bored, ill-educated teenagers, fuelled by drink, rule the streets through violence and go unpunished.
   They failed in school. And we are all paying the price.

(*Sun*, 27 January 2006)

 Activity 8.3 ⚬━

Identify stories on groups of social outsiders. How are these groups written about in terms of metaphor, transitivity and vocabulary?

Summary

Having looked at the way that the language of the news creates patterns of representation for an insider community, this chapter considers the ways in which outsiders to that community are represented. It looks at the various linguistic devices, such as lexical mapping, argumentation, macropropositions and metaphor, which combine to create a series of negative impressions of those not considered as belonging to the mainstream British community. The examples given illustrate continuities between the representation of those considered by the news media to be ethnic or religious outsiders as well as those social outsiders. The coverage tends inevitably towards a series of stereotypes which do nothing to help audiences deal with the complexity of ethnic and social realities but rather encourage them to interpret the world in terms of negative and simplistic categories.

Suggestions for further reading

Critcher, C. (2003) *Moral Panics and the Media*. Milton Keynes: Open University Press.
Dijk, T.A. van (1991) *Racism and the Press*. London: Routledge.

Hall, S. (1981) 'The Whites of Their Eyes'. In L. Bridges and R. Brunt (eds) *Silver Linings*. London: Lawrence and Wishart.

Lynn, N. and Lea, S. (2003) 'A phantom menace and the new apartheid: the social construction of asylum seekers in the United Kingdom', *Discourse and Society* 14(4): 425–452.

Richardson, J.E. (2004) *(Mis)Representing Islam: the Racism and Rhetoric of the British Broadsheet Press*. Amsterdam: John Benjamins.

Said, E.W. (1997) *Covering Islam: How the Media and the Experts Determine How We See the Rest of the World*. London: Vintage.

9 Debates on language in the news

Introduction

In addition to the stories of hard news, and commentary and opinion on that hard news, we need to understand that news cannot stand alone but that it is in constant communication with other forms of cultural information in a dynamic flow of influences which we might call 'cultural discourse' (Dahlgren, 1988). Such cultural discourse can take many forms. All of them tell us as much about the contemporary world as the hard news which they are complementary to. These forms can include commentary upon the language of the news and language conventions of the moment. They can also test the generic boundaries of news, for instance in the form of parody and irony as commentary on news. This chapter looks at the issues at stake in the hostility to the alleged practice of 'political correctness' in language, and examines responses to linguistic debate in the news in general. It considers the tension between appropriate cultural sensitivity in language and critiques broader liberal notions of free speech.

Political correctness: the language debate

Journalists are well able to engage in vigorous debate about the very stuff of their trade: the language of the news. Often key debates about the role and function of language are discussed in a way which illustrates that journalists are certainly not passive purveyors of language but actively aware of the potential within much of their output. At its most rigorous this debate is a popularized form of critical discourse.

One of the most absorbing recent debates about language has been conducted in the pages of the press. The whole issue of political correctness has attracted attention from elite to popular. It has provided an opportunity to witness a sustained debate on the use of language by columnists themselves. This chapter will begin by charting the emergence of the term in the mainstream British and North American press and highlight the differences in approach between journalists in the midst of what appears to be a normative, prescriptive intervention in language matters. It will consider other examples of language debate in the newspapers, from academics such as Jean Aitchison in Britain, Robin Lakoff in the United States and Jürgen Habermas in Germany, to columnists including Gary Younge and Decca Aitkenhead who draw upon critical linguistics in a populist idiom.

Political correctness: definitions and genealogy

Political correctness has emerged, for traditionalists and conservatives, as a crystallization of many of the liberal and progressive social and political attitudes of the late twentieth century. Fully in keeping with the tendencies of the linguistic turn, these critics see political and cultural dangers or opportunities (depending on their viewpoint) manifesting themselves in an increasing concentration on the use of language. It is important to remember that the knee-jerk response in much of our media to what they perceive as political correctness in language has had a long period of gestation. Before political correctness there were fears that policies which discouraged the use of discriminatory language, laws on racial equality, equal opportunities and positive discrimination could also destabilize traditional cultural behaviour and constituted a threat to convention.

Universities and schools from the 1970s attempted to design reading lists which reflected a better balance of non-white, female authors in what had been categorized as a literary canon which only dealt with dead, white Anglo-American males. Political parties in various countries attempted to produce employment and language codes which embedded a critical respect for cultural and ethnic difference into daily practice. From the 1970s onwards attempts to redesign university syllabuses and workplace practices from USA campuses to the Greater London Council tended to draw criticisms from conservative commentators who alleged that they posed a threat to free speech. Supporters of policies aimed at creating a language and a culture which went beyond passively accepting the discourse of equal rights and aimed at creating a more inclusive language and culture which actively promoted diversity while claiming that traditions of liberal free speech had often served to subtly deny respect or representation to many.

There have been a series of long-running social debates on how linguistic expression may reflect political preferences. The range of debate around issues of language seemed to confirm in material form the observations of a wide range of writers who had taken a special interest in the relationship between language and social power. Through the writing of writers as diverse as Foucault (1974), Fish (1994) and Bakhtin (in Holquist, 1994) the politics and philosophies of language have been brought into academic debate as never before, and these debates moved into the public sphere often in the pages of newspapers through the ways they reported and commented upon the importance of the use of language in the contemporary world. Foucault saw language as very much involved in maintaining the power structures of the social and political world. Bakhtin clarified the ways in which the very struggles waged over the meaning of particular words were what actually created the meaning of those words. From a liberal American perspective, Stanley Fish reflected on the impossibility of free speech, and argued that particularly within Western secular societies, freedom can only survive because language exists within rules which restrict absolute freedom. He pointed to the fact that restrictions on, for instance, racial abuse, were necessary for the development of the harmonious climate of tolerance and respect necessary for what we consider to be a free society. All of these viewpoints have been popularized within our news media as starting points for debate on the role of language in social life.

The anxieties of traditionalists gathered polemical coherence once an expression had been found to help identify and demonize such developments. They correctly perceived that an insistence on shifting language practice to help shape a new world threatened long-established conservative cultural patterns. The first indicator that a crystallization of these anxieties had occurred was when the Random House Dictionary listed political correctness as a new entry in the early 1990s: 'Marked by or adhering to a typically progressive orthodoxy on issues involving especially race, gender, sexual affinity or ecology'.

By 1993 the debate was in full cry and writers on the liberal left had identified the traditionalists' strategy in creating a bogeyman figure to focus the minds of those like-minded critics of ongoing language sensitivity and reform. Richard Gott, writing a review of Robert Hughes' *Culture of Complaint: The Fraying of America* in the *Guardian* used the opportunity to make a contribution to the wider usefulness of the term as a shibboleth of traditionalists when he expressed the paradox at the heart of accusations of political correctness as being their ability to mobilize antagonism and even prejudice against the phenomenon, while never needing to identify those responsible:

> **PC is a notional construct put together by the Right to create a non-existent monster on the Left that it can then attack. For although everyone knows the idiocies uttered in the name of PC, it is hard to find anyone who has actually heard them in person or even encountered them seriously in print.**

(*Guardian*, 1 June 1993)

As if to confirm the scepticism of the left of the existence of this conservative bogeyman, the left-wing magazine *Living Marxism* (December 1993) used an article by Frank Füredi to produce a similar assessment: 'Of course nobody is really PC'.

Debates on the significance of political correctness

Clearly any debate which appears to call into question the ways in which social change and resistance to that change are expressed in the language of our news media needs to be given serious consideration. Not only does it ask explicit questions about the very stuff of our public communication about the world we live in, it also risks delimiting what can be said about that world. We need to briefly sketch some of the important issues which criticisms of political correctness have raised as well as the benefits claimed by proponents of what they would consider a sensitive and constructive form of language awareness. The advocates of the latter see it as an insistence on respect for diversity reflected in language practice. It is easy to forget how it was quite recently acceptable to advertise accommodation for rent in Britain while stipulating 'No blacks. No Irish'. Legalized racial discrimination is far from being a distant memory in many Western democracies, including the USA. It took legislation to change this sort of language practice by making it illegal. Proponents of language awareness encourage a politicization of language as a form of active engagement in everyday politics and as a means of exposing liberal hypocrisy which bemoans the effects of inequalities while doing nothing concrete in terms of intervention in the practices of daily cultural life to create a climate in which attitudes can be radically challenged.

The range of interpretation could not be broader. To those who consider such interventions in language as political correctness it is a traditionalist's nightmare. Arguments range from the conservatives who fear an erosion of tradition to those who see this as a modern version of the Nazi book-burning mentality, an anti-liberal tendency which threatens freedom of speech or even, in concentrating on language, acts as a trivialization of allegedly more real political issues.

Political correctness in the news media

We have seen how the language of the news media acts as a formative social institution. It is therefore not surprising that there is a range of debate within the news which is based within wider concerns about political correctness. This particular debate on language use within the media and how the news media respond to what are represented as examples of political correctness provide an interesting account of a set of anxieties about language use and politics in the contemporary world. In some parts of the news media there is a great deal of suspicion, since drawing attention to language awareness can be considered a threat to certain traditionalist perspectives. This seems to confirm what Alibhai-Brown suggests is inevitable: 'the backlash comes when it gets serious' (1994: 57).

In the following examples, drawn from a variety of newspapers on a range of topics, political correctness can be used as a contextual signal, placing one story in terms of an accumulation of other such stories, as if to confirm both the prevalence of such activity in society and to reinforce the combined opposition of readers and newspaper to radical interventions through language. In the contextual setting, the phrase 'political correctness' acts as a reductive script. It signals a set position on the matter being presented and invites hostility and ridicule towards the event being covered. The reductiveness of debate clearly acts to make dealing with its core issues in anything other than a simple way much more difficult. Invoking 'political correctness' as a short-hand but complex term of abuse invites the reader to take up an automatic position concerning anything smeared with that description. In using this script, the newspaper can reduce complexity by implying that a whole range of divergent and complex social questions can be reduced to the allegedly politically motivated conspiracy of a small minority whom the newspaper seeks to discredit by association. It is in effect the politics of the smokescreen. It has become such an easy common denominator that it can be found in elite as well as in popular newspapers:

> **Even those of us who have come to despise the intellectual fascism of political correctness have to draw the line somewhere. And I have. I have no truck with cannibalism.**

> (Paul Weaver, *Guardian*, 4 May 1998)

It can also be found across the generic range of a newspaper. In this example it is used by television critic Charlie Catchpole to endorse the performance of a comedian who is praised in brutal terms as he is perceived to have 'delivered a 90-minute kicking to political correctness':

> ### Ricky's bad taste is really a breath of fresh air
>
> **Another week and another of last year's Christmas stocking fillers turns up on Channel 4 – Ricky Gervais. . . . A simply stunning, stand-up tour de force that delivered a 90-minute kicking to political correctness.**

> (*Daily Express*, 6 June 2005)

 Activity 9.1 ⊙━

Find references to political correctness in the newspapers. How is it described? What contexts and situations is it used in?

Linguistic sensitivity towards the feelings of members of other ethnic groups or religions outside the white, Christian mainstream in Britain is often a favourite target for those accusing individuals and institutions of conspiring against the interests of this mainstream, and it is routinely categorized as political correctness. In the next example, intervention is trivialized by the use of the word 'meddling' with its connotations of mischief. The report of the apparent decision not to place bibles in the sideboards of hospital beds is selected since it fits with the news values of the newspaper. It reinforces the value of this type of story by placing it in the context of a range of other stories which it identifies as having common ground with the script of the main story. The script of politically correct interference is thereby accentuated as if it emphasizes what is claimed to be a consistent attack on the values of the cultural and religious majority of the country and to further marginalize the invented community of the 'politically correct'. The spokesperson for the Muslim Council of Britain, Inayat Bunglawala, is reported as allying himself with the moral majority, who are represented as being the readers of this paper and, by inclusion, the national community. The 'politically correct', although they are said to be attempting not to cause offence, are represented as being involved in a whole range of activities driven by anxieties over representation of women, inclusivity of other faiths and concerns that Christianity is not being presented as the default religion in Britain. Instead of attempting to address the actual concerns which may underpin these sorts of decisions, decisions which are informed by a reasonable observation that the composition of British society has changed over time, the newspaper prefers a simplistic yet cumulative script which attempts to include Muslims in assertions that British society is better left well alone.

> ## Don't blame Islam for the religious meddling of the politically correct
>
> . . . All too often these gestures towards other faiths – particularly Islam – are initiated by the politically correct who seek not to cause offence. . . .
> Just over two years ago a primary school in Batley, West Yorkshire, made national news after the head teacher sent a memo to her staff instructing them not to use books using pigs when teaching the under seven classes in her school where two-thirds came from a Muslim background. . . . The following year Father Christmas was replaced by a woman in Telford, Shropshire, to help "recreate the figure in a more maternal image".

(*Daily Express*, 7 June 2005)

On other occasions there can be discussion of the usefulness of the expression itself. As 'political correctness gone mad' seems to be a phrase resorted to by both newspapers and members of the public whenever there is some change in cultural practice, whatever its motivation, one commentator chooses to contest the process through which this cliché is perpetuated. Daniel Finkelstein picks up on a report which suggests that the Scouts' oath which promises allegiance to God and the Queen is ripe for updating and pleads for readers to look beyond the cliché:

I swear it's not PC gone mad to change the Scouts' oath

. . . A public ban is due on people who use the phrase "it's political correctness gone mad". . . . My problem with "it's political correctness gone mad" is that on more than half the occasions on which it is used it isn't appropriate. It is attacking something that isn't politically correct and hasn't gone mad. . . . It's political correctness gone mad gone mad.

(Daniel Finkelstein, *Times*, 22 June 2005)

Occasionally, one reads a story which appears to have been selected specifically to reinvigorate the tradition of the political correctness script, so that it is not seen as becoming stale or dying out. In the next extract, an example of 'political correctness goes mad' is placed in the context of opposition from a host of organizations which, from this particular newspaper's perspective, are normally aligned with the liberal tendencies in society and which it usually assumes its readership is impatient of. The *Daily Express* reports on its front page that a nursery school has changed the words of a nursery rhyme from 'Ba Ba Black Sheep' to 'Ba Ba Rainbow Sheep'. As if to confirm how far out of line this particular nursery school is with regard to the newspaper's editorial views and the assumed consensus of the newspaper's readership, equal opportunity representatives, the Commission for Racial Equality and the Department for Education and Skills are all quoted as being opposed to the decision to vary the words of the popular nursery rhyme. The decision is abbreviated to a 'PC move' while the nursery is described as 'Government-backed' implying a link between the sort of public policy which the newspaper disapproves of and Government financial support for the nursery. The events at the nursery are conflated with the banning of conkers, the dropping of Seven Dwarfs from the title of Snow White and the removal of golliwogs from a shop window, as if to indicate a wider cultural conspiracy and to fit the decisions taken at the school into a longer chronology which is made to chime with readers' memories of other stories which the newspaper has categorized in this way.

When the words to the song are changed back to the traditional version the newspaper delights in puns and alliteration, 'fastest ewe-turn', 'Back to black sheep', 'Nonsense in the nursery'. The school has now been categorized on the basis of this one incident as a 'politically correct school' and it is the 'angry' and incensed' parents who have forced this 'victory for common sense'. The newspaper places itself on the side of this 'common sense' and on the side of the parents. Wider questions of attempts to engage with children of a wide range of cultural backgrounds are ignored as if they are not relevant to the traditions of Britain. The whole incident, which generates front-page spreads, illustrations of the words of the song, a brief history of how the words came about and leading articles over two days, indicates that this is not just a story about a song's lyrics as far as the newspaper is concerned. It is a part of a much more broadly perceived cultural threat – any change to traditional cultural practices. The fact that the newspaper chooses to bring in organizations of which it is usually sceptical or dismissive is an indicator of how seriously it takes these perceived threats.

Political correctness goes mad at the nursery

NOW IT'S 'BAA BAA RAINBOW SHEEP'

A NURSERY school was last night accused of 'ridiculous' political correctness after removing the word 'black' from a nursery rhyme.

Teachers at the Government-backed school were ordered to change the lyrics of the classic Baa Baa Black Sheep.

The idea was to 'avoid offending children' and keeping in line with equal opportunities. . . . In a move branded 'absurd' by politicians, equal rights groups and parents alike. . . .

It is also not the first time political correctness has led to alterations of traditional British songs and games. . . .

But the PC move to alter the words follows a welter of other bizarre decisions initiated by the politically correct brigade.

A few days ago, a shopkeeper in Hereford was stunned when police seized three toy golliwogs from his window display after a complaint that they were racist. . . .

Other examples include the Seven Dwarfs being dropped from the title of Snow White, the ending of the rhyme Humpty Dumpty being changed so as not to upset children and the banning of 'dangerous' conkers in playgrounds.

(*Daily Express,* 7 March 2006)

Nonsense in the nursery [Editorial]

POLITICALLY correct staff at the Sure Start nursery in Sutton Courtenay, Oxfordshire, probably do not have glittering careers ahead as lyricists. 'Baa, baa rainbow sheep' appears unlikely to catch on as the standard form of the much-loved nursery rhyme. At the risk of causing them offence, we must conclude it is a black mark on their records.

(*Daily Express,* 7 March 2006)

> **Back to black sheep [Editorial]**
>
> Rejoice, rejoice. The black sheep are back at the Sure Start nursery in Sutton Courtenay, Oxfordshire and the tots of Britain are reading from the same rhyme sheet once again. It might be the fastest ewe-turn in history.

(*Daily Express*, 8 March 2006)

> **The big climbdown on 'rainbow' sheep**
>
> Angry parents yesterday forced a politically correct nursery school to stop making their children sing Baa Baa Rainbow Sheep.
>   In a victory for common sense the nursery performed a U-turn under pressure from incensed mothers and fathers . . .

(*Daily Express*, March 8)

Paradoxically, the examples above demonstrate still further the social power of language. Language's power resides in how it acts historically and materially. The attempts by newspapers to close down the contestation of cultural change by ridicule and antagonism and by reducing serious and legitimate concerns about the role of language in a rapidly changing society demonstrates a resistance to these historical and material shifts. This in turn indicates perhaps how the newspaper would prefer their readers to be cocooned in an older, even safer and more traditional world, a world in which the words of nursery rhymes do not change. That there are readers out there who wish to inhabit this world means that these newspapers will continue to feed that static and backward-looking view of the world to this readership.

Verbal hygiene and liberal notions of free speech

One useful perspective on this range of language discussion and intervention has been provided by Deborah Cameron. She uses the expression 'verbal hygiene' to explain how in a tolerant society we should look to use language while respecting others' views and trying to minimize any offence that unthinking use of words might cause. She says that verbal hygiene is similar to washing one's hands; it may not eradicate all contagious diseases but it is a reasonable precaution to take. She claims that: 'the project is not a modernist attempt to construct a "perfect" language, but a postmodernist attempt to dramatize the impossibility of such a language' (1995, 155–156).

She stresses that language change does not in any simple way equate to or substitute for social change or political change but it might lead to a better awareness of certain social and political issues and thereby facilitate change. There is however a backlash, characterized by stories like those above, which is reinforced by anecdotal, everyday scripts which these stories succeed in connecting with. These include urban myths and rumours about the latest outrage committed by the 'PC brigade' which suggest that the fabric of our society is under threat because of the reconsideration of attitudes towards the relationship between language and cultural practice. The liberal notion of the self-regulating linguistic community disguises the differing philosophies of language which lie beneath the surface. It prefers the notion of a natural evolution to the idea that language can be in itself an agency of social change. Furthermore, prominent news coverage of the changing of the words of a nursery rhyme indicates the extent to which traditionalists in their turn also seek to politicize language. To return to semiology for a moment, the story is an example of how the sign, in this case a nursery rhyme, can be transformed through dialogue and social conflict into meaning, demonstrating that power over language is always contested even in a nursery rhyme. For the *Daily Express* and its readership the struggle is to maintain traditional values, even at the site of a children's song. This is no trivial matter for them, as the level of ridicule and editorial emphasis shows how important such small issues are when a community perceives that its values are under attack. By implication, the change is seen as a consequence of the presence of non-white children at the nursery. The multi-ethnic face of contemporary Britain has to be resisted and traditional white values maintained. The lack of overt racism does not make systematic discourses of exclusion any less potent, and these discourses include the flagging of change, however naive and trivial, as a significant threat to the presumed values of the dominant white majority. The story certainly does not deal with the change in lyrics in any way which could be described in Cameron's terms as seeking a civility and sensitivity towards a more mixed general culture. Instead it highlights angry parents on whose behalf it claims to speak, the criticism of liberal agencies and ridicule of attempts, however misguided, to develop strategies which can help a wider range of children to feel more included in British society.

Reflections on language and journalism in the press

In keeping with an age in which there is so much debate about language, it is hardly surprising that journalists themselves have begun to reflect upon the very stuff of their trade. Sometimes this can acknowledge broader linguistic debate in humorous fashion:

New war of words over Montgomerie allegations

Like God, the semantics of sport move in mysterious ways.

(*Guardian*, 30 May 2005)

On other occasions, the patterns of the language of journalism are commented upon explicitly and, in some cases, with an acknowledgement of how those patterns restrict what contemporary journalism has to offer:

Wyn's corner shop outshines Tesco any day

I was a young student at Lancaster University when I first heard the phrase: 'May you live in interesting times'. It is a journalistic commonplace, to be trotted out either as a grim comment in periods of political turmoil, war or natural disaster, or as a rueful reminder to be careful what you wish for. . . . Even the tireless *Daily Mail* is scraping the celebrity barrel – yesterday's front page story was: Jamie Oliver's wife Jools put on weight while pregnant. Wow, that's newsy.

(Vicky Woods Notebook, *Daily Telegraph*, 7 June 2005)

Why Watergate is still poisoning our political life

Let me break the sacred code of journalism and admit to a mistake: a very, very big one. I got Watergate wrong . . .

(John Humphrys, *Daily Mail*, 2 June 2005)

It is an unwritten law of journalism that a simple story always trumps a complex one . . .

(Mike Baker, Spin Watch, *Times Educational Supplement*, 10 June 2005)

Papers love simple slogans. Geldof provides

(*The Independent on Sunday*, 5 June 2005)

Activity 9.2 o┳

Can you find any examples of journalists highlighting the language or conventions of journalism in the newspapers?

Positive engagement with linguistic debate

On other occasions, journalists can take this process of commenting upon language use a step further. Then they can engage in discussion of the political implications of the use of language in the contemporary media in ways which draw upon popular versions of language criticism and which have the potential to draw wider audiences into such debate. One could not, for example, find a more stinging and concise judgement on the default use of the phrase 'political correctness' than in Gary Younge's piece, 'The Badness of Words' (*Guardian*, 14 February 2000): 'Political correctness is a phrase used to denigrate and contain true liberalism. We should not use it.'

Journalists and academics can both use the pages of a newspaper to make points about the politicization of language in the coverage of war. Decca Aitkenhead's piece 'Our Brave Boys, Their Lunatics' (*Guardian*, 26 April 1999), demonstrates from the headline onwards an awareness of the sort of simple binary categories which do so much to provide a solidarity towards British soldiers as well as a hostility to those portrayed as enemies. In doing so, it draws upon the sort of analysis developed by Hodge and Kress (1993). Professor of linguistics, Jean Aitchinson, has regularly taken the news media to task about the way in which they so easily adopt the euphemisms of war, which mask its horror and real human cost at the same time as they celebrate the success of military strategy and hardware. In the United States, another professor of linguistics, Robin Lakoff, has been a prolific contributor to public debate in the media about issues of language and gender, while German philosopher Jürgen Habermas has recently added a critical analysis in the press of the language used by the Pope on his visit to Auschwitz to his long list of interventions in discussion of the politics of language and the public sphere.

Charlotte Raven, in her piece 'One Night, Two Standards' (*Guardian*, 29 April 1997), looks specifically at the ways in which differentiated language use in the media with regard to male and female behaviour creates stereotypical images of women which are detrimental to social attitudes. She provides a wonderfully lucid analysis of the language of a specific television programme and uses her column in the newspaper to connect this to wider discussions of the impact of negative stereotypes in the media.

The final example of engagement by journalists with serious linguistic debate comes from a humorous perspective. Jeremy Hardy uses comic devices such as inversion, irony and hyperbole to deflate the rhetoric used, in this case in the *Daily Mail*, about political correctness:

Black people care about language – but they care more about justice

PC Plod learns PC

I'm never sure how worthwhile it is to relate things that have appeared in the *Daily Mail* but I have a morbid fascination with it. It is always breathtaking how 'political correctness gone mad' is the phrase used to describe all things eminently reasonable. I am not referring solely to the letters, which often appear to be transcriptions of the mutterings of traumatised people in their sleep. "The other day a woman in the supermarket called me 'love' and yet when I expose myself in the park I am the one accused of sexism."

This week's star offering was not a letter but a vast piece championing a dismissed policeman who had called a detained teenage boy a "black bastard". It seems his sergeant immediately upbraided him, saying: "Language!" The constable apologised, firstly to his superior and then to others present. The writer of the piece observes: "How vividly this illustrates the highly sensitised post-Stephen Lawrence anxiety over racial gaffes."

I am not sure whether he considers racist language *and* inaction in a murder case to be mere gaffes. But he appears to think racial abuse is a slip of the tongue that comes from nowhere. Even if for some weird reason you believe it to be part of everyday discourse, the point that seems to be constantly missed is that we pay the police to do a job. Maybe there is some public sector job in which freedom to racially abuse is part of the terms of employment, but I can't think of one. . . .

All these families have asked is that the police do their job and be held to account when they don't. But I suppose that would be political correctness gone mad.

(*Guardian*, 4 March 2000)

 Activity 9.3 o—⊤

Find examples of discussion of any linguistic point in the news media. How are arguments constructed to support or to criticize particular language use?

Implicit engagement with the language of news

Having considered the explicit engagement of journalism with linguistic debate, we will explore certain ways in which a more implicit approach to the language and genres of journalism has recently developed. The readership of newspapers has historically been considered as largely defined by notions of the public sphere (Habermas, 1992), a space for discussion open to all and in which the powerful can be held to reasoned account by the people. Identity within this public sphere has always been centred on concepts of the citizen, and its language was serious in tone and didactic in intent. In the popular press, there has been a century-long drift towards a more pleasure-based model for communicating with its audience. In the elite press, there has been a more recent trend towards the creation and representation of a new community of identity, based on irony and parody, which are at odds with more traditional views of the language of the press as serious, factual and literal. In short, there is a rebirth of irony and parody in our newspapers. These final sections will look at the implications that such a shift in the language within the elite press may have for conventional notions of the newspapers' public. They will concentrate on the representation of identity in the columnists and commentators of the elite press who articulate a cool and detached approach to these conventions of serious public-spiritedness. This will involve a discussion of the various forms and strategies of irony and parody and provide contemporary newspaper examples.

Irony

The simplest, yet incomplete, definition of irony is: saying one thing but meaning another. One of the problems associated with this sort of rhetorical playfulness is that people may not understand the fact that the author is being ironic, and take the message literally. In the world of music, Bruce Springsteen's *Born in the USA* was interpreted by right-wing Americans as a patriotic hymn, while its lyrics and intention were more an ironic criticism of American involvement in overseas military action. Randy Newman's *Short People* was taken as insulting to short people, whereas the author had intended it as a more general ironic commentary on irrational prejudice. There are many types of irony, some specific to particular literary genres, such as dramatic irony where a character makes a comment which has implications for the audience and perhaps other characters in a play or film which s/he is not aware of but which are obvious to other participants in the spectacle because of what has happened on stage without her/his knowledge. Irony of event refers to an occasion where one event may be happening which is undermined or discredited by another event – for example if somebody is declared bankrupt on the same day as they win the national lottery. Situational irony might be used to describe a pickpocket having his pocket picked while picking the pocket of some unsuspecting pedestrian. Both situational irony and the irony of events are commonly used in the cartoons illustrating the pages of newspapers.

The form which occurs most often in contemporary journalism is verbal irony. This form of irony allows a writer to say something which he does not believe in the hope that the reader can identify the inverted meaning within the text. It is a rhetorical device which counts on the reader being able to contradict what is asserted and this contradiction by the reader is in fact the real meaning of the author. It can also be used to make a moral point by presenting the incongruities in a situation or a lack of awareness in a character who we are expected to find objectionable.

Not taking things too seriously, using an ironic stance as a humorous position, is nothing new in either literature or journalism but it is something which has an increased prominence at the moment. Swift's *Modest Proposal* from 1729 was for the Irish to eat their over-abundant children as a means of avoiding famine. He clearly did not mean this, but was using an ironic conceit to draw attention to the horrors of famine and poverty in his native land, and to cause anger in his readers against the policies which could have made his ironic solution a 'modest proposal'.

What is the point of taking the risk of using a rhetorical device which can be misinterpreted and give offence? The main reason is that it provides an interesting variation on the maintenance of the bond between a particular audience and writers. The use of irony presupposes that there is a level of shared understanding, shared framework of references and shared moral values which can be played with in order to emphasize the worldview which audience and writer share. As Holland stresses, there is an enjoyable play in recognizing our place in the shared community of irony:

> We know that the *author* knew that we would know that the *author* must have intended *us* to recognize that *he* would never have doubted that we would know precisely that *he* . . .
>
> (Holland, 2000: 50)

How does irony fit into developments within contemporary journalism? As the need has declined for newspapers to provide the very latest news, given that other technologies such as the internet and rolling television news can provide this much more rapidly and efficiently, there is an increasing tendency for newspapers to provide commentary and opinion on news and even advice on how to conform to trends in lifestyle and fashion. These provide ample opportunity for the deployment of irony as a means of commenting on issues of the day, without the authors being drawn into taking things too seriously. Ironic commentary on current affairs can provide a critique while providing a lighter touch than the heavy, hard news. In doing so it must assume a similar mindset in its readers which can guarantee that the nuances of a particular ironic stance can be understood by its regular audience. Irony is one of the main indicators of the identity and tastes of a particular newspaper audience. Furthermore, in the contemporary news media, irony requires a level of detachment which is very in tune with our cool and detached era. To understand the particular form of irony and to accept it as a legitimate part of the newspaper's identity the reader must be part of that special constructed community.

There has been a long tradition of irony in news. John Crouch, a Royalist pamphleteer, used irony to present a version of the latest events in the English Civil War of the seventeenth century in a way which ridiculed the Republican side. The tradition continued within journalism through Jonathan Swift to contemporary exponents such as *Private Eye* and *The Onion*. It is used increasingly by contemporary columnists and political commentators who seem to lighten the political by sprinkling reports with ironic asides to entertain or better capture the attention of their audience. On other occasions, broadcast news can use images to produce an irony of situation, for instance when a recent report showed a mother duck leading her chicks across a pond as ironic commentary on the story about political leadership; shots of a roulette wheel spinning can be used as an accompaniment to news about the controversial trip of the British Deputy Prime Minister to the ranch of a wealthy American who wishes to obtain the licence to run the UK's largest supercasino in London.

In the first example below we see a columnist first claiming that it is easy to solve world poverty, which is clearly for the author and for the intended audience of the liberal, elite newspaper not something which they believe. Yet the irony is provocative in attempting to make the point that complicating the issue is not a solution. It is as provocative also in the advice the writer gives, based on ironic comparisons with anecdotal popular accounts of how debt collectors can best be avoided. He personalizes the relationship between the International Monetary Fund and the indebted countries of Africa in order to ridicule the high-flown political debates which have failed to alleviate the situation.

It's easy to solve world poverty

. . . So the most useful advice to Africa would be to try traditional methods of evading debt. When the IMF comes round for their payments, the whole country should turn off the lights and hide behind a settee. Maybe one person could wander past and say to the IMF bailiff: "Who you looking for mate? Ghana? Phhhh, haven't seen it round here for years, mate, I think they moved away."

(Mark Steel, *Independent*, 2 June 2005)

In the next example we can see how the author reinforces the identification of readers with the newspaper he is writing for by casting aspersions on the reliability of another rival elite newspaper, and then suggests ironically that he will be running a 24-hour competition for readers.

> Yes, it's time to test you on your knowledge of the news again. Every day lots of stories appear in the papers about man's idiocy and short-sightedness – but that's enough about the Bush administration. Today I am simply going to bring you four recent stories and tell you that one of them is genuine, in the sense that it was printed in the papers, and the other three are concocted in our secret laboratory where all week long we manufacture fake news stories and try to get them into *The Guardian*. Can you spot which is the genuine one? You have 24 hours to decide, starting now.

(Miles Kingston, *Independent*, 3 June 2005)

The irony in the following piece, about Osama bin Laden, is all the more striking for it appearing in an American newspaper, a country directly targeted by him. Under a headline which echoes many a music album title, the piece is prompted initially by an irony of event. A book recommended by the world's most wanted man has broken into the top ten on an online publisher's website. The author of this piece decides to take that irony further by embellishing the context imaginatively and considering what might be the next step in this set of developments. It is an ironic commentary on the interconnectedness of our contemporary media and political worlds and the often perverse place of celebrity and notoriety in those worlds.

> ## Osama's greatest hits
>
> Reading about the latest tapes by Osama bin Laden and his sidekick Ayman al-Zawahiri, my gut reaction is that they sound like a couple of burned-out rock stars who keep recycling their greatest hits in the hope of catching on one last time as the lounge duo in some Las Vegas hotel. "Now appearing at Caesars Palace. It's the Monkees! And at the Aladdin, Ayman and Osama."
> I will confess, though, that the fact that bin Laden could recommend a book in his latest video and then watch that book break into the top 10 on amazon.com within just a few days suggests that while he may not have much of a future as a terrorist, he could do a book club gig. When I checked Amazon, two of the top ten books were recommended by Oprah, and one was recommended by Osama. Now that's juice. I started to imagine bin Laden sitting in his cave in Pakistan and suddenly receiving all these books from publishers and agents . . .

(Thomas L. Friedman, *International Herald Tribune*, 26 January 2006)

Sometimes the irony can feature in the headline itself and proclaim the exact opposite of what the newspaper and readers believe, to prompt outrage and debate, especially in the burgeoning commentary pages of weekend newspapers, with a special brief to entertain a particular readership with accounts on the affairs of the past week which chime with a shared sense of the incongruities of public affairs:

Liars and cheats? Give them a medal.

(*Observer*, 15 January 2006)

 Activity 9.4 ⟳

Find an example of irony exploited in the news. What does it add to the composition of the news? What does it tell us about the relationship between the news medium and its assumed audience?

Genre, parody and intertextuality

News is comprised of many genres. These genres are stylistic and structural patterns which help us to recognize the meaning and purpose of particular writing strategies. In journalism, genre can be used to describe the conventions of hard news, soft news, celebrity news, sports news, features, editorials and commentary, to name but some of the more obvious. They all have recognizable structures which are embedded within the expectations of the audience. As such, these genres are forms of social contracts between writers and institutions and their publics. They form a bond of expectation and are an important part of the shared sense of community between the news and its audience.

Carolyn R. Miller (1994) sees genre in cultural terms. She argues that genre serves as a way of understanding how to participate in the actions of a community. Genre has particular functions which are located within a system of other cultural patterns. It therefore embodies various forms of knowledge about particular societies at particular times. Therefore we can ask ourselves what do we need to know about genres within the news in order for them to make sense to us in the early twenty-first century?

Although there is a hierarchy of importance between genres in journalism, with informational and explicitly persuasive genres such as comment or opinion traditionally more privileged and authoritative than, for instance, entertainment genres, these patterns are often disrupted by the use of irony and parody. They can fit within what Dahlgren has referred to as a 'cultural discourse' (1988) where the diversity of news demonstrates that it is not simply informational but a part of a broader set of symbolic representation which draws upon knowledge of other media and literary forms and upon the shared understanding of the audience of an increasingly flexible approach to genre.

Van Leeuwen has commented on the increasing flexibility and latitude within journalism's generic patterns:

> it can be seen that the social purposes of journalism are contradictory. Some are overt (entertainment, factuality, impartiality, objectivity), some covert (social control, ideological commitment, legitimation) and the overt and the covert purposes do not mesh easily. It is perhaps not surprising that in a situation of such contradictory generic demands a rich array of generic strategies has developed.
>
> (Van Leeuwen, 1987: 209)

Experimentation within genre can be seen as an illustration of what Bakhtin (1996) has referred to as heteroglossia, a variety of voices vying for the prize of authority within journalism. This variety of voices and generic experimentation does not mean that hierarchy and ideological preferences are not being maintained. This is achieved, as we have seen elsewhere in the book, by ordering, modality, the argumentative devices, categorization and news value, among other strategies, but the heteroglossia forms part of the news media's attempt to maintain its relationship with an increasingly astute set of cultural readers. One form of generic experimentation which allows a reconsideration of the hierarchy and credibility of genres within news media is parody.

Parody can be defined as a strategy which uses textual borrowing and echoing for critical or humorous purposes. It may, in the case of news, take any of the established patterns of news reporting and use them to humorous or critical effect. It can easily be combined with satire to enhance its political point for particular readers. It may take the shape of commentary, the status of commentators within journalism, or the conventions of truth telling within the news and play with the boundaries of these expectations.

A recently launched column by Armando Iannucci in the *Observer* follows the conventional pattern of political commentary and claims to include contributions written by people such as Tony Blair and David Cameron.

Broadcast news is also open to parody, as in the following television programmes: *Brass Eye*, *Broken News* and *The News Show with John Stewart*. They only function as humour because they are so close to the patterns of the news. They use parody to critique both the form and the content of contemporary news.

Activity 9.5 o—r

Find an example of parody in the news. How does it play with the conventions of news and, in your opinion, what effect does this have?

Intertextuality in its most obvious form is direct, attributed quotation within a larger text. It is an essential part of the composition of the language of the news. A news story is made up of many texts, interviews, reports and government pronouncements, for instance, which have to be combined into a presentable form for the particular news package. This is called external intertextuality as it is built upon elements which come from outside the news medium itself. Internal intertextuality, is comprised of issues such as the editorial decisions, institutional conventions, layout, location within a news package and by-line celebrity, which make up the generic/ideological contours of the news medium.

> Intertextuality is directly related to this type of complex communication model in its assumption that every text is embedded in a context and is synchronically and diachronically related to many other texts.
> (Titscher, Meyer, Wodak and Vetter, 2000: 24)

External intertextuality can also call upon the wider media knowledge of a readership and even its historical awareness within that knowledge. Like irony, it assumes a consensual and collective community of taste and identity in broad cultural matters. It can locate contemporary affairs within a more conversational style which makes comparisons and assumptions on the basis that the readership has a good recollection of a variety of cultural material, from Depeche Mode to *Yes Minister*, as cultural reference points. When used in the elite press it can form part of a less hierarchical style of cultural consumption:

God's sense of humour

It all started when Gideons International asked permission to replace the Bibles in Leicester hospitals. A basic familiarity with Oliver Twist would have told them not to ask for new stuff; it just gets you into trouble. Unfortunately, they were too busy – reading Bibles, probably. . . . One thing's certain. If Bibles really do spread MRSA then, to quote Depeche Mode, I don't want to start any blasphemous rumours but I think that God's got a sick sense of humour.

(Zoe Williams, *Guardian*, 7 June 2005)

Intertextuality can be used in an ironic and even parodic fashion in elite news-papers as well as in the popular tabloids, as illustrated in the following editorial from the *Guardian*:

Moments that matter

In a memorable episode of *Yes Minister*, the wily mandarin Sir Humphrey Appleby explains to hapless minister Jim Hacker that the purpose of British foreign policy for the past 500 years has been to create a disunited Europe. 'It's the old divide and rule, you see, that's why we want to break up the [European Union]. We tried to break it up from the outside, but that wouldn't work. Now we're on the inside we're free to make a complete pig's breakfast of the whole thing.' But if that is true, asks the aghast Hacker, why is the Foreign Office pushing for more countries to join in? 'I'd have thought that was obvious,' Sir Humphrey wearily responds. 'The more members an organisation has, the more arguments it can stir up, the more futile and impotent it becomes.' 'What appalling cynicism,' Hacker sighs. 'Yes, minister,' comes the ever silky rejoinder: 'We call it diplomacy.'

Plus ça change, they may angrily be muttering in parts of Europe. It is a fair bet that there are some capitals in which governments suspect that the spirit of Sir Humphrey is not just alive and well in London in 2005 but also purring with satisfaction at the confused condition of the European Union in the aftermath of last week's French and Dutch referendums.

(*Guardian*, 6 June 2005)

 Activity 9.6 o—r

Find an example of intertextuality. Which other texts does it draw on to illustrate a news story? What point does it make about the news it refers to?

Summary

This chapter has looked at explicit and implicit discussions of language in the news. It has considered the ways in which journalists as well as academics make use of the spaces of the news media to make interventions into topical debates on language and its functions in society and the political world. It has explored the issue of political correctness and how this is used within news media discussions as a litmus test of attitudes to language change and sensitivities to cultural change encoded in language. Finally, it has briefly touched upon the ways in which the language of the news can be used as an experimental area for testing the boundaries of generic convention through the use of irony, parody and intertextuality.

Suggestions for further reading

Cameron, D. (1995) *Verbal Hygiene*. London: Routledge.
Fish, S. (1994) *There's No Such Thing as Free Speech and It's a Good Thing Too*. Oxford: Oxford University Press.
Muecke, D.C. (1970) *Irony*. London: Methuen.
Williams, J. (1995) *PC Wars*. London: Routledge.

Bibliography

Alabarces, P., Tomlinson, A. and Young, C. (2001) 'Argentina versus England at the France '98 World Cup: Narratives of nation and the mythologizing of the popular', *Media, Culture and Society* Vol. 23: 547–566.

Alibhai-Brown, Y. (1994) "The Great Backlash'. In S. Dunant (ed.) *The War of the Words: The Political Correctness Debate*, pp. 55–74. London: Virago.

Anderson, B. (1986) *Imagined Communities*. London: Verso.

Austin, J.L. (1962) 'How to do things with words'. In Jaworski and Coupland (eds) *The Discourse Reader*, pp. 63–76. London: Routledge.

Bakhtin, M.M. (1996) *The Dialogic Imagination* (trans. C. Emerson and M. Holquist). Austin TX: University of Texas Press.

Bal, M. (1997) *Narratology: Introduction to the Theory of Narrative*. Toronto: University of Toronto Press.

Barber, B.R. (1995) *Jihad versus McWorld: How Globalism and Tribalism Are Reshaping the World*. New York: Times Books.

Barthes, R. (1974) *Mythologies*. New York: Wang.

Bell, A. (1984) 'Language style as audience design', *Language in Society* 13: 145–204.

Bell, A. (1991) 'Stylin' the News: Audience Design', in *The Language of News Media*. Oxford: Blackwell.

Bell, A. (1994) *Language in the News*. Oxford: Blackwell.

Berger, P.L. and Luckman, T. (1976) *The Social Construction of Reality*. London: Penguin.

Billig, M. (1995) *Banal Nationalism*. London: Sage.

Bishop, H. and Jaworski, A. (2003) 'We beat "em": nationalism and the hegemony of homogeneity in the British press reportage of Germany versus England during Euro 2000', *Discourse and Society* 14(3): 243–271.

Black, M. and Coward, R. (1998) 'Linguistics, Social and Sexual Relations: a Review of Dale Spender's "Man Made Language"'. In D. Cameron (ed.) *The Feminist Critique of Language*. London: Routledge.

Blumler, J. and Gurevitch, M. (1995) *The Crisis in Public Communication*. London: Routledge.

Brookes, H.J. (1995) 'Suit, tie and a touch of Ju-Ju – the ideological construction of Africa: A critical discourse analysis of news on Africa in the British press', *Discourse and Society* 6(4): 461–494.

Cameron, D. (1995) *Verbal Hygiene*. London: Routledge.

Cameron, D. (1996) 'Style policy and style politics: a neglected aspect of the language of the news', *Media, Culture and Society* Vol. 18: 315–333.

Chandler, D. (2006) *Semiotics: The Basics*. London: Routledge.

Chilton, P. (1982) 'Nukespeak: nuclear language, culture and propaganda'. In C. Aubrey and P.A. Chilton (eds) *Nukespeak: The Media and the Bomb*, pp. 94–112. London: Comedia.

Chippendale, P. and Horrie, C. (1992) *Stick It Up Your Punter*. London: Mandarin.

Chomsky, N. (1972) *Language and Mind*. New York: Harcourt Brace Jovanovitch.

Clark, K. (1998) 'The Linguistics of Blame'. In D. Cameron (ed.) *The Feminist Critique of Language*. London: Routledge.

Cohen, S. (1980) *Folk Devils and Moral Panics: The Creation of Mods and Rockers*, Second Edition. New York: St Martin's Press.

Cole, P. (2004) *Diversity in the Newsroom: Employment of Minority Ethnic Journalists in Newspapers*. Cambridge: Society of Editors.

Collins, J. and Glover, R. (eds) (2002) *Collateral Language*. New York and London: New York University Press.

Conboy, M. (2002) *The Press and Popular Culture*. London: Sage.

Conboy, M. (2004) *Journalism: A Critical History*. London: Sage.

Conboy, M. (2004a) 'Heroes and demons as historical bookmarks in the English popular press'. In R. Phillips and H. Brocklehurst (eds) *History, Nationhood and the Question of Britain*. Basingstoke: Palgrave.

Conboy, M. (2006) *Tabloid Britain: Constructing a Community Through Language*. London: Routledge.

Creedon, P.J. (ed.) (1989) *Women in Mass Communication: Challenging Gender Views*. London: Sage.

Critcher, C. (2003) *Moral Panics and the Media*. Milton Keynes: Open University Press.

Curtis, L. (1984) *Nothing But The Same Old Story: The Roots of Anti-Irish Racism*. London: Information on Ireland.

Dahlgren, P. (1988) 'What's the meaning of this? Viewers' plural sense-making of TV news', *Media, Culture and Society* 10: 285–301.

Dijk, T.A. van (1991) *Racism and the Press*. London: Routledge.

Dijk, T.A. van (1993) *Elite Discourse and Racism*. London: Sage.

Dijk, T.A. van (1999) 'Media, Racism and Monitoring'. In K. Nordentreng and M.Griffin (eds) *International Media Monitoring*. Cresskill, NJ: Hampton Press.

Dijk, T.A. van (2000) 'New(s) Racism: A Discourse Analytical Approach', in

Cottle (ed.) *Ethnic Minorities and the Media: Changing Cultural Boundaries,* pp. 33–49. Buckingham: Open University Press.

Dunant, S. (ed.) (1994) *The War of the Words: The Political Correctness Debate.* London: Virago.

Eagleton, T. (1992) *An Introduction to Ideology.* London: Verso.

Easley, A. (2000) 'Authorship, gender and power in Victorian culture: Harriet Martineau and the periodical press'. In L. Brake, B. Bell and D. Finkelstein (eds) *Nineteenth Century Media and the Construction of Identity.* Basingstoke: Palgrave.

Engel, M. (1996) 'Papering over the cracks', *Guardian* 2, 3 October: 2–4.

Entman, R.M. (1993) 'Framing: toward clarification of a fractured paradigm', *Journal of Communication* 43(4) 51–58.

Fairclough, N. (1989) *Language and Power.* London: Longman.

Fairclough, N. (1995) *Media Discourse.* London: Arnold.

Fairclough, N. (2000) *New Labour, New Language?* London: Routledge.

Fish, S. (1994) *There's No Such Thing as Free Speech and It's a Good Thing Too.* Oxford: Oxford University Press.

Foucault, M. (1974) *The Archaeology of Knowledge,* trans. A.M. Sheridan-Smith. London: Tavistock.

Fowler, R. (1986) *Linguistic Criticism.* Oxford: Oxford University Press.

Fowler, R. (1991) *Language in the News: Discourse and Ideology in the Press.* London: Routledge.

Galtung, J. and Ruge, M. (1973) 'Structuring and Selecting News'. In S. Cohen and J. Young (eds) *The Manufacture of News: Social Problems, Deviance and the Mass Media.* London: Constable.

Gilroy, P. (1987) *There Ain't No Black in the Union Jack: The Cultural Politics of Nation.* London: Hutchinson.

Gledhill, C. (1997) 'Genre and gender: The case of soap opera'. In S. Hall (ed.) *Representation: Cultural Representations and Signifying Practices.* Milton Keynes: Open University Press.

Goatly, A. (1997) *The Language of Metaphors.* London: Routledge.

Gripsrud, J. (1992) 'The aesthetics and politics of melodrama'. In P. Dahlgren and C. Sparks (eds) *Journalism and Popular Culture.* London: Sage.

Habermas, J. (1992) *The Structural Transformation of the Public Sphere.* Oxford: Polity.

Hall, S. (1973) 'Encoding/decoding'. In S. Hall, D. Hobson, A. Lowe and P. Willis (eds) *Culture, Media, Language.* London: Hutchinson.

Hall, S. (1978) 'The Social Production of News'. In S. Hall, C. Critcher, T. Jefferson, J. Clarke and B. Roberts (eds), *Policing the Crisis: Mugging, the State and Law and Order.* London: Macmillan.

Hall, S. (1981) 'The Whites of Their Eyes'. In L. Bridges and R. Brunt (eds) *Silver Linings.* London: Lawrence and Wishart.

Halliday, M.A.K. (1978) *Language as Social Semiotic: The Social Interpretation of Language and Meaning*. London: Arnold.

Harcup, T. and O'Neill, D. (2001) 'What is News? Galtung and Ruge revisited', *Journalism Studies* Vol. 2 (2): 261–280.

Harris, M. and Lee, A.J. (1978) *The Press in English Society from the Seventeenth to the Nineteenth Century*. London and Toronto Associated Presses.

Hodge, R. and Kress, G. (1993) *Language as Ideology*. London: Routledge.

Holland, P. (1983) 'The Page 3 Girl speaks to women too', *Screen* Vol. 24 (3): 102.

Holland, P. (1998) 'The politics of the smile: 'soft news' and the sexualization of the popular press'. In C. Carter, G. Branston and S. Allan (eds) *News, Gender and Power*. London: Routledge.

Holland, G.S. (2000) *Divine Irony*. London: Associated University Presses.

Holquist, M. (1994) *Dialogism: Bakhtin and his World*. London: Routledge.

Keeble, R. (1998) *The Newspapers Handbook*. London: Routledge.

Keeble, R. (2005) 'New Militarism, Massacrespeak and the Language of Silence', *Ethical Space: The Journal of Communication Ethics*. Vol. 2 (1): 39–45.

Kieran, M. (ed.) (1998) *Media Ethics*. London: Routledge.

Kitis, E. and Milapedes, M. (1997) 'Read it and believe it: how metaphor constructs ideology in news discourse', *Journal of Pragmatics* 28(5): 557–590.

Kress, G.R. (1985) *Linguistic Processes in Sociocultural Practice*. Geelong: Deakin University Press.

Langer, J. (1998) *Tabloid Television: Popular Journalism and the 'Other News'*. London: Routledge.

Law, I. (2002) *Race in the News*. Basingstoke: Palgrave.

Lynn, N. and Lea, S. (2003) 'A phantom menace and the new Apartheid': the social construction of asylum seekers in the United Kingdom, *Discourse and Society* 14(4): 425–452.

Matheson, D. (2000) 'The birth of news discourse: changes in news language in British newspapers, 1880–1930', *Media, Culture and Society* Vol. 22 (5).

McDowell, P. (1998) *The Women of Grub Street*. Oxford: Oxford University Press.

McLuhan, M. (1995) *Understanding Media*. London: Routledge.

Miller, C.R. (1994) 'Rhetorical community: the cultural basis of genre'. In A. Freedman and P. Medway (eds) *Genre and the New Rhetoric*. London: Routledge.

Mitchell W.J.T. (ed.) *On Narrative*. Chicago: University of Chicago Press.

Montgomery, M. (1986) 'Language and power: a critical review of *Studies in the Theory of Ideology* by John B. Thompson', *Media, Culture and Society* Vol. 8: 41–64.

O'Connor, T.P. (1889) 'The new journalism' in *New Review* 10 October.

Ogden, C.K. and Richards, I.A. (1985), *The Meaning of Meaning* [1923]. London. Ark.

Page, R.E. (2003) '"Cherie: lawyer, wife, mum": contradictory patterns of representation in media reports of Cherie Booth/Blair', *Discourse and Society* 14(5): 559–579.

Preston, P. (1999) 'Time to be Brutally Honest', *Guardian*, 1 March.

Propp, V. (1968) *The Morphology of the Folk Tale*. Austen: University of Texas Press.

Reah, D. (2002) *The Language of Newspapers*. London: Routledge.

Richardson, J.E. (2004) *(Mis)Representing Islam: The Racism and Rhetoric of the British Broadsheet Press*. Amsterdam: John Benjamins.

Romaine, S. (1999) *Communicating Gender*. Mahwah, NJ: Lawrence Erlbaum.

Said, E.W. (1978a) *Orientalism*. London: Routledge and Kegan Paul.

Said, E.W. (1978b) 'The problem of textuality: two exemplary positions', *Critical Enquiry* 4: 673–714

Said, E.W. (1993) *Culture and Imperialism*. London: Chatto and Windus.

Said, E.W. (1997) *Covering Islam: How the Media and the Experts Determine How We See the Rest of the World*. London: Vintage.

Saussure, Ferdinand de (1974) *Course in General Linguistics*. London: Fontana/ Collins.

Schudson, M. (1978) *Discovering the News: A Social History of American Newspapers*. New York: Basic Books.

Searle, C. (1989) *Your Daily Dose: Racism in the Sun*: London: Campaign for Press and Broadcasting Freedom.

Simpson, P. (1993) *Language, Ideology and Point of View*. London: Routledge.

Smith, A. (1978) 'The long road to objectivity and back again: the kinds of truth we get in journalism'. In G. Boyce, J. Curran and P. Wingate (eds), *Newspaper History from the Seventeenth Century to the Present Day*. London: Constable.

Sommerville, J. (1996) *The News Revolution*. Oxford: Oxford University Press.

Spencer, P. and Wollman. H. (2003) *Nationalism: A Critical Introduction*. London: Sage.

Spender, D. (1980) *Man Made Language*. London: Routledge and Kegan Paul.

Titscher, S., Meyer, M., Wodak, R. and Vetter, E. (2000) *Methods of Text and Discourse Analysis*. London: Sage.

Todorov, T. (1993) *On Human Diversity: Nationalism, Racism and Exoticism in French Thought*. Cambridge MA: Harvard University Press.

Toolan, M.J. (1998) *Narrative: A Critical Linguistic Introduction*. London: Routledge.

Toulmin, S. (1958) *The Uses of Argument*. Cambridge: University of Cambridge Press.

Tuchman, G. (1978) *Making News: A Study in the Construction of Reality*. New York: Free Press.

Tuchman, G. (1981) 'The symbolic annihilation of women by the mass media'. In S. Cohen and J. Young (eds) *The Manufacture of News: Deviance, Social Problems and the Mass Media*. London: Constable.

Tunstall, J. (1996) *Newspaper Power*. London: Clarendon.

Van Dijk, T.A. (1991) *Racism and the Press*. London: Routledge.

Van Dijk, T.A. (1993) *Elite Discourse and Racism*. London: Sage.

Van Leeuwen, T. (1987) 'Generic strategies in press journalism', *Australian Review of Applied Linguistics* 10 (2): 199–220.

West, R. (1913) 'Mr. Chesterton in hysterics', *The Clarion* 14 November.

White, H. (1984) 'The value of narrativity in the representation of reality'. In W.J.T. Mitchell (ed.) *On Narrative*. Chicago: University of Chicago Press.

Williams, J. (1995) *PC Wars*. London: Routledge.

Winterson, J. (1988) *The Passion*. London: Penguin.

Wodak, R. and Matouschek, B. (1993) ' "We Are Looking at People Whose Origin One Can Clearly Tell Just By Looking": Critical Discourse Analysis and the Study of Neo-Racism in Contemporary Austria', *Discourse and Society* 4(2): 225–248.

Wykes, M. (2001) *News, Crime and Culture*. London: Pluto.

Younge, G. (2000) 'The Badness of Words'. *Guardian*, 14 February.

Index